Two week loan

Please r
date
Ch.

2 -

POVERTY DYNAMICS: ISSUES AND EXAMPLES

Poverty Dynamics: Issues and Examples

ROBERT WALKER in association with Karl Ashworth
Centre for Research in Social Policy
Department of Social Sciences
Loughborough University

Avebury

Aldershot · Brookfield USA · Hong Kong · Singapore · Sydney

Published by
Avebury
Ashgate Publishing Limited
Gower House
Croft Road
Aldershot
Hants GU11 3HR
England

Ashgate Publishing Company
Old Post Road
Brookfield
Vermont 05036
USA

British Library Cataloguing in Publication Data

Walker, Robert
    Poverty Dynamics: Issues and Examples
    I. Title II. Ashworth, Karl
    362.5
    ISBN 1 85628 929 X

Library of Congress Cataloging-in-Publication Data

Walker, Robert, 1949-
    Poverty dynamics: issues and examples / Robert Walker
    in association with Karl Ashworth
        p.   cm.
    Includes bibliographical references and index.
    ISBN 1-85628-929-X: $59.95 (est.)
    1. Poverty--United States. 2. Public welfare--United States.
    I. Ashworth, Karl II. Title.
    HC110.P6W24 1994
    362.5'8'0973--dc20
                                                    94-26650
                                                    CIP

Printed and bound by Athenæum Press Ltd.,
Gateshead, Tyne & Wear.

Contents

Figures and tables

Acknowledgements

This book builds more than most on the work of other people. Jill Vincent contributed to the initial versions of Chapters 3, 4, 5 and 7. Similarly Alan Deacon, Katie Brittain and Jennifer Park helped with Chapter 7. Martha Hill jointly authored the conference papers from which Chapter 6 evolved and, as a collaborator and friend, has contributed more than she can be aware to the genesis of this book.

David Ellwood's pioneering work on poverty dynamics ignited our interest in the subject and subsequent conversations with him were an inspiration. Alan Deacon, Anne Corden, Greg Duncan, Stefan Leibfried, David Rose, Jacqueline Scott and Wolfgang Voges are among the many others who also provided great encouragement.

The work reported in Chapters 3, 4, 5, 8 and 9 derives from studies commissioned by the Department of Social Security, while the Joseph Rowntree Foundation funded the study reported in Chapter 7. The views expressed are, of course, those of the authors alone and not necessarily those of the Department of Social Security or the Joseph Rowntree Foundation.

A great deal of painstaking work went into preparing the manuscript for publication and our heartfelt thanks go out to Karen Kellard, Sharon Walker, Nigel Bilsbrough and Rosie Woolley.

1 The forgotten dimension of time

Time seldom features in debates about poverty. Yet, without taking time into account it is impossible fully to appreciate the nature and experience of poverty or truly to understand the level of suffering involved. Equally, it is impossible to develop policies that successfully tackle the multiple causes of the problem or offer lasting solutions.

Regrettably we are not in the position to tell the complete story about the interaction of time and poverty. Appropriate information is only just becoming available with the advent of panel surveys and longitudinal administrative data. Computers have only recently acquired the power needed to handle the mathematics involved. The concepts with which to handle the complexity of thinking in another dimension are still embryonic and scattered across a range of disparate disciplines. Moreover, we stumbled into the area quite unprepared for the enormity of the intellectual task ahead.

We are publishing this book, therefore, as a progress report long before we have answers to most of the important questions. The intention is to encourage others to join us in the quest to incorporate time into our understanding of poverty for, like Piachaud (1987), we believe that poverty brings with it the imperative to act. Greater understanding of the problem should mean that we are better equipped, and perhaps more motivated, to find the necessary solutions. At worst it removes ignorance as an excuse for inactivity.

1

It would be wrong to suggest that time has been totally ignored in accounts of poverty in Britain. Time may not be made explicit in the basic definition, but it is certainly important in the measurement of poverty: families are described as poor if their resources fall short of needs, and both resources and needs have to be measured over a predetermined period of time. However, two supplementary questions of untold importance have rarely, if ever, been asked. First, how sensitive are measurements to variations in the period over which needs and resources are compared? The answer turns out to be 'very sensitive'. Secondly, and of even more significance, analysts have not generally asked for how long families remain poor. Instead, a rather static view of poverty has been adopted in which the poor are contrasted with the non-poor as if the membership of the two groups remained very much the same. The concomitant policy response is to focus on the relief of poverty rather than its prevention or cure. Whether the failure to ask these supplementary questions is the child or parent of British policy is a moot point for others to discuss.

When the questions are asked, as in Chapter 2, the answers generate new insights and stimulate further questions and reflection. First, most spells of poverty are found to be short and poor families frequently exchange places with the formerly non-poor. But, poverty is nevertheless very inequitably distributed and is highly concentrated even within the subset of families who are ever poor.

Secondly, the way in which poverty is distributed over time affects the distribution of poverty within a society. If most spells of poverty are long, prevalence - the proportion of the population that experiences poverty in any given period - will be low. Where spells are short, prevalence will be higher. Just how high depends on the extent to which people repeatedly experience spells of poverty.

Similarly the distribution of poverty within a population is likely to affect the nature of poverty. If poverty is highly concentrated, affecting very few individuals, it will occur as long unbroken spells from which few people ever escape. Short spells of poverty, on the other hand, are associated with a greater prevalence of poverty within the population. Moreover, long periods of poverty are inherently different from short spells and repeated spells of poverty - which imply a degree of prevalence between the extremes - differ from a single spell of poverty even if the duration is the same. In this way it becomes apparent that there may not be one kind of

2

poverty but many, each different in their aetiology, their effect and in terms of the most appropriate policy response to them.

These and a number of other issues concerned with the conceptualisation and measurement of poverty are discussed in Chapter 2. Chapter 3 takes the relief of poverty and the prevention of dependency as objectives of social security provision and explores the substantive and policy implications of making the consideration of time explicit. The recognition that most spells of poverty begin and end directs attention to the circumstances associated with people becoming poor and to the factors that cause spells of poverty to end. Under this paradigm, as already noted, the objectives of social security policy are likely to shift away from relief towards prevention and intervention.

But this is not all. The evidence is that many people experience the coincidence of circumstances associated with poverty without themselves becoming poor. The search for the root explanation of poverty is thereby shifted away from the events that trigger a spell of poverty towards the prior circumstances which allow the occurrence of an event to bring about a shortage of income in relation to need. There may here be a basis for developing a united theoretical structure that links micro and macro-analyses and reconciles structural and personal models of causation. Such analyses may, in turn, provide the foundation for the evolution of policies that offer true protection against the risk of poverty.

Three objectives, more characteristic of the social security systems of continental European countries, are the subject of Chapter 4. The maintenance of living standards, compensation and redistribution are all informed by adopting an explicitly temporal perspective. Incomes and needs are shown to fluctuate so markedly over time that few people experience stable living standards for very long. While there are persistent patterns associated in particular with stages in the life-course - patterns that may have changed little since Rowntree (1901) first identified them at the turn of this century, variations in living standards cannot be accurately predicted statistically. Nor can they be foreseen in detail by an individual. This is taken as strong support for the principle of social insurance as a mechanism providing for compensation and income maintenance.

Turning to redistribution, it is shown that the apparent degree of inequality in living standards decreases as the period over which it is measured is extended from a year or less to a life time. This is due to the averaging out of short term fluctuations. However, it also appears that governmental attempts to redistribute income vertically from richer to poorer are more effective when recorded over the life time than over shorter periods. This is because vertical and horizontal transfers partly equate to redistribution across the life-course. This does not mean, however, that social security mechanisms that aim to assist the individuals more efficiently to manage their life time resources to meet periods of need could not be improved substantially.

In Chapter 5 the emphasis shifts from consideration of the objectives of social security policy towards issues of implementation, notably targeting and administration. It is shown that the failure to take thorough cognizance of time, due primarily to an absence of suitable data, results in erroneous or misleading assumptions about the nature and extent of need leading, in turn, to inefficient procedures for targeting and promoting benefits. Existing statistics tend to understate the turnover of individuals with short spells of benefit entitlement and receipt, underestimate the number of individuals falling within the scope of particular schemes and inflate estimates of take up. They also down play the rate of change in people's circumstances and give too great a weight to the one-off nature of need.

The dynamic nature of benefit populations, which continually alter in response to socio-economic forces and the changing circumstances of individuals, has implications for the targeting of benefits at all levels. It has meant that strategic decisions, concerned with the allocation of resources between groups with different needs, have necessarily been based on relatively weak, explanatory models and have not taken full account of variations in the persistence of need.

Finally, it is shown that a more detailed knowledge of benefit dynamics: changes in the circumstances of recipients; time spent on benefit and movements between benefits would provide a better understanding of the functions that benefits actually perform, and therefore improved means of assessing the extent to which individual policy objectives are met.

Examples

The concepts and issues introduced in the first section of the book are, wherever possible, illustrated by examples drawn from experience in Britain, the USA and elsewhere. However, given the breadth of coverage it is rarely possible to consider the examples themselves in great detail. This is not the case in the second section in which four examples, or case studies, are presented as mechanisms for exploring and further elucidating some of the issues raised earlier in the volume.

Chapter 6 takes the example of childhood poverty in the United States. The underlying premise will, by now, be familiar: time is crucial to the conceptualisation of poverty and the patterning of spells of poverty can be employed to differentiate the poverty experience. Taking data from the Panel Study of Income Dynamics, a cohort of children is followed for the first sixteen years of life and six types of poverty are defined, a priori, on the basis of the number, duration and spacing of spells. Each is found to be associated with a different level of economic welfare, measured over childhood, and the chapter documents the unique socio-demographic profile that characterises the six types of poverty. Although a small step in the differentiation of poverty, the analysis presented in this paper graphically illustrates the potential of the approach and the dangers of assuming that one person's poverty is identical to another's.

The analysis of single homelessness, presented in Chapter 7, has its origins in a project to establish the consequence of closing a resettlement unit at Alvaston, Derby in 1992. Despite their name, resettlement units primarily provide direct access accommodation for homeless men and constitute one of the last vestiges of the system of outdoor relief that operated under the Poor Law. By applying a dynamic analysis that took account of the patterns of stays at Alvaston, it was possible both better to evaluate the consequences of closing the hostel and to begin to categorise the different life-styles of the men who stayed there during the twelve months before closure.

The focus moves from poverty to benefit dynamics in Chapters 8 and 9 with two complementary analyses of Family Credit, a British income tested benefit targeted on working families with dependent children. Both analyses use data derived from administrative records and cover the 45 month period following the introduction of the scheme in April 1988.

Chapter 8 reveals that most families receiving Family Credit claim it for short periods but that long term recipients will gradually accumulate in the system and come to account for a substantial proportion of overall expenditure. For the majority of recipients, therefore, Family Credit offers a transitory supplement to tide them over a short-lived set of circumstances. But, in expenditure terms, the principal function of Family Credit has rapidly become the long term subsidisation of wages.

The process by which this accumulation of long term recipients of Family Credit occurred is described in Chapter 9. As would be expected, with a new benefit, the caseload increased throughout the study period despite very significant month to month variations in the flows on and off benefit. Recipients of larger awards are more likely than other groups to remain on benefit for long periods and there were small changes in the characteristics of new recipients which had larger long term effects.

The effects of national advertising campaigns were also examined. Their apparent success varied but, in general, they appeared to work by encouraging existing recipients to renew their awards when they expired rather than attracting new applications. Indeed, the number of applications from families who had never before received Family Credit declined steadily which is consistent with other (cross-sectional) evidence that points to the attainment of high levels of take-up. Unfortunately, no evidence is available to facilitate comparison of the dynamics of the claimant population with those of the target population which would enable the veracity of such an assumption to be established.

Finally, in Chapter 10, a number of the main themes are brought together to show how taking account of time affects the definition and measurement of poverty and changes our understanding of the causes of poverty and the appropriate policy responses. Equally important, Chapter 10 draws attention to the many new questions that now require answers.

Explaining US poverty

One of the case studies and many of the examples cited in the first part of the book are drawn from the United States. This reflects both a long history of panel studies - surveys in which the same individuals are interviewed at regular intervals - which permit temporal processes to be studied directly and a policy commitment to interventionist strategies in the social assistance field. Britain and the United States both have benefit systems that rely heavily on means-tested assistance aimed primarily at the relief of poverty (Lodemel and Shulte, 1992). This means that many of the US studies have a direct bearing on policy issues in Britain. Moreover, most of the examples serve to illustrate universal truths that follow logically from premises basic to the argument. However, there are a host of important differences between the two countries that need to be discounted by the reader when deciding how to map the examples into the British context. Two important institutional differences are outlined below.

First, unlike Britain, the USA has for a long time adopted an official definition of poverty which is used both for statistical purposes (to specify poverty thresholds) and to determine whether a person is financially eligible for assistance or services under a particular Federal programme (poverty guidelines).

The original conceptual work was undertaken in 1964 by Mollie Orshansky of the US Social Security Administration who prepared a set of income thresholds varying by family size and composition (Orshansky, 1969). The thresholds were based on the estimated weekly food costs of individuals, derived from the US Department of Agriculture's 1961 economy food plan, grossed up to an annual estimate and expanded by the application of a set of weights to cover non-food expenditures. Currently thresholds are prepared annually for 48 different household types based on equivalencies originally calculated by Orshansky. Since 1963 the thresholds have simply been uprated in line with the consumer price index rather than by taking into account changes in the cost of food included in the food plan. Information on household income composition is collected each year in the March sample of the continuous Current Population Survey. As yet no account is taken of non-money income in calculating the official poverty thresholds.

Certain technical changes and improvements have been implemented since the poverty statistics began in 1959, most notably in 1967 and 1980, so that in the very strictest sense they do not constitute a continuous series. Nevertheless, in all its basic essentials the official definition has remained unchanged for about 30 years. It should be stressed, also, that, unlike the Supplementary Benefit/Income Support standard often used in the United Kingdom, the official US definition of poverty is a subsistence not a relative one. This means that the poverty threshold income would purchase the same volume of goods in 1993 as in 1959. It also means that the US definition implicitly denies poor people the right to share in the improvements in living standards enjoyed by the society as a whole. Nevertheless, the standard, though open to criticism on a number of grounds, is widely accepted in the USA and provides a particularly secure basis for assessing trends over time.

In terms of purchasing power, US poverty thresholds are roughly equivalent to Income Support rates, though with some variation between types of household. However, in relative terms, when set against per capita consumption expenditure, the US poverty thresholds are between one and two-fifths lower than the British benefit safety net.

A second difference is that most benefits in the United States are categorical, aimed at particular circumstances or demographic groups, and there is no universal safety net such as that offered by Income Support in Britain.

Means-tested programmes in the United States providing assistance in case and in kind are often grouped together under the term 'welfare'. The most important programmes are Medicaid, Food Stamps, Supplemental

Security Income (SSI) and Family Support Payments (FSP). Certain smaller schemes exist and the destitute may be able to obtain a measure of financial assistance at state level.

Medicaid, which provides medical services and is intended to meet the medical costs of certain low income families, is the largest programme and costs two and a half times more than any of the other three which are of roughly equal size. Entitlement to Medicaid is, in large measure, conditional upon receipt of SSI or FSP. The Federally administered system of Supplemental Security Income provides income support for the aged, blind and disabled. FSP - principally Aid to Families with Dependent Children (AFDC) - is a joint Federal-State programme designed to meet the financial needs of families where there is at least one child aged under 18 'who is deprived of parental support or care' for any of a prescribed set of reasons. Most recipients of AFDC are lone parents and most of these are female. Finally, the Food Stamp programme provides coupons which are redeemable for food at most retail stores. Food stamps are received by most SSI and AFDC recipients but are also available to other households with gross incomes below 130 per cent of the Office of Management and Budget (OMB) poverty guidelines provided that they have disposable assets of less than $2000 (or $300 in households with an elderly member).

Thirdly, there is an important difference in terminology. While in Britain 'Social Security' is used to refer to means-tested benefits, social insurance and, even, aspects of occupational welfare, in the USA 'social security' relates solely to insurance based provision provided through the public sector. As noted above, means-tested benefits are typically termed 'welfare'.

Finally, the British reader should be aware that many of the American studies cited use information derived from the Panel Study of Income Dynamics (PSID) based at the Survey Research Center, University of Michigan. This has been repeated each year since 1968. In the original design, lower income and minority families were over-sampled. Since the first two years of the survey sample attrition has been small so that reliable national estimates can be constructed adjusting for the original over-sampling and for differential response. Each year one adult from the original families that have remained intact is interviewed (usually the head of household), together with an adult from each family that contains a member of the original families. This procedure produces an unbiased sample of between six and seven thousand families. Because of more complete information, poverty estimates based on PSID data tend to be lower than those prepared by the US Social Security Administration (Duncan, Coe and Hill, 1984).

TAKING ACCOUNT OF TIME:
ISSUES

2 Definition and measurement of poverty

Time is seldom taken fully into account in the definition and measurement of poverty. This omission is important. Time is not simply a further dimension over which poverty can be measured. It is the medium within which poverty occurs and shapes the experience of being poor.

Poverty is normally defined in terms of a shortfall in resources in relation to a set of legitimate needs. Much has been written about the appropriate specification and measurement of needs and also about the suite of resources which should be taken into account. However, the simple act of asking over what period personal income should be set against needs reveals the limits of the paradigm within which poverty is usually discussed. If any answer at all is forthcoming it is likely to be couched in terms of what is possible with the 'available data'.

Yet the difference between a shortfall in resources to needs lasting a few hours and that lasting a few months, or years, is clearly important even if the precise consequences of the difference are not self-evident. They are not self-evident because poverty is experienced as a shortfall in the resources to needs (severity) which lasts for a period of time (duration): a short bout of severe poverty may be just as troublesome to the individual (and for society at large) as a longer but less severe spell. Furthermore, while the severity of a spell of poverty can always be assessed (at least theoretically) the duration of a spell cannot be determined until it is over. This uncertainty as to the duration of poverty is arguably a key element in the experience of poverty.

The intention in this chapter is to explore some of the implications of explicitly considering time in the definition and measurement of poverty.

11

Where possible, the arguments will be illustrated with reference to empirical examples which, as noted in Chapter 1, are necessarily drawn mainly from the US where longitudinal studies of poverty are more abundant. The chapter divides into five sections. The first shows that all definitions of poverty contain inbuilt assumptions about time, while the second presents evidence about the distribution of poverty over time. There then follows a discussion of attempts to link duration and severity in approaching a definition of poverty that more accurately captures the meaning inherent in the experience of poverty. Certain measurement issues are covered in the fourth section before, finally, rehearsing some of the implications of adopting a temporal perspective of poverty.

Time in poverty

The aim in this section is to clarify the assumptions about time which are implicit in existing measures of poverty and to consider the consequences of different assumptions on the poverty rate and the presumed characteristics of the poor.

The accounting period

The operational definition of poverty is invariably expressed in terms of a shortfall in resources in relation to legitimate needs where both elements are measured over a period of time which is usually referred to as the accounting period. The accounting period adopted is normally assumed to be the same for both resources and needs, although this assumption is sometimes violated.

The accounting period is generally determined by the information available. To take some examples from Britain, the UK Family Expenditure Survey (FES) collects financial data linked to the periodicity of payment so that wages are recorded weekly and salaries monthly. Income information from the FES is used for the purpose of preparing the official 'Households Below Average Income' (HBAI) tables when it is converted to a weekly basis, which is the period used for the purposes of the HBAI tables. Analyses using information derived from administrative social security records typically relate to the assessment period used to calculate benefit entitlement. The official analyses of income distribution undertaken by the Central Statistical Office (CSO, 1991) use an annual accounting period since they are based on data from the Survey of Personal Incomes collected in relation to annual tax liability.

Occasionally more thought is given to the choice of accounting period. Four different income periods were considered ahead of introducing the HBAI statistical series : annual; quarterly; 'normal'; and 'current' which was eventually chosen (DHSS, 1988). Quarterly income was recognised as being 'ideal' in that it was "long enough to avoid very short-term fluctuations but not so long as to run the risk of producing an averaged figure that may not reflect reality at any particular point in time". (DHSS, (1988) p. 20) Clearly this begs the questions of what 'reality' means and who is to define it. In some circumstances the accounting period may need to be very short to capture the reality of poverty as it is experienced by poor families. This is illustrated in Britain by the large number of crisis loans which are made to cover the living expenses incurred by families awaiting their first payment of Income Support (Walker, Dix and Huby, 1992).

Quarterly income was ruled out because of the need to avoid overloading the Family Expenditure Survey with additional questions. Annual income, which is used by the US Census and many other surveys in the United States, was dismissed partly because it would 'conceal significant fluctuations' but, more importantly, because the FES collects little information on changes in household circumstances and other factors over the year as a whole.

The earlier statistical series on 'Low Income Families' employed the concept of 'normal income'. In practice this meant adjusting for the likely impact of changes in employment circumstances in the three months preceding an interview. Where people had become sick or unemployed their previous income in employment was taken, although no corresponding adjustment was made for individuals who had recently returned to work after a long spell of unemployment. The result was that the number of cases recorded as having low income was less than if current income had been used.

The poverty rate

The assumptions about time which are inherent in the various operational definitions of poverty are important because they affect measures of the incidence of poverty and conclusions about the nature of poverty.

Lengthening the accounting period reduces the apparent poverty rate. This is because averaging incomes (and needs) over time evens out the temporary mismatches between incomes and needs, lessens the degree of dispersion in the population and hence reduces the proportion of individuals appearing in the tails of the statistical distribution of income over needs. Moreover, there is an asymmetry built into the averaging process because windfall income will inflate the average income of a low income person rather more than a temporary shortfall will reduce the average income of a wealthy person (Walker, 1991).

Table 2.1 shows the effect of altering the accounting period between one month and one year using data derived from the Survey of Income and Programme Participation (SIPP) in the United States : the poverty rate falls from 14 per cent to 11.3 per cent. (Other examples are given in Walker, 1991.) Turning to Britain, the use of current income in the HBAI tables, the shortest accounting period which it is possible to derive using the FES, locates the HBAI series towards one end of the spectrum of possible measures. Reverting to the use of normal rather than current income in the HBAI analyses would increase the proportion of families with incomes below half average income from 7.7 to 8.1 per cent, an increase of about 200,000 individuals (Johnson and Webb, 1989).

The effect that altering the accounting period has on measures of poverty is dependent on the extent of income volatility and other relevant changes in circumstance. The greater the income volatility, the larger the difference in the estimates that results. Unfortunately there is virtually no hard evidence on the extent of income fluctuations in Britain (see below). However, the American evidence is that fluctuations are very important, and there are reasons for suspecting this may also be the case in Britain (Walker, Ashworth and Vincent, 1991).

There are also grounds for believing that the incomes of lower paid workers are more variable than those of other groups. Table 2.2 shows that, in the United States in the early 1970s, income instability was three times higher among the lowest paid than among those earning more than average wages. In Britain, sickness and unemployment are known differentially to affect low income groups while the small sums that Income Support claimants are permitted to earn may typically derive from lump sum payments rather than a regular work commitment. Salaried groups have less scope for overtime than other workers, although this may partly be offset by irregular income from perks (Smail, 1988).

The poor and persistently poor

The choice of accounting period is important for another reason. As the period is extended, with the result that the temporarily poor are excluded,

14

poverty measures yield increasingly better approximations of the extent of persistent or permanent poverty. At the same time the profile of characteristics associated with the people defined as being poor becomes a more accurate description of those who are poor on a long-term basis.

Table 2.1
Accounting period differences in poverty and crisis measures (1984)

Accounting period[a]	Percentage in poverty (a)[c]	Percentage in crisis[d] (b)	$\frac{a - b}{a}$ (c)[b]
1 month	14.0	11.0	21.4
4 months	13.2	11.3	14.0
1 year	11.3	10.4	8.0

[a] The four month figures are the averages derived from three four month periods and the monthly figures the average of three monthly periods.

[b] C = 100 (a - b/a); i.e. the difference between the proportions in poverty and experiencing crisis expressed as a percentage of the former.

[c] Ruggles and Williams (1987) provide abstracts of 13.7 per cent for the average of 12 monthly rates and 11.0 per cent for the annual rate based on the same survey.

[d] Without assets that would meet needs during the accounting period.

Source: David and Fitzgerald (1987) based on an analysis of a longitudinal sample from SIPP.

This effect can be illustrated with US data. Table 2.3 records the incidence of poverty among American women over a six year period in the early 1980s. On the basis of annual income 27 per cent of poor women were white. When the accounting period is lengthened from one to six years the proportion of white women falls to about 15 per cent. This accords closely to the proportion of white women among those who were poor continuously during the six year period.

Table 2.2

Annual income instability by five-year average income level, USA, 1970s (same household head and in labour force at least 1500 hours all five years)

Average Earnings of Head	Percent	Instability Level (S.E.E.)*
Less than $2000	1.6	.221
$ 2000 - 3999	7.6	.140
$ 4000 - 5999	15.1	.106
$ 6000 - 7999	19.8	.080
$ 8000 - 9999	19.1	.065
$10000 - 11999	13.9	.062
$12000 - 14999	11.6	.056
$15000 - 19999	6.5	.061
$20,000 or more	4.7	.078
TOTAL	100.0	.081

* 'Standard error of estimate for each individual after regressing individuals' residuals from an expected cohort earnings equation against time.

Source: Benus, (1974)

Calculated from figures in Duncan and Rodgers, (1990)

Table 2.3
Impact on increasing the accounting period on the composition of the female poor, USA, 1980s

Percentages

	Black women	White women	All
Average of single year poverty rates	72.8	27.2	100.0
6 year income less than poverty threshold	85.2	14.8	100.0
Poor in all 6 years	84.6	15.4	100.0

The precise effects of adjusting the accounting period depend on the composition of the population, the relative size of the constituent groups and the degree to which the groups differ in terms of the stability of their financial and household characteristics. The choice of an absolute or relative measure of poverty is also important. The move from 'normal' to current income which occurred with the introduction of the HBAI tables is analogous to shortening the accounting period. Had incomes been measured against an absolute poverty standard, the impact of this change would have been to emphasise the characteristics of the temporarily poor; the proportion of pensioners, chronic sick and lone parents counted as poor would have decreased relative to other groups, reflecting the fact that their circumstances are likely to be relatively stable. In practice, the HBAI tables use a relative standard and, while the incomes of pensioners were not affected by the move away from normal income, the average income of the population as a whole rose. Hence, the proportion of pensioners with below average incomes increased.

While a long accounting period yields much better descriptions of the characteristics of the permanently poor, this does not mean that statistics based on a short accounting period accurately reflect the characteristics of the short term poor. This is because people who are poor for long periods have a greater chance of being included in a survey than those who are poor for short spells. For example, it has been estimated that over half of the non-elderly Americans who are in poverty at any given time are in the midst of a spell lasting over nine years (Bane and Ellwood, 1986 - See also Table 2.5 below). This means that US estimates of poverty that are based on cross-sectional statistics effectively assign a weight of around eight to the characteristics of the long-term poor.

To summarise, a picture of the characteristics of the poor which derives from cross-sectional data is likely to be much influenced by the attributes of the long term poor. The effect is greatest when a lengthy accounting period is used. The choice of accounting period also affects the poverty rate: other things being equal, the longer the period, the lower the apparent poverty rate. The precise effect of altering the accounting period depends on the stability of incomes and needs in the population, something which can only be determined if longitudinal data are available.

Poverty in time

Having shown that any discussion of poverty is likely to be premised on assumptions, usually implicit, about time, it is necessary to explore how the explicit consideration of time influences the definition, measurement and, indeed, the conceptualisation of poverty.

In Britain poverty is usually conceptualised as an 'either/or' state with people considered to be poor or not poor. Some interest has been shown in the idea of a poverty gap, a shortfall in income, both as a measure of financial severity and relative deprivation (Atkinson, 1989). However, hardly any attention has been paid to the duration of poverty or to distinctions between long-term, recurrent and transient poverty. This may simply reflect the absence of longitudinal data.

The result is to risk making too great a distinction between the poor and the not (currently) poor, to treat poverty as a state rather than as a process (with the concomitant policy imperatives that this implies) and to neglect the inextricable link between the distribution of poverty and the experiences of the poor.

Prevalence

The prevalence of poverty is defined as the proportion of a population that experiences a spell of poverty during a given period. Prevalence provides a key to understanding the distribution of poverty when viewed longitudinally

18

and helps focus attention on the link between the distribution and experience of poverty.

Prevalence is determined by the total volume of poverty, the length of spells and the extent of recurrent spells. The lower bound is set by the situation where the same group of people is in poverty continuously. The upper bound describes a situation where poverty approaches a once in a life time event and where spells of poverty are as short as the global sum of poverty allows. Values in between imply that a variable proportion of the population is experiencing repeated spells of poverty of various lengths.

Low prevalence provides conditions consistent with the development of an underclass[1]. The poor would have no chance of escape and little in common with the wider community, while those who were not poor would have no personal experience of the problems faced by those in poverty. High prevalence, given the same aggregate amount of poverty, would be consistent with situations where distributional justice of the kind proposed by Rawls (1973) prevailed and where the chances of experiencing poverty were more equally shared. Moderate prevalence, again with the same fixed sum of poverty, implies something in between these two extremes: with people differing in terms of the constancy or intermittent nature of their poverty. Moreover, the precise way in which repeated spells are distributed over time might forge different experiences of poverty. Long spells of poverty separated by short spells of relative affluence could well be very different from a norm of affluence interspersed with short bouts of poverty.

Prevalence is analogous to the poverty rate as measured with cross-sectional data and the two measures are equivalent in the unique case where all the poor are always poor. In reality, this situation never occurs and prevalence generally exceeds the cross-sectional poverty rate by a considerable margin. Table 2.4, for example, shows that over a decade during which the annual poverty rate in the United States never exceeded 10 per cent, the prevalence of poverty, the proportion of families where annual income fell short of needs in at least one year, was 24 per cent. Therefore, in America at least, the minority of people who ever experience poverty is much larger than the proportion who are poor at any given time. This means that there is some movement across the poverty divide and hence some basis for shared experience.

One difficulty in operationalising the concept of prevalence is the choice of period over which it is measured. The longer the period chosen, the larger the recorded value is likely to be because of the enhanced opportunity to observe a greater proportion of short-term poverty. Typically the length is

19

Table 2.4
Durations of poverty, USA, 1969-78

% poor for:	
Never Poor	75.6
1 or 2 years	13.6
3 - 7 years	8.1
8 - 10 years	2.6
All 10 years	0.7

Source: Hill, (1981)

determined by the window of opportunity provided by the duration of a longitudinal survey, 10 years in the case of the example used in Table 2.4.

A more satisfactory approach is to choose a period that has social and personal meaning. Rowntree (1901), as early as 1899, identified five stages in the life of a British labourer (characterised as contrasting periods of 'want and comparative plenty'): childhood, early working adulthood, child rearing, working life after children have grown up and old age. Hindu culture (Sen, 1961) allows for four stages (asramas). O'Higgins et al (1988) recognise 10 stages while Duncan (1988) has defined 10 life-cycle categories defined solely in terms of age and sex. Others (e.g. Elder, 1988) have argued for the existence of multiple, interlocking trajectories (marriage, working life, parenthood, and the like) each comprising sequences of states and events. Setting the observation period to coincide with a life state means that any spell censorship[2] that occurs coincides with a socially meaningful event or transition. As a consequence it becomes reasonable to talk about the extent of poverty in childhood, working life or old age.

Ashworth, Hill and Walker (1991), observing a cohort of children born in the USA between 1968 and 1972, found the prevalence of poverty in the fifteen years of childhood to be 38 per cent (see Chapter 6). Prevalence for black children exceeded 79 per cent compared with 30 per cent for white children.

Duration

Duration has been used in the literature to refer to the length of individual spells of poverty and to the total duration of poverty experienced over a given period (here termed 'accumulated duration'). Both aspects are important attributes of the personal experience of poverty. Long spells of poverty may be assumed to be worse than short ones. However, if an individual experiences a series of short spells, accumulated duration may be high. Moreover, it is not self-evident, a priori, that the welfare implications of a single spell of poverty lasting five out of ten years are necessarily worse than five separate spells of one year. There is, for example, evidence that some households favour low but stable incomes over higher unstable ones (McLaughlin, Millar and Cooke, 1989).

Little is known about the duration of poverty in Britain although there is increasing debate about the existence of an underclass and a dependency culture (Field, 1989; Murray, 1990), ideas that are both predicated on long durations of benefit receipt. Statistics for the United States, presented in Table 2.4, show that most people who experienced poverty during a 10 year period had incomes below the poverty line in only one or two years, although one in seven were poor in eight or more years. Measures of accumulated duration are extremely sensitive to the length of the observation period and it is again desirable that this should correspond with a life state or trajectory (see Chapter 5). The same problem occurs when observing the duration of individual spells since some will start before the period of observation ('left-hand censorship') and others finish after observation has ceased.

However, techniques are available to simulate the length of completed spells (see Annex A) and Table 2.5 presents the results of such an analysis based on US data (Bane and Ellwood, 1986). In this case the unit of analysis is a spell. The table shows, in column 2, that, while 45 per cent of spells last for a single year, 12 per cent last for nine years or more. The average length exceeds 12 years.

The third column shows that, although individuals destined to remain poor for a long time constitute only a small proportion of those who become poor, the permanence of their position means that they come to constitute a large proportion of the poor observed in cross-sectional data. This is the same point as made earlier in the context of the choice of accounting period.

It remains to consider how poverty is patterned over time. The two extremes are permanent poverty (Table 2.4 shows that 0.7 per cent of Americans were 'permanently' poor over a 10 year period) and a short once-

21

Table 2.5
Exit probabilities and distribution of completed spells of poverty (USA)[a]

Spell length years	Exit probability (1)	Distribution of completed spells for	
		Persons beginning a spell (2)	Persons poor at a given time (3)
A. The Non-elderly			
(1970-81)			
1	0.445	44.5	10.6
2	0.285	15.8	7.6
3	0.246	9.8	7.0
4	0.208	6.2	5.9
5	0.197	4.7	5.6
6	0.145	2.8	4.0
7	0.128	2.1	3.5
8	074	1.0	2.0
9	083	1.1	2.3
9-29(9+)[2]	0.100	12.0	51.5
30	1.000		
(Average)[b]		4.2	12.3

[a] See Annex B for discussion of the underlying methodology.

[b] Bracketed labels refer to distribution of completed spells.

Source: *Bane and Ellwood (1986)*

in-a-life-time spell. In between there is a large set of other possibilities each of which may constitute a different kind of poverty experience.

Interesting work in this area has been undertaken by Charles Murray (1986) of 'Losing Ground' fame. With his characteristic commitment to showing that things are not quite what they seem, he constructed case-studies of 'anomalous populations' from the US Panel Study of Income Dynamics. Two examples of this work are shown in Tables 2.6 and 2.7.

The first considers the trajectory of persons who were poor in 1980 but who had seemingly been prosperous (annual income three times the poverty level) at some point during the preceding decade. Such people were rare, comprising just 1.4 per cent of the population, and their experiences proved to be very disparate. The largest group that Murray identified consisted of individuals undergoing a long term fall into poverty. In reality, there appear to be at least two distinct patterns of experience within this group. The first comprises individuals who suddenly fall into poverty and remain poor for several years before the data is censored. The second includes people who suffer a gradual but remorseless drop in living standards which eventually takes them below the poverty threshold.

The next two groups by size are quite similar to each other. In both cases individuals moved into poverty in 1980 and remained poor the following year. Those experiencing 'a reversal of fortune' had previously enjoyed a long spell with moderate to high incomes; those with a 'spike' had received slightly lower incomes during the preceding decade.

For some individuals 1980 was the only year in which they were poor and by 1981 many had recovered some of the lost ground. Yet others experienced still more fluctuating circumstances that took them into poverty and relative affluence at least twice. Finally, Murray suggests two patterns which are 'deceptive' with, in one case, 1980 constituting a freak, perhaps inexplicable, departure from a life of comparative affluence and, in the other, a single prosperous year in the 1970s standing out from a life lived below or close to the poverty line.

The other example from Murray's work concerns the trajectories of the working poor. Murray found 88 males defined as such by PSID data for a single year (1970) and tracked their progress over a decade. Murray concluded that by 1980, 39 per cent were 'making a comfortable living', 20 per cent were 'getting along' and 41 per cent were 'still in trouble'. Most of the men in the last group were relatively old and poorly educated but the pattern of their experience was often quite different as is indicated by the selection of year to year profiles included in Table 2.7 and chosen to illustrate this point.

Table 2.6
Income patterns of people poor in 1980 who had a middle class* income during the 1970s

Income Pattern	Percentage of PSID sample (weighted)	Number	Simple unweighted percentage of group
'Deceptive affluence'	0.09	7	9
'Short spike from a usually non-poor baseline'	0.28	12	16
'Two-peaked prosperity'	0.11	5	7
Reversal of fortune in 1980	0.34	16	22
Temporary set-back with recovery in 1981	0.16	5	7
Deceptive poverty	0.18	9	12
Long term fall into poverty	0.27	20	27
TOTAL	1.43	74	100

* Greater than three times the poverty line in at least one year

Source: Adapted from Murray (1986)

Perhaps above all else, therefore, Murray's analyses illustrate the almost unbelievable instability of people's financial circumstances. Murray's examples were chosen because they were 'anomalous' but they nevertheless echo the experience of anyone who has worked with panel data. It is also evident how widely different one person's experience can be from another's

Table 2.7
US males working full time but poor in 1970

	By 1980, they were:		
	'making a comfortable living'	'getting along'	'still in trouble'
Examples of year-to-year profiles*	09899999995 01121144776 00000689963 06922458895	00111422159 00000114213 01000269781 02221344361	00100061002 00000000000 01241134222 03335499950
% in each group (N=82)	39	20	41

* 0 = at or below poverty index (PI) 3 = 151-175% PI 6 = 226-250% PI
  1 = 101-125 % PI   4 = 176-200% PI 7 = 251-275% PI
  2 = 126-150% PI   5 = 201-225% PI 8 = 276-300% PI
                                                       9 = >300% PI

Source: adapted from Murray (1986)

and, therefore, the difficulty of devising typologies that accurately and meaningfully group people with similar patterns of economic well-being. For example, there is very little difference between the individuals that Murray classified as experiencing a 'temporary set-back' and those who were described as in 'deceptive poverty': while the latter were (presumably) singled out because they had marginally higher incomes in an arbitrary reference year (1981), both had suffered a single year's poverty in an otherwise prosperous decade.

On the positive side, one can see in Murray's work the value of concepts such as the level, instability and trend in economic well-being that Ray (1975: Ray et al., 1991) has employed in developing systematic approaches to the grouping of temporal patterns. In an illustrative example, using data from a panel survey in Lorraine (France), the above three concepts were respectively operationalised as mean equivalised income, the coefficient of variation, and the slope of the linear trend (together with the adjusted Rsquared coefficient to provide an indication of the year to year scatter around the trend line). Applying principal components analysis and a hierarchical grouping routine, Ray was able to derive six groups of people with similar profiles. (In this way Ray (1991) was able to show that beneficiaries of the French social assistance scheme, RMI, had less stable profiles than non-beneficiaries.)

Ray (1992) has also highlighted one of the major problems in using traditional taxonomic procedures to elucidate temporal patterns of poverty: the totally rigid implementation of time. So, for example, the following two profiles, where 0 indicates a year in poverty and 1 a year not poverty:

Individual A = 01010101010101
Individual B = 10101010101010

will be treated as totally dissimilar. This is to neglect the fact that the two individuals share a common pattern of income instability and is only reasonable if historical time is crucial for the analysis (for example, if one was trying to establish the impact of the implementation of a particular policy).

Ray's response to this problem has been to develop summary indicators, such as the four used above in the Lorraine study but of increased sophistication, which are input directly into standard clustering routines. Other approaches have been suggested, such as S and T mode factor analysis (CRSP,1991) but unfortunately the technical problems of characterising temporal patterns have yet to be satisfactorily resolved.

Mention should also be made of an approach, discussed in more detail in Chapter 6, which falls midway between those of Murray and Ray. Ashworth, Hill and Walker (1991) argued that there is an intrinsic difference in the nature of continuous and intermittent poverty. Moreover, the instability associated with the latter, perhaps manifest as repeatedly frustrated hopes and great difficulty in planning, might mean that it was not necessarily preferable to the former. They also drew attention to the length of spells between bouts of poverty and suggested that periods of comparative prosperity might significantly affect families ability to cope financially when times were very hard. This might, in turn, affect the way in which spells of poverty were approached and experienced.

Cognisant of these ideas Ashworth and his colleagues developed a six-fold classification through inspection of the PSID dataset which distinguished between transient, occasional, recurrent, persistent, chronic and permanent poverty. Finding that each category had a unique socio-demographic profile, and was associated with a different level of economic welfare when measured over a life-stage, they concluded that it might be best to think of poverty taking not one but many forms.

The various methods of classifying temporal patterns of poverty share a common assumption, at least at a technical level, that each spell of poverty is independent of ones that precede it. There is, though, considerable evidence that this is not so and, indeed, this is implicitly accepted in the Ashworth typology which defines occasional poverty as 'repeated short spells'. Work by both Ellwood (1986) and Burstein and Visher (1989), for example, shows that people with prior experience of poverty are more at risk of poverty than people who have never been poor. However, it is far from clear whether poor people are simply more prone to experience poverty than others (the 'heterogeneity effect') or whether poverty itself materially increases risk of experiencing another spell ('state dependence').

An attempt to disentangle these factors has been made by Hill (1981). It suggests that the heterogeneity effect may be the more important. She calculated, on the basis of data for the 1970s, that the odds of being poor in one year were increased by a factor of 40 if the person was poor in the preceding year. Once the effect of individual characteristics were taken into account, however, the increased odds fall to a factor of four. So, on the basis of this evidence, it appears that individual specific differences in the propensity to be poor are much the more important. Nevertheless, there does appear to be a real causal link between poverty status at one time and the future likelihood of being poor. Whether this is because of an effect on the individuals' attitudes or behaviour, or whether it reflects the attitudes and behaviour of employers and others in a position to effect individuals' movement out of poverty is unclear. What is clear, however, is that work on temporal patterns would gain from the existence of better causal theory.

Linking severity and duration

Nicholson (1979) and Atkinson (1984) have suggested that a truly satisfactory measure of poverty would need to combine lack of resources and duration. There is, Atkinson argued, 'some level of income deficiency which is serious enough even for short periods and a lesser extent of deprivation which becomes serious if it lasts long enough' (Atkinson, 1984: 15).

Nicholson proposed a generic formulation of poverty measured over time:

$P = YT$

where Y is the income deficient and T is duration.

Adopting different terminology and notation Ashworth, Hill and Walker (1991) provide a more specific definition of what they term absolute cumulative poverty.

$$Y^*_i = \sum_{t=1}^{T} \ [(e_{it} - y_{it})|x = 1] \qquad (1)$$

Y^*_i = absolute cumulative poverty

y_{it} = income in year t

e_{it} = needs in year t

T = observation period (ideally a life stage or other intrinsically meaningful period)

$x =$
1 if in poverty

0 if not in poverty

This formulation, following Nicholson, makes no allowance for the fact that the same absolute shortfall in income will impose different financial constraints depending on the needs and size of the household unit. One response to this deficiency is to adjust the absolute measure by the equivalence scale implicit in the original measure of needs. Equivalised cumulative poverty. Y^{**}_i, is defined:

$$Y^{**}_i = \sum_{t=1}^{T} \ [((y_{it} - e_{it}/c)|x = 1] \qquad (2)$$

$c =$ an equivalising constant representing the needs of a male and female couple aged 21 - 35; = \$9272.51 (1987 US dollars).

A more readily interpretable approach, which achieves the same effect, involves summing (1 - (income to needs ratio)) for years in poverty to yield, Y^{***}_i, the cumulative income deficiency ratio:

$$Y^{***}{}_i = \sum_{t=1}^{T} \; [1-(y_{it}/e_{it})|x=1] \qquad\qquad (3)$$

A value of unity indicates that a shortfall in income equivalent to the needs for one year has been experienced over the period observed. It can be shown that $Y^{**}{}_i$ and $Y^{***}{}_i$ have identical distributions.

None of the above measures takes account of spells of relative prosperity experienced during the observation period. This can be achieved by removing the conditioning from the above equations so that each entity is cumulated over the entire observation period rather than over episodes of poverty:

$$D_i^* = \sum_{t=1}^{T} \; (e_{it} - y_{it}) \qquad\qquad (4)$$

where D_i^* is the absolute life-stage income deficit

$$D_i^{**} = \sum_{t=1}^{T} \; [(e_{it} - y_{it})|c] \qquad\qquad (5)$$

where D^{**} is the equivalised life-stage income deficit
and

$$D_i^{***} = \sum_{t=1}^{T} \; [1 - (y_{it}/e_{it})] \qquad\qquad (6)$$

where D_i^{***} is the life-stage income deficiency ratio

A final measure, P, life-stage poverty, records instances where equivalised income during the observation period falls short of needs, that is:

$$P_i = \; D_i^{**} > 0 \qquad\qquad (7)$$

The results of applying these various measures to American data on the financial circumstances of children are presented in Table 2.8. The data derive from the Panel Study of Income Dynamics, childhood is defined as the first 15 years of life and the accounting period for income and family needs is 12 months. Care should be taken in interpreting the maximum and

29

minimum values which sometimes appear as outriders to the distributions. The first five measures relate only to children who experience some poverty; the prevalence of poverty among the group is 38 per cent.

Comparing the first two columns shows that taking account of family size substantially reduces the apparent level of cumulative poverty. Because childhood poverty is more frequent in large families than small ones, the equivalisation process also has the effect of slightly reducing the apparent inequality in the distribution of cumulative poverty (the Gini coefficient falls from 0.62 to 0.56). Even so, it is clear that poverty, measured as the cumulative shortfall in income, is far from equitably distributed even among those children who experience some poverty. (By way of comparison, the Gini coefficient for household money income in the USA was 0.40 in 1987.)

The cumulative income to needs ratio highlights the pattern of inequality. The mean value of the ratio is 1.99, indicating a shortfall in income during periods of poverty which is very nearly equivalent to the income required to meet the needs of a family for a two year period. However, the distribution is very skewed and the median value is only 1.0; on the other hand, the corresponding value for the first quintile is 3.63.

The final three columns in Table 2.8 take account of the income received during periods of relative prosperity which, for all but 25 per cent of children who suffer poverty, more than compensates for the shortfall in income experienced whilst in poverty. (It should be noted that no account is taken of the sequencing of periods of poverty and relative prosperity.) It can be calculated from Table 2.8 that, for the average child experiencing poverty, family income during childhood exceeds needs by about 64 per cent. For children in the fifth decile this value exceeds 120 per cent.

In the final column of Table 2.8 the accounting period is effectively set equal to childhood. The result is that the prevalence of poverty falls to 9.4 per cent. (Even so, a figure of this order might cause some consternation if it were found to apply in the United Kingdom.) The distribution is less skewed than for the other measures. The deficit for those in the fifth quintile roughly equates with the annual needs allowance for a two parent, two child household, while that for the first quintile is four times as great.

There are unresolved difficulties with the composite measures of poverty presented above. For example, it is self-evident that the consequences of a shortfall equivalent to annual needs that is concentrated in one year are likely to be more severe than the same shortfall read over several years.

However, all the measures treat a given shortfall in the income to needs ratio as equivalent irrespective of the length of time over which it occurs. A

Table 2.8
Temporal measures for poverty for children in the USA

Quintiles	Absolute cumulative poverty $	Equivalised cumulative poverty $	Cumulative income deficiency ratio	Equivalised childhood income deficit $	Childhood income deficiency ratio	Childhood poverty $
Max	13	9	0.00	-1,262,014	-136.10	49
4th	3,499	2,904	0.33	-166,996	-18.01	15,112
3rd	9,501	6,484	0.70	-87,397	-9.43	34,029
2nd	21,468	13,880	1.50	-34,864	-3.76	44,319
1st	51,336	33,671	3.36	14,186	1.53	58,205
Min	285,917	112,205	12.10	112,205	12.10	112,205
Mean	32,732	18,472	1.99	-89,761	-9.68	39,931
Median	15,692	9,272	1.00	-62,148	-6.70	40,661
Prevalence	38	38	38	38	38	9

Source: Calculations from the Panel Study of Income Dynamics based on a cohort of children born between 1968 and 1972 and followed until aged 16. The poverty measure used is about 25 per cent above the official US datum.

more fundamental criticism derives from the logic of arguments presented earlier. If poverty is no longer to be conceptualised as a single phenomenon but differentiated according to temporal patterning (among other attributes) then it is inappropriate to conflate the different types by use of a single measure. Rather attention would be better focused on establishing the incidence and distribution of the different kinds of poverty experience.

Measurement issues

Finally, it is necessary to mention some of the more important measurement problems that arise when attempting to take account of the temporal characteristics of poverty.

Unit of observation

It is traditional in atemporal studies of poverty to treat the household as the unit for both measurement and analysis. The reasoning is that resources are generally shared within households such that members share a common standard of living. Even if there is evidence that this assumption may not hold (Pahl, 1989) the operational difficulties of doing otherwise mean that the fiction is generally maintained (but see Coulter and Jenkins, 1990).

With longitudinal studies the individual is usually the unit of analysis while the household is the primary unit of measurement. The same, questionable, assumptions are made about the sharing of resources within households but, because households are dynamic, incessantly splitting and reforming in unpredictable ways, the only meaningful strategy is to track the experience of individuals whatever household they happen to be in at the time. Moreover, the precipitating event at the beginning or end of a spell of poverty experienced by individuals may itself be linked to a change in household.

While treating the individual as the unit of analysis is the only practical approach, some caution is necessary. For instance, it may not be appropriate to treat as equivalent changes in the income to needs ratio caused by the arrival or departure of another family member, those caused by variations in the earnings of the individual or by variations in other sources of income (Bane and Ellwood, 1986). On some occasions the individual under study is an active participant in change but in others he or she may be a more or less passive victim of it.

32

All surveys are prone to error. Sampling error is covered in many statistical texts on sampling and non-sampling error has been a subject of increasing interest over the past two decades (O'Muircheartaigh, 1977, 1986). However, temporal studies call for repeated observations which generate many more variables and substantially increase the scope for error. Moreover, the focus is often on change, the difference between two measures, each subject to error, made at various times.

In measuring movements in and out of poverty a trade off between precision and reliability is required. This is illustrated by the operational definition of poverty adopted by Bane and Ellwood (1986). They sought to 'adjust' for measurement error and for 'pure randomness', that is movements across the poverty line that happen 'even though no change of any significance to the individual involved' occurs. They did this by eliminating one year spells of poverty or relative prosperity if the spells either began or ended with an income change that was less than one-half of the needs standard (Bane and Ellwood, 1986: 7). This adjustment reduced the number of people experiencing poverty during the thirteen-year observation period by 5.5 per cent and the number of people having multiple spells by 12 per cent.

Measures to cope with sample attrition over the life of a survey also typically have the effect of reducing the amount of change which is recorded. Observations on individuals who are not present in every year are usually omitted although their absence from the survey may well be explicable in terms of some relevant change in their circumstances. Alternatively missing observations may be replaced by estimates resulting from some smoothing or averaging procedure.

Arbitrary poverty levels

Poverty lines are essentially arbitrary thresholds imposed on a distribution of income to needs ratios[3]. The higher the poverty line is placed in relation to the median of the distribution, the higher the likelihood that a person's income/needs ratio at any point will fall beneath it and that they will be defined as being poor. Table 2.7 demonstrates this effect for a sample of Americans observed over a 16 month period commencing in 1984. When the poverty threshold was set at 50 per cent of the official standard, poverty was experienced by only 16 per cent of individuals. However, the proportion rose to 30 per cent and 58 per cent when the threshold was raised to 100 per cent and 200 per cent respectively.

Table 2.9
Percent of population with spells of low-income, by percentage of monthly poverty thresholds (1984-5)

Percentages

Spell duration:	Percent of poverty threshold:					
	50%	75%	100%	125%	150%	200%
No spell	84.0	77.1	70.0	62.8	55.8	42.4
Spell of 6 months or less	11.3	14.5	17.3	19.9	22.1	25.0
Spell of 7 to 12 months	3.1	4.8	6.6	8.6	10.6	14.5
Spell of more than 12 months	1.6	3.6	6.1	8.7	11.5	18.1
Total with spell	16.0	22.9	30.0	38.2	44.2	57.6

Source: Calculated from a 16 month sample drawn from the first five waves of the 1984 Panel of the Survey of Income and Program Participation. Spells shown are those observed during the 16 month period, with no adjustments for censoring. (Ruggles, 1988)

Altering the poverty line will also affect classifications of temporal patterns such as those of Ray and Ashworth discussed above. Table 2.10 presents a sensitivity analysis of the Ashworth, Hill and Walker (1991) typology which shows the effect of altering the poverty line by 25 per cent. While the rank ordering by size of the six categories remains constant (as does the socio-demographic profile of each group which is not shown in the table, see Ashworth et al. (1992)), the number of children suffering permanent, chronic and recurrent poverty falls noticeably. Moreover, while most children appear in the same or adjacent category when the level is

34

Table 2.10
The effect of lowering the poverty threshold   Percentages

Types using Official Definition		Types using PSID Poverty Definition						Ever Poor
	No Poverty	Transient	Occasional	Persistent	Recurrent	Chronic	Permanent	
No poverty	100	48	16	7	1			29
Transient		52	49	27	7			10
Occasional			35	4	12			19
Persistent				52	22	0		36
Recurrent				9	58	81	19	2
Chronic						19	24	3
Permanent							58	
TOTAL	100	100	100	100	100	100	100	100
Ever Poor	-	27	8	14	41	5	5	-

changed, children classified as persistently poor when a high threshold is used typically experience a single transient spell rather than the expected series of short ones when the threshold is lowered (see, also, Hill et al, 1993).

Generally lowering the poverty threshold results in a fall in the average spell length. In practical terms, this means that spells of intense poverty tend to be *comparatively* brief. Even so, Table 2.5 shows that in the USA about a third of individuals with incomes below 50 per cent of the official poverty threshold remain in poverty for over six months.

The 'fractal' effect

Whenever the period of observation is expanded, and/or the accounting period is reduced, the greater number of observations means that the chances of recording a fluctuation in the income/needs ratio increases. This phenomenon is perhaps best viewed as being the temporal counterpart of the topological concept of fractals (Mandelbrot, 1972). In biology, for example, it has been shown that the surface area available for living creatures expands as the resolution of the observation (or magnification) is increased (Lawton, 1986). Similarly, analyses in the USA based on the Survey of Income and Program Participation are beginning to show that the long spells of uninterrupted poverty identified using annual information, mask substantial variations from month to month. The process could be continued to absurdity. For example, if an hourly standard was used, a millionaire who wished to make a purchase but who had forgotten his or her wallet might be counted amongst the poor. What this example makes clear, however, is that the choice of time period is important, and that the choice should fit the purpose of the investigation.

Conclusion

Time is important in the definition and measurement of poverty irrespective of whether its role is made explicit. However, making time explicit offers new insights into both the nature of poverty and its social and personal meaning.

Cross-sectional data can be likened to a single frame extracted from a motion picture. The frame may be studied in detail but the social processes that drive the story line are lost. The danger is that conclusions derived from studying the frame misrepresent the true nature of the plot. Thus, as has been shown above, any picture of poverty which is derived from cross-sectional data will be heavily influenced by the characteristics of the long-term poor. Moreover, the empirical evidence reported from the United States suggests that the distortion which is associated with cross-sectional analyses can be considerable. This is because the people who are temporarily poor, or poor for repeated short spells, far outnumber the permanently poor and differ from them in terms of social-demographic characteristics.

Further distortion, or uncertainty, can be introduced by the process of stilling the dynamics of social life in order to facilitate measurement. The choice of accounting period will determine the extent of poverty recorded. The longer the accounting period, the less the amount of poverty that is recorded; the precise relationship is determined (in part) by the volatility of incomes.

Uncertainty and distortion are inevitable in cross-sectional analyses and there is little that can be done to improve the situation[4]. The lesson to be learnt is that of awareness: awareness of the factors that might lead to distortion and of the need to be careful in the deductions that are drawn from the data. For example, the shift in targeting away from pensioners in favour of families which was intended by the 1988 social security reforms in the UK was influenced by changes in composition of the lowest quintile of the income distribution. The formative analysis was based on the cross-sectional Family Expenditure Survey and different conclusions might have been drawn had dynamic income data been available (see Chapter 3). Many of the families appearing in the lowest quintile were affected by unemployment and most spells of unemployment are known to be short. On the other hand, pensioners' incomes are presumed to be much more stable (though see Coe, 1988) with the result that more can be expected to have remained poor for long periods.

These methodological problems are not entirely solved by panel studies nor by the explicit consideration of time. Indeed, some new difficulties emerge. Panel studies involve repeated measurements which increases the likelihood of measurement error. The individual has to be taken as the unit of observation because of the instability of families over time. However, this is not always ideal since living standards are usually determined by 'black box' transfers within the family or household unit. More fundamentally, there are no clear guidelines as to the choice of observation period or accounting period. Because different choices yield different answers, it is appropriate to vary the periodicity of measurement according to the purpose of the analysis but this is often impractical.

The principal reason for taking account of time is that the concept of poverty is incomplete without doing so. Setting out for the first time to describe poverty one would ask whether income falls short of needs and, if so, by how much and for how long. Strangely, for reasons which presumably have much to do with the difficulty and expense of longitudinal surveys, attention in Britain has tended to focus on the first question, seldom addressed the second and rarely, if ever, considered the third. The result is a static, undifferentiated concept of poverty which feeds through to a rather fatalistic policy response (see Chapter 3).

The tendency has been to contrast the poor with the non poor and to assume that the poor seldom exchange places with the non poor. This is well illustrated by the search for a poverty threshold, a discongruity in behaviour which can be employed to distinguish people who are poor from those who are not (Townsend, 1979; Hutton, 1991). In its least sophisticated form, this approach is entirely atemporal. It takes no account of the duration of poverty or of people's prior experiences. Rather it assumes considerable homogeneity within the poor and the non poor and heterogeneity between them. The explicit hypothesis is that the poor constitute a distinct group separate, in behavioural terms, from the rest of society. The implicit assumption is that the membership of each group is more or less permanent.

In practice, of course, a proportion of the poor do switch places with the non-poor. For the vast majority of people who ever suffer poverty the experience is not long lived, although the US evidence is that the experience is often repeated. Indeed it is suggested above (see also, Chapter 6) that the different patterns of poverty that individuals experience over time may point to differences in kind rather than simply in degree. It may be that a single transient movement into poverty has a different personal and social significance from either long term unremitting poverty or repeated movements across the poverty divide which is experienced as spells of want interspersed with times of relative prosperity.

Individual spells of poverty should also be differentiated according to their duration and severity. Most people would probably recognise a long spell of poverty as being worse than a short one for it is evident that the shortfall in income accumulates over time. However, the precise nature of the relationships between duration and severity and with personal well-being is open to question. The US evidence suggests that financial severity increases steadily during the first decade of poverty and escalates thereafter

38

(Ashworth, Hill and Walker, 1991) but that any links between duration and well-being, both in the short and long-term, appear complex. During spells of poverty psychological well-being may reflect a complex interplay between factors that change with time: frustrated expectations and stress caused by the need to budget on an exceptionally low income for long periods, contrasting with growing expertise in what may be relatively stable financial circumstances. The inherent uncertainty about whether poverty will ever end is a further consideration that needs to be taken into account.

Finally, to return to a theme developed above, there are important linkages between the temporal patterning of poverty, the distribution of poverty and its social significance. In societies where poverty is highly concentrated among individuals and families that are poor for long periods, the scope for the development of a culture of poverty, isolated from mainstream society, is much greater than elsewhere.

The distribution of the different types of poverty within societies can have equally profound social implications. American data on childhood poverty illustrate this point in dramatic fashion (see Chapter 6). The total duration of poverty suffered by white children is such that every single child could expect to experience one year of poverty. In reality the prevalence of poverty among white children is 30 per cent, not 100 per cent. However, when compared to the experience of black children, the relatively small amount of poverty suffered by white children is spread quite widely. The ratio between annual incidence and prevalence is relatively high (1:3.36) indicating that the durations of individual spells of poverty are quite short. And, while repeat spells are common, 36 per cent of the children who experience poverty once, are poor for a single year.

The picture for black children is very different. So great is the total duration that each black child could expect to experience 6.6 years of poverty. In fact 79 per cent of black children suffer an average of 8.4 years. However, the ratio between incidence and prevalence is only 1:1.77 and just 5 per cent of black children who experience poverty are poor for a single year. It appears, therefore, that black children who are poor for long periods suffer a greater proportion of the total sum of childhood poverty than is the case with white children. This, in turn, is partly because childhood poverty in America is heavily concentrated in the black community.

It is difficult to exaggerate the social and political significance of sub-societal differences of this order. However, the point to be emphasised, is that the differences are apparent only because the temporal dimension of poverty has been made explicit.

Notes

1. Poverty is of course unevenly distributed in space as well as time and this is important in any discussion of the underclass (Wilson, 1991; Adams and Duncan, 1990; Walker and Huby, 1989; Walker and Lawton, 1988).
2. Sample censorship occurs when a spell of poverty occurs before the observation begins (left hand censorship) or ends after observation is completed (right hand censorship).
3. It is recognised that Townsend (1979) and others argue that the poverty thresholds revealed by behavioural measures are not arbitrary.
4. It is possible to use single surveys to collect longitudinal data by means of retrospective questioning but the likelihood of recall errors are generally considered to be very high.

3 The relief of poverty and prevention of dependency

The aim in this and the subsequent two chapters is to explore the consequences of explicitly considering time, and the changes which people experience over time, when thinking about the design and implementation of social assistance and social security schemes. The relief of poverty and the prevention of dependency are considered first. Then Chapter 4 addresses other strategic objectives of social security that have perhaps played a more central role in the development of policy in other European countries: the maintenance of living standards, compensation for income loss and income redistribution. In Chapter 5 the focus shifts to the more practical, but no less important, issues of targeting and benefit administration.

This chapter divides into two. The first part concerns the most important strategic objective to shape British social security, namely the relief of poverty. In the second, space is taken to comment on the issue of benefit dependency which has, over the last few years, become an increasingly important element in policy thinking, certainly as judged by the pronouncements of Ministers.

The chapter begins at the point where Chapter 2 ended: having thought anew about the nature of poverty, how should this affect our policy responses to it?

The relief of poverty

The relief of poverty has always been a central objective of the British social security system. The language used has evolved. Beveridge, in 1942, talked of 'want' and 'squalor' while the 1985 'Reform of Social Security' White Paper (HMSO, 1985) refers to 'meeting genuine need'. Moreover, no administration since World War II has been prepared to countenance the introduction of an official definition of poverty as in the United States. Nevertheless, the greater emphasis given to income testing in Britain than in most other parts of Europe serves as evidence of the greater importance attached to this objective as against, for example, the enhancement of social solidarity (Walker, Lawson and Townsend, 1984; Simpson and Walker, 1993).

No doubt reflecting the emphasis given to the relief of poverty as a policy objective in Britain, considerable attention has been paid to the definition and conceptualisation of poverty in the academic literature (Rowntree 1901; Townsend 1979; Mack and Lansley, 1985; JSP 1987, Atkinson, 1989). Certainly, when editing a book on responses to poverty in Europe during the early 1980s, this British author was shocked by how rarely poverty featured in the intellectual and policy debates of our continental partners (Walker, Lawson and Townsend 1985). Yet despite the increasingly erudite exchanges in scholarly journals the treatment of time has been far from sophisticated.

Indeed, as was demonstrated in Chapter 2, time has been very largely ignored. Estimates of poverty have almost always been based on cross-sectional data and little thought has been given to the choice of accounting period. There must therefore be considerable uncertainty as to the proportion of the British population that has been touched by a personal experience of poverty and some doubt about which groups are most at risk.

The lack of attention paid to time is accompanied by an essentially static conceptualisation of poverty. The definite article used when talking about 'the' poor serves to underline an assumption that the group is unchanging, behaviourally separate from the rest of society, and welded into a class structure that is itself rigid and susceptible only to minor changes.

Debates about the causes and distribution of poverty have also tended to take for granted this static view of poverty and have, in fact, served to reinforce it. At one end of the spectrum are those who view human frailty as the root cause of poverty. Individuals are believed to be poor as a consequence of their own capacities, attitudes and behaviours which have to change if they are to become non-poor. Few proponents of this view hold out much hope that this change will occur. Certainly in the short term or without major social changes that involve the dismantling of the welfare state, the reconstitution of the nuclear family, the promotion of traditional family values and the coercive application of moral rectitude (Green, 1992). Indeed, a number of authors have gone on to argue that the poverty is self-perpetuating and passed from one generation to the next (Joseph, 1972).

The political significance of individualisatic models of welfare have ebbed and waned over the last fifteen years despite receiving little empirical support. But even critics of this approach, who tend to emphasise the structural causes of poverty, offer little real hope that poverty will end or that poor people will be able to make good financially.

Again at considerable risk of over-simplification, the structuralist view is that poverty reflects the existence of low paid jobs in the labour market and in the contractions of the labour market that push workers into unemployment and economic inactivity. Precisely who suffers poverty has much to do with the all embracing effect of class which exerts its influence over income, wealth, education, career, family formation and inheritance. The result is that poverty is largely confined to the working class with the effects of class being mediated and largely compounded by race and gender. As a consequence:

> The majority of the poor today walk along economic paths that are familiar to their parents and which, most probably, will be trodden by most of their children as adults and parents in the future. (George and Howards 1991, p.119)

What neither view of poverty takes sufficiently into account is that spells of poverty begin and end. Moreover, most spells appear to be relatively short; probably very few people remain poor throughout their lives. Focusing on the factors that appear to trigger spells of poverty would seem to open a more productive line of enquiry that may eventually provide a basis for developing a united theoretical structure that reconciles structural and personal models of causation. The empirical foundations for such a theory require the identification of the kinds of event that trigger spells of poverty, specification of the distribution of these events within the population as a whole, and measurement of the differing risk that the events will result in poverty. The set of factors affecting the incidence of poverty generating events and the likelihood the occurrence will precipitate a spell of poverty may possibly turn out to contain both personal characteristics and structural determinants.

Causes, resolution and policy

It is only recently, with the advent of longitudinal data that it has become possible to examine the direct causes of poverty by focusing on transitions in and out of poverty and investigating the conjunction of events that occur

43

at the transition. Needless to say, we are still a long way from developing the integrated theory that is the goal of our enquiry and which might provide the intellectual framework for a positive policy response.

On the causes of poverty

Much of the research to date has focused on the events, or triggers, that immediately precede spells of poverty. Analysis based on PSID data for the USA (Bane and Ellwood, 1986) is reported in Table 3.1. The most important factor associated with the start of a spell of poverty, not surprisingly, is a fall in the earnings of the household head. But, the feature revealed by the table which generated most surprise in the USA was the high proportion of poverty spells which could be linked to other causes, and especially to changes in household composition. Over eight per cent of poverty spells are immediately preceded by the arrival of a child and 11 per cent by the transition to a female headed family. Overall nearly half the spells started with a change in family structure or transition in the life cycle. The publication of similar statistics which showed the dominance of changes in family composition over labour market events as direct precipitants of AFDC receipt (75 per cent were linked to relationship breakdown or the birth of a child) caused equal surprise (Duncan and Hoffman, 1986; Bane and Ellwood, 1986).

However, the impact of even major upheavals in household circumstances does not necessarily have an immediate impact on the risk of poverty. For instance, Bound et al (1989) examined the experience of 571 women of all ages widowed in the PSID sample. Only 19 per cent of the episodes of poverty experienced by these widows began in the first year of widowhood. Fifty-nine per cent began later (the residual 22 per cent of spells relate to those women who were already poor at the time that they were widowed). While the death of a partner will often reduce household income, it also reduces the need for consumption which limits the number of cases in which death is the immediate cause of poverty. Indeed, widowhood can bring financial advantages (life insurance pay-outs, for example) and Bound found that a quarter of the women who were poor prior to being widowed succeeded in escaping poverty in the subsequent five years. This unexpected finding may not, in fact, be linked with insurance since the incomes of the widows involved were seldom a great deal above the poverty line and poor families are typically under-insured.

In 19 per cent of cases the onset of poverty among widows was triggered by a substantial fall in asset income and, in 12 per cent, by a drop in pensions or social security payments. Some of this lost income would have been earned in the dead partner's name and could, therefore, be directly or

44

Table 3.1
Causes of poverty spells, USA

Percentages

| Primary Reason for Beginning | All Persons | Male Headed | | | Members of Families with Children | | | | Single Heads With No Children | | Other Relative of Head |
| | | | | | Female Headed | | Married Couples With No Children | | | | |
		Heads	Wives	Children	Heads	Children	Heads	Wives	Males	Females	
Earnings of head fell	37.9	58.1	57.5	57.1	14.1	14.5	40.1	38.9	32.4	24.6	8.5
Earnings of wife fell	3.7	6.5	6.8	5.6	-	-	7.0	11.4	1.6	-	2.2
Earnings of others fell	7.7	4.5	4.7	4.9	10.1	14.0	3.6	8.5	3.5	8.1	19.5
Unearned income fell	8.0	4.6	7.0	6.1	9.7	11.0	6.7	9.3	4.3	9.9	15.2
Needs/poverty level rose	8.2	15.7	8.7	10.9	7.1	7.6	10.0	2.7	3.8	0.7	7.6
Child* became head or wife	14.7	10.6	13.4	-	20.7	-	32.6	29.2	54.5	41.9	-
Wife became female head	4.7	-	1.9	-	38.3	-	-	-	-	14.8	-
Child of male head became child of female head	6.4	-	-	1.5	-	33.9	-	-	-	-	-
Child was born into poverty	8.6	-	-	13.8	-	19.0	-	-	-	-	47.0
Percent of all beginnings	100.0	8.8	9.5	26.4	8.1	17.8	4.2	4.7	7.3	9.8	3.4

*Includes child and grandchild and other relative of head
Source: Bane and Ellwood (1986)

indirectly attributable to the partner's death. On the other hand, 14 per cent of spells began when the widow reduced her hours of work and 10 per cent when another family member moved out. Moreover, in 52 per cent of cases the poverty was triggered by one of a multitude of disparate factors that defied simple coding.

Similarly, retirement does not necessarily trigger poverty in the ways that might be expected. An analysis, based on the Retirement History Study in the USA (Burkhauser, Holden and Feaster, 1988), found that just over half of the 10.5 per cent of couples who fell into poverty during the first decade of the male's retirement did so immediately. In three-quarters of the cases where couples were separated by death during the survey period any poverty experienced was not connected to retirement. But equally widowhood was implicated in less than a third of cases. The erosion of financial assets was a more important factor, affecting 35 per cent, inflation took nine per cent below the poverty threshold and in 15 per cent of cases the poverty was attributable to a fall in the wife's wages (in some cases her retirement).

In many instances, even events that have dramatic and direct traumatic financial consequences do not cause families to become poor. So, for example, Bound's study of American widows, discussed above, found that although widowhood was associated with a 37 per cent fall in average family income, only a quarter of widows were forced into poverty during the five years following the death of their husband. Similarly, while divorce doubles the risk of poverty among women in America, 87 per cent of divorced women escape poverty altogether in the years immediately following the divorce. For men the poverty rate actually falls from six to four per cent.

These findings are typical of many American studies which in aggregate show that the kind of events likely to be associated with the beginning of spells of poverty are much more common than most observers would have expected but that only a minority result in poverty and destitution. Duncan (1988) discovered that, during the decade 1969-70, well over a third of Americans suffered a fall of 50 per cent in their household income-to-needs ratio from one year to the next but in only a third of cases was poverty the result.

Table 3.2 documents the events implicated in these developments. Labour market events are obviously very important with unemployment accounting for a fifth of the transitions of prime age working males and retirement almost a quarter of those of men aged 56-65. Older men and women who are financially more dependent on their savings, were more susceptible to the effects of falls in asset income, while children and women were more often affected by the financial implications of divorce.

Although not shown in the table, forty per cent of transitions experienced by young people aged between five and 24 were associated with leaving home and becoming a household head or wife.

The frequency with which a life event, or any other form of economic trauma, results in poverty clearly depends on a number of factors including, individuals' prior financial circumstances, their ability and willingness to prepare for such contingencies, and the effectiveness of the social security system in responding to the need. (How far events are predictable and to what extent social security can be focused on them are topics to be discussed in Chapter 4.) One factor which is important is the time which has elapsed since the previous experience of poverty and the characteristics of that earlier episode. This is considered later in this chapter.

The recognition that poverty inducing events are widespread but relatively rarely result in poverty, means that any full explanation of the incidence of poverty has to take account not only of the probability that any particular event occurs, but also of the probability that the event triggers a spell of poverty. Both probabilities are likely to vary dramatically between (groups of) individuals for reasons to do with personal characteristics and the plethora of structural factors associated with their prior social position and spatial location.

Duncan and Hoffman (1985), again in the United States, found that the living standards of 80 per cent of women and children involved in divorce or separation fell in the following year. In a quarter of cases living standards dropped by a third or more and falls of this magnitude were most frequent among black women and those white women who had previously enjoyed high incomes. Despite the fact that both groups of women were particularly susceptible to large falls in income resulting from divorce, we can safely assume that the risk of experiencing poverty as a result was far higher among the first group than among the second (see Chapter 6).

Longitudinal data reveal that the prevalence of predisposing circumstances and the differential incidence of trigger events also combine to determine the risk of poverty among the elderly (Burkhauser, Holden and Feaster, 1988). Couples in the US who retired in the 1980s with an occupational or insurance pension found their incomes dropping by an average of 20 per cent on retirement; nevertheless, living standards were still generally around five times the poverty level. Incomes gradually fell in the first decade of retirement but only five per cent were poor at any time during this period. Even couples who retired without a pension averaged a living standard four times the poverty level and an income no less than 75 per cent of what it had been prior to retirement. Depreciation was no worse than for other groups but because their incomes in work

Table 3.2

Persons in age group with a 50 per cent decrease in the income-to-needs ratio associated with various life events, USA, 1969-79 (percentages)

Demographic status in 1969	Family composition events					Labour market/health events					
	Divorce/ separation of spouse*	Death of spouse*	Birth of a child	Person became household head or wife	Major reduction in work hours of head due to retirement	Major unemployment of household head	Major work loss due to illness of household head	Decrease in work hours of wife	Decrease in work hours of other family members	Large decrease in asset income	Any of the 10 events
Under 5 years old											
White	10	1	9	0	1	16	5	3	6	2	50
Black	11	8	6	0	6	13	7	2	11	0	37
All	10	3	8	0	2	16	6	3	7	2	48
25-45 years old											
Men	5	0	9	2	3	19	9	4	10	8	58
Women	9	3	3	1	4	10	5	3	17	5	52
56-65 years old											
Men	1	0	2	0	23	0	2	15	13	9	58
Women	1	5	0	6	19	1	2	8	10	11	60
66-75 years old											
Men	0	8	0	0	5	0	0	0	7	23	49
Women	0	12	0	14	0	0	0	0	11	22	48

Source: Duncan (1988)

* For persons under 5 years old, these events refer to parent rather than spouse.

and subsequently in retirement had initially been lower, the risk of experiencing poverty in the first decade of retirement rose to virtually one in five. If the husband died his widow faced a one in three chance of being poor.

Social policies are, of course, a mediating influence on the probability of becoming poor as a consequence of some precipitating event. They may also complicate attempts to establish the probabilities involved. For example, Smeeding (1986) has drawn attention to the plight of 'tweeners', elderly Americans who are neither poor nor particularly affluent. Because they cannot afford the health insurance premiums paid by their more affluent peers and do not have access to the means-tested insurance available to elderly people with below poverty cash incomes, they face a level of economic insecurity contingent on poor health far greater than for the other two groups. In Britain, too, significant numbers of people on low to middle incomes find on retirement that their occupational pension contributions and savings have served only to deny them access to housing benefit and other income tested benefits, including residential and community care, and failed to add to their living standards (Walker, Hardman and Hutton, 1989).

So, to conceptualise poverty as occurring in finite spells is to direct attention not only to the events that trigger poverty, but also to the distribution of such events within the population, and to the differing risk that they will result in poverty. In this way the root explanation of poverty is extended backwards in time: poverty is understood not simply as a shortage of money, or the occurrence of an event that leads to a shortage of money, but in terms of the prior circumstances which allow the occurrence of an event to bring about a shortage of income in relation to needs. Translated into policy, this conceptualisation shifts the focus from amelioration towards prevention. In the United States the results of empirical analyses are beginning to identify ways in which prevention may be achieved (Ellwood, 1986: Burstein and Visher, 1986).

Ending poverty

The same conceptualisation of poverty leads to a focus on the factors associated with the end of spells of poverty. Again analyses in the United States created much surprise although the results of those studies are now familiar in Britain. The classic analysis of spells of AFDC receipt is reproduced as Table 3.3 and shows that 35 per cent of spells end with marriage.

Attention has been drawn above to the fatalism that can afflict policy making if a static view is taken of poverty. Longitudinal data rapidly

Table 3.3
Factors associated with the end of spells of poverty

Primary Reason for Ending	All Persons	Members of Families with Children									Other Relative of Head
		Male Headed			Female Headed		Married Couples With No Children		Single Heads With No Children		
		Heads	Wives	Children	Heads	Children	Heads	Wives	Males	Females	
Earnings of head rose	50.2	64.4	59.7	56.2	33.0	26.1	63.8	48.7	80.2	48.7	16.3
Earnings of wife rose	7.2	10.6	12.2	11.7	-	-	12.0	13.8	3.8	0.9	3.5
Earnings of others rose	15.8	12.8	12.1	18.6	18.4	26.2	3.1	5.1	2.7	8.5	37.3
Unearned income rose	13.8	7.7	8.6	8.0	19.0	20.1	16.8	24.4	9.0	20.8	25.4
Needs/poverty level fell	2.5	4.2	0.9	0.9	3.3	3.4	4.4	3.6	4.3	2.3	2.9
Female head became wife	4.7	-	5.9	-	26.4	-	-	3.6	-	18.9	-
Child of female head became child of male head	5.4	-	-	4.7	-	23.2	-	-	-	-	10.7
Child* became head or wife	0.4	0.3	0.5	0.0	-	1.1	0.0	0.8	0.0	0.0	3.9
Percent of all endings	100.0	9.5	10.3	28.2	7.9	16.3	4.5	4.8	6.1	9.6	2.7

*Includes child and grandchild and other relative of head

Source: Bane and Ellwood (1986)

convinces one that few people's financial circumstances are static even those of the 'poor'. People are moving out of poverty all the time and it may be possible to draw policy lessons by contrasting the experiences of those who leave and those who remain behind (though not necessarily for long).

Perhaps the most persuasive evidence of the dynamics of poverty comes from American studies of people poor in old age (Coe, 1988; Burkhauser, Holden and Feaster, 1988). Mostly outside the labour market and living on pensions or other income derived from assets one would have predicted most of them to be permanently poor. Table 3.4 shows that 71 per cent of the elderly who are poor at a given point in time are likely to be poor for a decade or more and that this is much above the corresponding figure for the non-elderly (52 per cent). However, 42 per cent of the elderly who are ever poor are poor for a year or less and only a quarter remain so for a decade or more.

Table 3.4
Length of poverty spells among the US elderly

Percentages

Spell length (years)	Distribution of completed spells for:	
	Persons beginning a spell	Persons poor at a given time
1	42.3	8.0
2	13.3	5.0
3	9.5	5.4
4-9	8.8	10.6
10+	26.1	71.0
	5.3	N/A

Coe (1988)

Similar evidence is available for widows who experience poverty in the United States. Over a third of widows who become poor upon widowhood have escaped poverty within two years (Burkhauser et al 1986) and half of the spells of poverty ever experienced by widows are over within a similar time frame (Hurd and Wise 1987). Bound et al (1989) found that in 22 per cent of cases a widow's move out of poverty coincided with an increase in income from assets, often following the sale of a house or business, while on 20 per cent of occasions it followed receipt of state pensions or means tested income. In twelve per cent of cases the widow was able to earn her way out of poverty but, for nine per cent, the relative prosperity only

51

occurred when a family member came to live with her frequently as a result of failing health. Perhaps, not surprisingly, the time spent in poverty after widowhood seems to increase with the age at which the widow is widowed.

The policy imperative which follows from analyses of the ending of spells of poverty is again proactive. Poverty is not a permanent state to which the appropriate response is amelioration through the provision of benefit to (help) make up the shortfall in income. The task for policy is to devise ways of bringing the spell to an end.

The Clinton administration in the United States is committed to limiting periods of AFDC receipt to two years and his aides are making clear that this does not mean simply withdrawing benefits and leaving families to fend for themselves. Rather the pledge is to put more money into education and training programmes, to give lone mothers child care and transportation to facilitate their working, and perhaps to substitute AFDC with the offer of public sector employment. Also under consideration are options to increase workfare obligations and improve the collection of child maintenance payments from absent parents (DeParle, 1993).

It is not, though, specific policies that flow from a recognition of the dynamics of poverty and of the fact that poverty occurs in spells that begin and mostly end. Instead, it is a change in the objectives of social security policy, away from the relief of poverty towards prevention and active intervention to bring about its end.

Reducing dependency

The prevention of welfare or benefit dependency is not a primary objective of the social security system. Rather it is a secondary objective concerned with adverse consequences that potentially flow from the very existence of social security and from the success that is achieved in attaining the primary objectives. It has to do with social control, with maintaining labour market discipline and with the allocation of limited resources.

Dean and Taylor-Gooby (1992) link the increased salience of the concept in Briain to long-term changes in employment and family structures and to a new right administration keen to cut welfare and reinforce the supremacy of the market and family institutions. The former changes have increased the number of working people who are vulnerable to poverty and are ill-defended by the traditional structure of insurance-based welfare. The term 'benefit dependency', however, did not feature much in debates about the 1985 reforms of social security and it was not until 1987 that Ministers were openly talking about 'dependence' which 'in the long run decreases human happiness and reduces human freedom' (Moore, 1987, p4). By 1993 the reduction of dependency, followed by the encouragement of self-reliance, came top of the list of objectives that successful reform of the social security system could achieve (Lilley, 1993).

Dependency is an over-identified term, meaning different things to different writers, (Dean and Taylor Gooby, 1992; Deacon 1993). (Many of the most influential, even in the British debate, are American.) Some argue that the existence of benefits set at high levels relative to wages makes it rational for people to choose not to work but to live on benefits (Murray, 1984, 1990). Others suggest that benefits facilitate those not wanting to work not having to (Mead, 1984). Yet others have proposed that being on benefit itself generates a dependency culture, strong enough to be passed from one generation to the next (Lewis, 1966; Joseph, 1982), that erodes values of self-reliance and self-sufficiency and engenders, at best, feelings of despondency and a loss of self esteem and, at worst, creates a counter culture, an underclass, based on drugs and crime (Auletta, 1982).

There is a sense, too, in which the term is demeaning almost regardless of how it is used. While any society comprises a network of mutual interdependencies, dependency on the state is associated with personal failure. In Britain, Dean and Taylor-Gooby (1992) found that the word most frequently used by long-term benefit recipients to describe their relationship to the state was 'degrading'. Under the Poor Law system this sense of degradation was deliberately created as a deterrent or rationing device through imposition of the less-eligibility principle. Indeed, Dean and Taylor-Gooby would argue, following Foucault (1977), that dependency is used symbolically to 'divide and brand' as part of the exclusionary processes of class-based societies:

> 'Independence implies the norm of the wage relation and the mutually self-sufficient family; dependency implies the 'abnormal' and, in particular, unemployment or single parenthood and the receipt of welfare benefits' (Dean and Taylor-Gooby, 1992, p.45).

One common element embodied in the use of the term dependency is a concern with duration, long durations in poverty and especially on benefit. This is so even in Britain where official usage of the term is perhaps primarily driven by a concern at the overall level of spending. While most analyses are based on point of time estimates, with all the inherent inaccuracy that implies (see Chapter 2), Ministers clearly believe that increasing durations were a 'powerful factor' in the growth in social security expenditure in recent years (Lilley, 1993). Given that this is the case, it may be helpful briefly to consider what longitudinal studies can reveal about the existence, or otherwise, of what has been called welfare dependency.

A distinction is made between long-term dependency, repeat spells of receipt (termed 'recidivism' in the United States) and intergenerational transmission of dependency. As noted above the term dependency is troublesome in that it implies social failure, delinquency or antisocial behaviour. In reviewing the research which focuses on the duration of benefit receipt, 'reliance' on benefit is perhaps a more accurate term to use than dependency.

Long-term receipt

The three important empirical questions to ask are:

a)   What proportion of people spend substantial periods in receipt of benefit?

b)   Is there any relationship between the time spent on benefit and the chances of moving off benefit?

c)   Do long-term recipients have characteristics that distinguish them from other recipients? and, if so,

A fourth question has as much to do with values as fact:

d)   Do the characteristics constitute 'justifiable' reasons for remaining on benefit?

These questions clearly need to be asked in the context of policy objectives. It may, for instance, be considered appropriate for some groups of benefit recipients (pensioners and people with disabilities for example) to remain on benefit for long periods. In this case other questions would need to be asked relating to the adequacy of benefits to sustain the living standards of recipients for long periods and the social status accorded to long term recipients, etc.

Table 3.5 shows the duration of AFDC receipt derived from an analysis of the PSID data using the 'spells' methodology described in Chapter 2. It shows that, while the median spell length for women is in the order of two years, an eighth of spells last for a decade or more. When account is taken of women who experience more than one spell on benefit the median durations increase noticeably: the median time spent on benefit is around four years and nearly a quarter of women receive benefit for 10 years or more. Because of the accumulation of long term recipients within the system they constitute the majority of the case load at any one time (see Chapter 8).

Table 3.6 provides similar information for the US Food Stamp programme. This benefit is intended for short term use and mean spell length is under two years. However, even for this benefit, one spell out of every 15 lasts for a decade or more.

On this occasion there is some evidence on British claimants. The recent DSS study of lone parents (Bradshaw and Millar, 1990) was able to estimate the length of time for which lone parents received Income Support or supplementary benefit. Unfortunately the estimates were derived from a cross-sectional sample and therefore understate, to an unknown but probably considerable extent, the number of lone parents who spend only a short time on benefit. The simulations indicate that the median length of time spent on benefit by the 'average' lone parent was twelve years. Similarly, it is known that 7.5 per cent of the people currently registered as unemployed have been unemployed for over three years. (In April 1990, the corresponding figure was 11.5 per cent, EG. 1991). Chapter 8 shows that while most claims for Family Credit are short, those staying on benefit for six years or more will soon account for 30 per cent of the caseload.

While only a minority phenomenon, long-term reliance on welfare benefits would nevertheless appear to be important. Analysis of the dynamics of AFDC (Ellwood, 1986)) showed that longer durations were systematically related to claimant characteristics. Longer periods of benefit receipt were associated with poor education, limited work experience, single status, and having three or more children and possessing a disability which limited employment. Mothers with children under school age also experienced slightly longer spells (with a child under three the average period of receipt was 4.8 years compared to 3.2 years when the youngest child was aged 6-10) but this factor seemed less important than the others.

Similar factors were associated with long spells of Food Stamp receipt in America. In this case, however, spells were longest among elderly couples and single people, although lone parents also tended to claim food stamps for longer periods than average. Food Stamp recipients who were also receiving AFDC typically used Food Stamps for up to two and a half years longer than other groups. Where local unemployment rates were higher, durations were longer: an increase of a percentage point increased average durations by between five and eight months for households without children.

The factors which appear to be associated with long spells of Supplementary Benefit receipt by British lone parents are similar to those found with respect to AFDC receipt in the US: large families, long term

Table 3.5
Expected total time on AFDC & exit rates for female AFDC recipients

Expected total time on AFDC	Women beginning a first spell of AFDC	Length of first spell	Women receiving AFDC at any point in time	Exit rates
1 Year	15.7	29	2.4	.27
2 Years	14.1	19	4.3	.28
3 Years	9.4	10	4.3	.19
4 Years	10.9	11	6.5	.29
5 Years	5.1	3	3.8	.08
6 Years	8.3	7	7.5	.32
7 Years	5.9	5	6.2	.26
8 Years	3.8	3	4.6	.15
9 Years	3.3	2	4.5	.15
10 or more Years	23.5	12	56.0	.15
TOTAL	100.0	100	100.0	
Average years of AFDC receipt	6.6(4)*	(2)*	11.6	

Source: *Ellwood (1986)*   *Median length
            Ellwood n.d.*

illness and disability and lack of educational qualifications, although the presence of under school age child appeared to be more important. The receipt of maintenance payments was associated with short spells. Remarriage or cohabitation was associated with 57 per cent of lone parents coming off benefit although only two thirds of these gave reconstitution as the reason. Twenty six per cent of reconstituted families remained in receipt of Income Support.

The fact that specific individual characteristics are associated with particularly long spells of benefit receipt is important in that it points to the possibility of selective targeting (see Chapter 5, and Voges and Rohwer, 1991). However, it does not in itself provide evidence of causation. For example, it is sometimes claimed - albeit with little hard evidence - that the type of person who is attitudinally inclined to remain on benefit may also be more likely to become unemployed or a single mother.

Table 3.6
Lengths of spells of food stamp receipt

Number of years	%	Cumulative %
1	43.0	43.0
2	21.8	64.8
3	9.0	73.8
4	7.0	80.8
5	4.2	85.0
6	1.8	88.5
7	1.8	88.5
8	1.6	90.1
9	2.4	92.5
10	2.0	94.5
11+	5.5	100.0

Mean length in years:	3.22
Unweighted number of spells:	8,627

Source: Burstein and Visher, (1989)

Another question is whether the time spent on benefit makes it increasingly difficult to attain financial independence. This could happen, for example, if people lost heart and ceased looking for work, or if their increasing detachment from the labour force was perceived to be a problem by employers. If this were the case, one would expect to find the chance of a person coming off benefit falling with time (Ellwood, n.d.). One would expect to find a similar result (at a group level) if some people were attitudinally inclined to remain on benefit. This is because over time such people would constitute an increasing proportion of those remaining on benefit. Table 3.5 shows that this does not happen which suggests that, at least in the case of AFDC, people neither become trapped on benefit nor self select to remain on benefit for long periods:

'They remain on benefit a long, long time. Yet they may be stuck there as much because of lack of alternatives than because they have become passive or unmotivated.' (Ellwood, n.d., p. 70).

57

The tables discussed above were sufficient to convince many US commentators that long term reliance on benefit, and welfare dependency, were serious policy problems. Certainly the evidence for AFDC indicated that the majority of current recipients were long term and that the bulk of expenditure was going to meet their needs. Long durations, the persistent claiming of benefits, are necessary, though not sufficient, conditions for the existence of a 'benefits' or 'under' class, the members of which are detached from legitimate employment and may exhibit, or acquire, social mores inconsistent with those of mainstream society. The debate concerning the existence of an underclass in the United States is continuing, but the preliminary evidence from longitudinal studies (Ruggles, n.d.; Wilson, 1991; Hughes, 1988) suggests that the significant number of recipients who claim benefits for long periods results from a lack of opportunities rather than from choice. Long term receipt of benefits by lone parents and the unemployed in Britain has also been cited as a cause for policy concern although there is, as yet, little reliable evidence about the size of the phenomenon (Lilley, 1993).

Repeated claims

It is clear from the previous section that it is not unusual for people to claim benefit more than once. Forty per cent of former AFDC recipients will eventually make another claim, and taking this into account has the effect of doubling the proportion of AFDC recipients who receive benefit for over a decade (Table 3.5). Likewise, Burstein and Visher (1989) found that 32 per cent of recipients who left the Food Stamp programme claimed again within the space of two years.

The fact that considerable numbers of individuals experience repeated spells of benefit receipt leads one to ask whether, for any of a range of reasons, these people are simply prone to experience bouts of poverty, or whether the experience of receiving benefit itself increases the probability that they will need to claim again. These two possibilities, respectively termed the 'heterogeneity effect' and 'state dependence', are difficult to disentangle (See Chapter 2).

The phenomenon of repeat spells of claiming is not confined to the US welfare system. In Germany the families affected have been terrmed 'oscillators' (Butir et al., 1989). In Britain, too, there is evidence of considerable flows of people moving on and off benefit, often quite rapidly. Indeed the extent of repeat claims has placed considerable strain on administrative systems. The Housing Benefit system, fully implemented in 1983, involved the transfer of information between the local offices of the national Department of Health and Social Security and local authority

Housing Benefit sections. The 'on-off' problem, as it came to be known, helped to generate such an administrative overload that the system had to be reformed (Walker, 1985). Likewise the UK system of Social Fund loans was predicated on the assumption that families would only need one loan at a time. In fact multiple loans are extremely common and add greatly to administrative costs (Walker, Dix and Huby, 1992).

Ellwood (1986) has examined whether the characteristics of earlier spells of AFDC receipt materially affect the likelihood of future spells. He discovered that there was no clear pattern between the length of the first spell and the likelihood of repeat claims. Multiple spells appeared more likely among short term AFDC recipients than among long term ones - a quick escape from benefit receipt may not constitute a lasting solution - but rates of reapplication were also high among some individuals with long spells on benefits. However, he did find that the odds of repeat claims declined very sharply as the time since the last spell of receipt increased. So former claimants have almost a one in five chance of returning to benefits within a year of claiming but only a very small, 'essentially zero' chance of returning after seven or more years (Ellwood, 1986, p. 12).

Similar findings have been reported for Food Stamp receipt. If a repeat claim is not made within a few months, a case is much less likely to be reopened at all. Repeat claims were significantly more likely in areas with high unemployment rates. Younger people and families were more likely to make several claims although, in part, this may simply reflect death as a reason for closure among cases involving elderly recipients. Likewise, in Britain, it appears to be the most disadvantaged families that are likely to claim Family Credit on separate occasions; notably those with the lowest earnings, especially lone mothers (Chapter 8).

The reasons why people need to make repeated claims have yet to be studied in detail. In part the phenomenon may simply reflect technical factors such as a person's benefit being withheld while seeking further information, although the analyses reported above have sought to exclude repeat spells of this sort. (Factors linked to benefit administration, which result in a process described as 'churning' in the United States, are discussed in the next chapter). In some cases people's incomes may have moved so marginally above means tested thresholds that the smallest drop in income may cause the person to fall back onto benefit. Some individuals may misjudge their own earning potential or find it difficult to hold down the new job.

Unfortunately the analyses of repeat claims have not attempted to distinguish between the heterogeneity and state dependence effects identified by Hill. Consequently it is still far from clear what processes link the repeated spells of time on and off benefit. Nevertheless, the studies do identify repeated claiming as an important feature of welfare use in America. Indeed Ellwood (1986) has calculated that AFDC roll could be reduced by more than 20 per cent if repeat spells were cut by a half.

Benefit careers

Researchers in Germany have made constructive use of the concept of a benefit career to link evidence on long term and repeated receipt with the notion of welfare dependency or its partial opposite, individual autonomy. They recognise five types of career (Buhr et al., 1989). 'Bridgers' experience a single short spell on social assistance, suffer only a temporary loss of social status and no substantial loss in autonomy. In Germany, bridgers often turn out to be people receiving social assistance for the short period while their claims for insurance benefits are being processed. As such they are only momentarily, if ever, truly dependent whereas 'escapers', the second career type, do spend considerable periods in receipt of social assistance but nevertheless manage eventually to move off benefit. Buhr et al cite examples of people who manage to gain educational qualifications while on social assistance, others who marry out of benefit and yet others who move first into supported employment and then off benefit altogether. Nevertheless, relatively few welfare recipients appear to experience such a successful end to their benefit career.

'Oscillators', who move back and forth onto benefit, face the imminent loss of their autonomy. In the German context, many oscillators appear always to be at financial risk, inhabiting the world of ever more precarious employment and suffering repeated spells of unemployment.

Socially there is little difference between the oscillators and those who have already lost status and autonomy and become 'marginalised'. In Germany one symbol of having become marginalised is a gradual reduction in the notes attached to a person's social assistance files. When new to benefit, files are replete with details of support measures offered and implemented but later the picture shifts to the routine handling of clients, almost a matter of shifting paper.

Buhr and her colleagues distinguish between the marginalised, who suffer a loss of status, from other long term recipients which, in Germany, do not. This latter group, which Buhr et al (1991) term the 'externalised', comprises principally old-age pensioners who are no longer engaged in gainful employment. These pensioners are generally not expected to move off welfare and are not the target of policies that have this as their goal. Therefore, rather than suffer dependency as a result of claiming social assistance, welfare payments in this case actually serve to enhance autonomy by supplementing low pensions.

The work of Buhr and her colleagues is important in drawing attention once again to the positive role of welfare benefits, bridging short or long spells of deprivation, while eventually allowing individuals to return to their expected life-course trajectory. The down side, marginalisation, is also recognised and appears to be particularly prevalent in the German system where social assistance is very much residualised. This, and the distinction made between the 'marginalised' and the 'externalised' which has to do with social expectations rather than objective circumstances, serves to emphasise social not personal determinants of dependency.

Benefit receipt across generations

Welfare reliance and poverty extending across generations has attracted considerable attention in both the USA and Britain (Corcoran, et al, 1987; Goldberger, 1989; Duncan, Hill and Hoffman, 1988; Atkinson, Maynard and Trinder, 1983).

Table 3.7 shows the intergenerational pattern of AFDC receipt based on the daughters of welfare families. Medium and high receipt is defined in terms of any AFDC income being received during 2 or 3 years of a 3-year period. The first period coincided with the time when the daughters were aged between 13 and 15 when benefit would have been paid to their parents. The second covered the period when they were aged between 21 and 23 and so would have received the benefit in their own right. The limitations of this comparison are important: observation periods are very narrow and adequate account is not taken of the intermittent nature of AFDC receipt described above. Bearing these restrictions in mind, the table shows that the chances of receiving AFDC were six times higher for women whose parents had been highly dependent on AFDC. Even so, four out of five of the daughters of families on welfare did not receive AFDC during the observation period (Duncan, Hill and Hoffman, 1988).

Other studies have found similar, but not overwhelming intergenerational effects. Hill and Ponza (1983) found that long-term welfare receipt as a child was associated with long-term receipt among white families but not among black ones, while Corcoran et al (1987) found that children from families that had received some form of means tested benefit often exhibited lower educational performance and obtained lower paid jobs.

Table 3.8 compares the earnings of fathers and sons derived from a 1976 follow-up of Rowntree's 1950 survey of 'working class families' in York, England. Rowntree's initial sample does not match up to modern standards and tracing the children of the original respondents proved difficult so that the overall response rate was not high. Nevertheless, the pattern is not dissimilar to that found in the USA.

Table 3.8 shows that the probability of having a wage in the bottom quintile of the earnings distribution is 45 per cent for sons with fathers who earned similarly low wages and only 2 per cent for those with fathers in the second quintile of earnings:

'The [correlation] coefficient relating to earnings of fathers and sons (adjusted for age) is of the order of 0.4 - 0.5 (the latter making allowance for possible measurement error). In this case, it is close to that found for heights and other physical characteristics, but whether it is large or small is a matter for the reader to judge.' (Atkinson, Maynard and Trinder, 1983, p. 179).

An obvious problem in relying on figures such as those presented in Tables 3.7 and 3.8 is that they make no allowance for other relevant characteristics of the individual, family or local environment. When this is done, results are often inconsistent and unstable between one study and another (Ellwood, 1987). There is, though, evidence that part of the

Table 3.7
Intergenerational patterns of AFDC receipt (23)

Dependence of parents (%)	Dependence of daughters (%)				Unweighted number of cases
	No	Moderate	High	Total	
No	91	6	3	100	811
Moderate	62	22	16	100	127
High	64	16	20	100	147

Source: Duncan, Hill and Hoffman (1988)

apparent effect of benefit receipt is simply due to the effect of a low income environment on the socio-economic achievements of children. Duncan et al (1988) examined the experiences of daughters from families that, while not reliant on AFDC, nevertheless had low incomes. They found that 7 per cent received AFDC as adults. For daughters from mother-only families, the percentage relying heavily on AFDC doubled again to 14 per cent.

A recent study (Hill and Ponza, 1989) has sought to explore different definitions of 'dependency' and to take account of neighbourhood and familial influences. In summary, it showed that:

parent to child transmission of welfare dependency ... exists, but its magnitude is small to moderate. The key factor in transmission is the dichotomy of ever receiving welfare, with the level of dependency of welfare recipients secondary in importance. Welfare dependency is difficult to predict, and parental welfare dependency is one of the few identifiable predictors. However, other factors such as parent's education and county unemployment rate are of comparable importance; (Hill and Ponza, 1989, p. 7).

It is appropriate to this section to reference Ellwood's (1985) extensive review of the American literature on welfare 'dependency'. He concluded that there was a modest connection across the generations with the offspring of families relying heavily on benefits more likely to become welfare recipients themselves. He noted, also, that it would in fact be astounding to discover that economic mobility across generations was complete and so some relationship was to be expected. What could not be assumed, however, was any precise pattern of causal links although 'the proposition that heavy dependency almost inevitably leads to dependency of the children because of the cultural links between parent and child (could) be rejected' (p. 56) in the American context.

Ellwood's review addressed each of the three aspects: long-term receipt, repeated claims and receipt across generations of reliance on benefits covered in this section: it also sought to evaluate various theoretical models that have been used to explain dependency against the available empirical evidence, much of it stemming from longitudinal studies. He concluded that choice models, which emphasise the limited options open to AFDC recipients and the adverse incentives which they face, equate best with the available evidence: 'work often makes little sense unless (1) the woman works full-time, (2) she commands a wage well above the minimum (3) day care costs are low, (4) available benefits are low' (p. 24). Expectancy models, which attach weight to limited self confidence, poor information and perceived lack of control, and cultural models, which stress deviant values and cultural mores, received much less empirical support.

Interim conclusions

Taken together with findings from Chapter 2, the policy implications that result from adopting a temporal perspective on the relief of poverty and the prevention of dependency are clearly profound. While they do not

Table 3.8
Transition matrix: fathers and sons

Age-adjusted hourly earnings

Income-range for fathers	Income-range for sons					
	Top 20%	Second 20%	Middle 20%	Fourth 20%	Bottom 20%	Total
Top 20%	-	-	-	-	-	-
Second 20%	2	2	3	5	2	14
	(14.3)	(14.3)	(21.4)	(35.7)	(14.3)	
Middle 20%	8	8	18	11	6	51
	(15.7)	(15.7)	(35.3)	(21.6)	(11.8)	
Fourth 20%	23	23	40	47	40	173
	(13.3)	(13.3)	(23.1)	(27.2)	(23.1)	
Bottom 20%	12	23	19	21	61	136
	(8.8)	(16.9)	(14.0)	15.4)	(44.9)	
Total	46	56	82	84	109	374

Notes:

1) The figures in parentheses are the percentages for the row.
2) There are two reasons for the difference in the sample size between the top and the bottom tables. First, age information is missing for one case. Second, the age adjustment reduces the number in the top 20 per cent of fathers, so that omission of this group leaves out three rather than five cases. There is therefore a net increase of one case.

Source: *Atkinson, Maynard and Trinder (1983)*

necessarily point to a specific policy agenda (see Chapter 10), they certainly demand a new way of thinking.

The poor are seen not to be a discrete group separate and disconnected from the rest of society. The evidence, albeit mostly from the USA, is that most spells of poverty are short. Moreover, there is very little empirical support for cultural models of benefit dependency. This is the case despite the fact that poverty is very inequitably distributed with some people spending long periods living on inadequate incomes and claiming benefits.

Poverty is dynamic. The formerly poor are continuously switching places with (a relatively small proportion of) the formerly non-poor. Poverty, however, is harmful with some long term effects, certainly at a personal and, arguably, at a societal level too. But since the poor are always changing, change is clearly possible. Moreover, it should prove possible to learn from the changes that occur. The reason for so doing is to develop policies that seek not reactively to relieve poverty but proactively to prevent and curtail it.

Longitudinal analysis demonstrates that spells of poverty are triggered by a range of different kinds of event, some of which are avoidable and others which, though not, can be ameliorated in their effect. Prevention emerges as an appropriate and attainable goal. Likewise, it is clear that most spells of poverty eventually end and that many people escape from poverty for long periods, perhaps, for ever. Identifying the factors that provide the keys to escape, especially if they are amenable to policy intervention, adds another pro-active policy objective to prevention, namely to bring spells of poverty to an early end.

Poverty can be differentiated according to cause and type. The factors that trigger poverty are almost infinite but may, in the first instance, be viewed as reducing the family's resources, increasing claims on the family budget or both. The probability that a trigger occurs is related to a person's position on a number of socio-economic dimensions relating to class, gender, ethnicity, locality etc. Whether a trigger results in poverty similarly depends on the cultural, personal and financial networks in which those affected are located and the financial, personal, intellectual and emotional resources that the persons can call upon.

Most spells of poverty are over quickly - though this depends on the precise cause - and some people are never again poor; indeed the risk of further poverty rapidly subsides as the time since the last spell increases. Many experience repeated spells for it seems that the risk of poverty is significantly increased by a previous spell. Whether this effect arises from an erosion of the financial, emotional or social and family resources that serve to protect people from poverty is not yet clear. (Indeed, one of the major contributions still to be made by longitudinal studies is to document the long-term, and not so long-term, effects of poverty.)

Thankfully, the number of people who suffer poverty continuously for long periods would appear to be very small although the accumulation of these families in cross-sectional data, and in social security casefiles, serves to exaggerate their prevalence. However, their importance in policy terms may be difficult to exaggerate. Not only do they account for a disproportionate amount of social security expenditure, a necessary consideration if Treasury officials are to support policy development, certainly in the US they represent a level of personal suffering inconsistent with advanced western societies (Chapter 6). While it would be wrong to ignore the other kinds of poverty, and still worse to design policies to benefit the long term poor at the expense of other groups of poor people, the long term poor have to be a policy priority.

Indeed with poverty occurring in so many guises the challenge is to tailor policies to meet the different needs. This may not be a problem unique to anti-poverty programmes. Indeed, Williams (1991, p.8) presents it as the fundamental issue for modern social policy:

> 'to resolve the tensions between universal principles and policies, on the one hand, and the recognition of diversity, on the other. In other words, how to have welfare provision which is universal in that it meets all people's welfare needs, but also diverse and not uniform, reflecting people's own changing definitions of difference, and not simply the structured differentiation of the society at large.'

4 Income maintenance, compensation and redistribution

This chapter examines three other objectives of social security: compensation; maintenance of living standards; and redistribution. Once again the aim is to explore the consequences of making temporal considerations central to our thinking.

Compensation and the maintenance of living standards are considered together in the first part of the chapter. At various times both have been major and explicit objectives of British social security policy although the importance of both may currently be on the wane. Neither, however, has ever received the same emphasis as in countries where policies obtain their impetus from the tradition of Bismarck rather than from that of Beveridge with its focus on the relief of poverty (Pieters, 1991; Walker, Lawson and Townsend, 1985).

Redistribution is examined in the second part of the chapter. Social security almost inevitably achieves some measure of horizontal and vertical redistribution. Vertical redistribution has rarely featured as a central component in the social security agenda of any British government, yet the evidence from cross-sectional studies is that social security provisions are far more effective than fiscal policy in this regard (CSO, 1992). Moreover, as the direct tax system became less progressive over the 1980s, so the redistributive contribution of social security became ever more important. The trend was exaggerated by the recession of the early 1990s which substantially increased the numbers in receipt of benefits. With moves further to enhance the role of indirect taxation, which is at best neutral in terms of its redistributive impact and frequently regressive, the importance of social security in this regard looks set to increase in Britain.

Compensation and the maintenance of living standards

There was a period, most noticeably during the 1970s, when the objective of employing the social security system to help maintain living standards was more clearly evident in Britain than it is today. At that time, for reasons that probably had more to do with attempts to constrain expenditure than with matters of high principle, unemployment benefit and national insurance pensions had been made earnings related. Higher waged workers paid larger premiums in exchange for better benefits. Although a measure of redistribution in favour of the lower paid was retained, the structure had much in common with continental systems of social insurance that emphasise social solidarity and the maintenance of living standards.

Since then, in response to the same concern about expenditure and a new sensitivity to the possible work disincentive effects of higher benefit levels, earnings related unemployment benefit has been abolished and the earnings related component of the state pension (SERPS) downgraded. Nevertheless, some remnants of this philosophy are still apparent in what remains of SERPS and especially in occupational pension schemes that almost always link pensions to final salary.

Compensation for loss of faculty and loss of income are important goals in British industrial injuries and war pension provisions and have been so for a very long time. With the expansion of coverage to non industrial injuries and disabilities, a feature of the 1970s, and the increased uptake of these benefits throughout the 1980s, there has been increased debate about the way in which these objectives are interpreted. Moreover, a third compensatory element, to cover the increased direct and indirect costs associated with the incapacity, has become more evident. At the time of writing (July 1993), however, more concern is being expressed about the growth in expenditure on disability benefits than about their success as tools of compensation.

A key task in the implementation of income maintenance benefits is to determine the level of income or living standard previously attained by the applicant. The corresponding task in relation to compensatory benefits is to assess the income or living standard that would have been achieved were it not for the injury or incapacity that is the cause of the claim for compensation. Time engages in these parallel tasks in three principal ways.

First, living standards are shown to fluctuate as a result of variations both in income and needs. Secondly, incomes and living standards tend to be characterised by secular trends related, at a societal level, to economic growth but also, at an individual level, to progress through the life course.

68

Even so, much of the fluctuation in living standards that is observed appears to be unexpected and unpredictable. Finally, current living standards are influenced by past decisions and experiences.

Fluctuating incomes and needs

In operationalising social security schemes which seek to maintain incomes a key question becomes 'which income to maintain?'. The conceptual and measurement issues discussed in relation to poverty (Chapter 2) apply equally to longitudinal data relating in income and needs. (Indeed, the discussion on poverty was limited to the small subset of income fluctuations which took individuals across a poverty threshold.) Increasing the observation period and reducing the accounting period are both likely to increase the degree of instability recorded. Table 4.1 presents data on annual earnings for American males for the period 1967 to 1978. Unfortunately more recent data is not readily available. What the table reveals is a degree of change that in the early 1980s would have 'come as a shock to the analyst brought up seeing smooth, parabolic wage-earning profiles of the "typical" worker' (Duncan and Hoffman, n.d. p. 49). Less than two fifths of Caucasian Americans and a half of Afro-Americans ended the period in the same earnings quintile as they had begun. Not only were income shifts ubiquitous, many were substantial. Almost a quarter of Caucasians moved at least two quintiles as did an eighth of Afro-Americans.

If longitudinal data have revealed large variations over time in the level of earnings, the evidence of change is even more striking with respect to needs. Take, for example, family composition. By the eighteenth year of the Panel Survey of Income Dynamics in America, two-thirds of families were headed by someone other than the person who had headed the 'same' family when the survey began (Duncan and Morgan, 1985). For this reason almost all recent longitudinal studies, including the British Household Panel Study, have chosen the individual rather than the family as the unit of observation.

a)   Permanent income. When discussing fluctuating incomes Friedman (1957) made a distinction between permanent and transitory income. The latter can be likened to the scatter around a trend line which designates permanent income. Permanent income is presented as a more important determinant of expenditure and living standards than transitory income and theoretically, therefore, a better datum against which to assess earnings replacement through the benefits system. Assumptions about the level of 'permanent' income are frequently incorporated into macro economic models used to predict future consumption (Christiano et al, 1991). The problem is how to establish the trend line.

Table 4.1
Earnings mobility between 1967 and various years, by race, USA*

Mobility between 1967 and:	Proportion in same quintile		Proportion moving at least two quintiles	
	Caucasian	Afro-Americans	Caucasian	Afro-Americans
	%	%	%	%
1968	58.8	64.9	7.5	8.1
1970	52.7	53.9	12.4	11.3
1972	47.3	51.3	14.1	10.6
1974	46.1	56.0	18.2	13.0
1976	39.0	38.2	23.0	18.6
1978	38.7	48.6	23.0	13.7

Source: *Duncan and Hoffman (1981)*

*   For all male household heads, age 25-50 in 1968 with 500 hours worked each year between 1967 and 1978.)

In the absence of longitudinal information on earnings the traditional approach has been to rely on theoretical models which attempt to explain differences in the level of earnings. One early, though still influential, human capital model is that proposed by Mincer (1974) which postulated that income was a function of educational attainment, labour market experience and an error term. The error term was taken to embrace transitory earnings. However, models based on cross-sectional data such as Mincer's cannot incorporate variables which change over time: period variables for example, which relate to the prevailing economic conditions at the time; or cohort variables which index the unique circumstances which face persons born at a given time, such as the quality of schooling they receive, or the state of the labour market at the point when they leave school.

To take account of these factors requires panel data. One approach is that adopted by Gottschalk (1982) which can be used when the run of longitudinal data is short. This involves regressing actual earnings against time. The slope coefficient is then interpreted as the secular trend indexing permanent income and the error term as transitory income. Gottschalk found that the trend of the permanent earnings profile was flattest for those on middle incomes and steepest for those on highest and lowest incomes. The steeper trend at lowest incomes no doubt reflects people in the first years of their career. Those with permanent low incomes had socio-demographic characteristics associated with the long-term American poor (see Chapters 2 and 6).

Panel data also enable permanent income to be measured more directly. With sufficiently long runs of data it is possible to specify separate earnings equations for each individual so as to determine their personal life time trajectory and to identify transitory changes in incomes. So far this has not been attempted. However, Figure 4.1a plots the family incomes of individuals in the PSID sample at various points in the life course. This is achieved by averaging incomes over an eleven year period (1969-1979), inflating incomes to 1985 levels and differentiating individuals according to their age in 1969 and their sex. Family incomes peak when individuals are in their prime earning years and subsequently fall as they retire. Incomes increase during childhood because, as they get older, childrens' incomes add to those of their parents that tend to be higher than those of younger parents. This pattern is echoed in the life course analysis undertaken for Britain using the Family Expenditure Survey which is reported in Figure 4.2 (broken line).

The pattern of rising and falling income during the life course is well appreciated and is often viewed as the outcome of conscious choices made by family members in relation to labour supply, reflecting personal investment in education, training and work experience (Duncan, 1988). Labour market income is a crucial component in the family income mix and increases in response to investments in training etc. in the early years. The decline in earned income later in life is partially compensated for by income from earlier voluntary and compulsory savings, the latter being determined by a mixture of state, occupational and commercial schemes.

The American evidence reveals that the gap between the family incomes of men and women increases substantially over the life cycle as a result of the increased number of women without spouses who come to head their own families (Burkhauser and Duncan, 1989). Figure 4.3 confirms the disadvantaged position of women but shows that the pattern of disadvantage emerges during the early years of adulthood. The figure is based on a quasi cohort analysis of young people in Britain, in which the circumstances of

Figure 4.1a
Eleven-year average total family income by age and sex (1969-79)

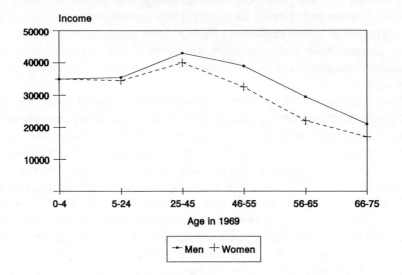

Figure 4.1b
Eleven-year average total family income-to-needs by age and sex (1969-79)

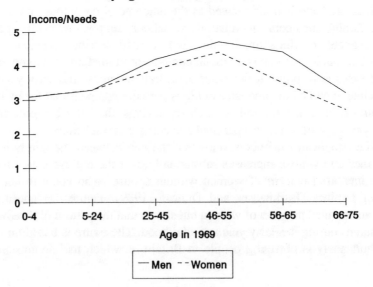

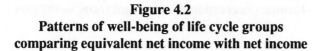

Figure 4.2
Patterns of well-being of life cycle groups
comparing equivalent net income with net income

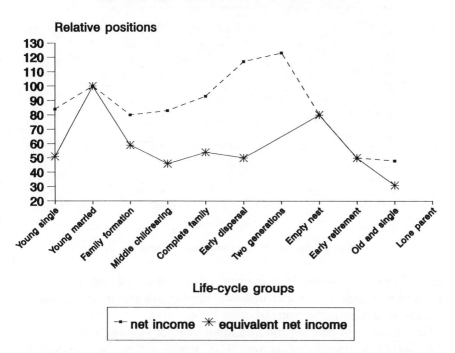

individuals aged 16-20 included in the 1963 Family Expenditure Survey are compared with those of individuals aged 21-25 in the 1968 survey, those aged 26-30 in the 1973 survey and so on (Hutton, 1991). It shows that the average personal income of the cohort of young men grew rapidly, starting some way below average male earnings, exceeding it by the age of 30, and continued to grow thereafter until the data series ended. However, no such 'career' is evident for women. Instead, their incomes accurately reflect the overall growth in female earnings with the result that, while, at age 16-20, female incomes averaged 69 per cent of male, by age 41-45 they had fallen to only 40 per cent. The reasons for this lie partly in the home care responsibilities assumed by women, and a consequent fall in labour market participation, but also in the segmented labour market which means that women tend to work in jobs with limited career prospects (Hutton, 1991; Glendinning and Millar, 1987).

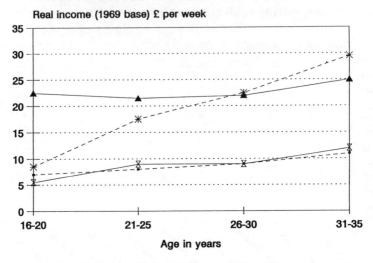

Figure 4.3
Income progression for men and women, 1973-88

Real income (1969 base) £ per week

Age in years

▲ Men ⊼ Women ✳ Trend line men ⁻⁺⁻ Trend line women

b)   *Transitory income.* If it is seemingly possible to detect a pattern of permanent income which nevertheless varies through the life cycle, what is the nature of transitory income?

One approach to defining and measuring transitory income is that adopted by Gottschalk mentioned above. This involves first determining the empirical relationship between time in employment and the earnings. From the resultant equation it is then possible to examine the variability of each individual's earnings over time and to calculate the proportion which would be explained by a person moving along his or her own trend line. The residual is interpreted as transitory changes in income. In Gottschalk's sample of middle-aged US males during the period 1966 to 1975, 70 per cent of variation in income appeared to be due to transitory fluctuations. When Gottschalk averaged individual's income over the survey period, he found that transitory, unpredictable changes in income were most marked among those groups of men with the highest and lowest average earnings.

An important feature of transitory income is its unpredictable nature. As a consequence it may have lower utility since it denies people the opportunity to plan and to borrow on the basis of assured cash flows. Benus (1974) established a trend line based on the wage progression of cohorts of individuals defined in terms of race, sex, years of schooling and work

74

experience, and then decomposed individual variations about this line into a constant trend reflecting individual characteristics and residual unpredictable variation. Unpredictable income was common in the lowest quarter of the income distribution, fell throughout the middle ranges of income and rose again (albeit to proportionately lower levels) only around the top decile. This confirms the U-shaped relationship between income instability and average income found by Gottschalk. Indeed, Benus found that average income was in fact the best predictor of income instability. It was followed by occupation (very high among the self-employed, farmers and to a lesser extent, labourers), age (highest when young and old) and the local unemployment rate.

To summarise, it would appear that there is a patterning of income fluctuations associated with progression through the life cycle which may well differ between men and women. However, at the individual level this patterning is confused by seemingly random, or at least unpredictable, changes in income.

c)   *Changes in living standards.* Given that income and family composition both fluctuate rapidly, it is not surprising to find that the same is true of living standards which are typically defined in terms of the relationship between income and needs, the latter indexed by household composition. Moreover, it would appear that there are again changes that are linked to movements through the life course which are in broad terms predictable, and those which are not. The effect of shifting from a simple measure of income to an index of living standards based on the income-to-needs ratio is evidenced by comparing Figure 4.1a with 4.1b and the broken and solid lines in Figure 4.2. The relative position of families whose children have left home is enhanced while the position of pensioners falls in relation to that of children. The pattern of relatively low living standards in childhood, during child-rearing and throughout old age is the same as that documented by Rowntree (1901) in York at the turn of the century.

This description of the changes in living standards that occur over the life course is based on group averages and requires considerable qualification when the same individuals are followed over time. Age related movements in living standards remain evident but equally there are substantial variations that are seemingly not related to age. This is clear from an analysis of 11 years of the US Panel Survey of Income Dynamics during the 1970s (Duncan, 1988). It revealed the expected improvements in the living standards of children and men aged 25-40 and corresponding falls in living standards around retirement and during old age. These movements were

75

considerable. Increases in living standards averaged three per cent per year, or 40 per cent over the 11 year period. Living standards fell by an average of one third between age 55 and 65.

However, life course dynamics were not the only cause of substantial movements in living standards. Table 4.2 records the percentage of men and women who experienced very rapid increases or reductions (averaging 5 per cent each year) in their standards of living over the same 11 year period. Changes of this magnitude mean either a 70 per cent increase in living standard or a fall in the region of half. The chances of substantial improvements in living standards were highest in early life and lower later, but counter-intuitive movements were far from rare at any stage.

Table 4.2 also records cases when the income-to-needs ratios of individuals in the PSID sample fell by half or more between one year and the next. Falls of this order occurred in a substantial 31 per cent of cases and, while the incidence was greatest for people around retirement age and least for men in the prime working years, the patterning across the life cycle was not very marked. Table 3.2, in the previous chapter, lists the factors which appear to be associated with the falls in living standards. Some of these vary with life course position: falls in wage incomes at retirement and during the pre-retirement years, household formation among young people, child birth affecting families and especially other children in the family and divorce among young women. Others were linked to labour market factors and to sickness and were not clearly related to the life course.

Well over three-quarters of all individuals in the PSID sample experienced one of the events listed in Table 3.2 (Chapter 3) during the 11 year period. Whether the event resulted in a substantial drop in living standards and whether this fall was long lasting depended in part on prior income, age and gender. The living standards of divorced women fall on average by two thirds in the year following divorce. If they do not remarry their living standards vary little in the next five years, while the economic position of those women who remarry is typically higher than before the divorce. Income from employment is important in protecting living standards and so is alimony or maintenance. However, alimony paid by ex-husbands from previously high income marriages falls precipitously so that after five years payments are, on average, less than those made by low income husbands (Burkhauser and Duncan, 1987).

Pension income cushions the fall in living standards and retirement but, in America, the depreciation in pension income is relentless. Nevertheless, the

Table 4.2
**Fraction of various age cohorts of individuals
with various changes in income-to-needs (1969-1979)**

Demographic status in 1969	Percentage with income/needs:				
	Keeping up with inflation (>)%)	Growing very rapidly (>5%) per year	Declining very rapidly (<-5%) per year	Doubling at least once	Falling by 50% or more at least once
Less than 5-years old					
All	60	23	11	30	27
5-24 years old					
Men	71	38	11	42	33
Women	66	35	13	44	39
25-45 years old					
Men	71	35	6	25	18
Women	67	32	10	27	24
46-55 years old					
Men	61	22	13	25	26
Women	55	21	20	28	33
56-65 years old					
Men	26	7	38	16	38
Women	30	6	35	21	39
66-75 years old					
Men	34	6	17	24	27
Women	37	11	16	26	27
All ages	62	29	14	33	31

*Source: Duncan (1988)
Panel Study of Income Dynamics*

risk of poverty is highest in the year following retirement and subsequently declines for pensioner couples (see Chapter 3). For those who will become widows, the risk of poverty is the same as for other couples in the first year after retirement, but thereafter continues to increase.

Other work has pointed more explicitly to the role of savings in maintaining living standards following traumatic events. The previously mentioned studies included income from savings when calculating falls in the income-to-needs ratios. Adopting a different approach, David and Fitzgerald (1987) found that savings could generally only protect people for limited periods. They calculated that 21 per cent of people who were classified as poor on the basis of their monthly income, net of assets, had sufficient income to tide them over for a month, but only 8 per cent defined as poor on the basis of annual income could support themselves for a year solely by depleting their assets. Mayer and Jencks (1988), in a recent study in Chicago, found that low income families with relatively high earnings in the previous year encountered less hardship (measured on the basis of 10 indicators of budgeting and material stress) because they had been able to accumulate savings or informal credit upon which they could draw. Similarly, in Britain, Heady and Smyth (1989) found that:

> 'Families varied considerably in the living standards they were able to maintain while the head of the family was out of work. ... Two major reasons for this variation in living standards were families' differing stocks of 'domestic capital' and the role that people's savings played in sustaining their levels of current consumption.' Heady and Smyth, (1989)

To summarise, the evidence from longitudinal studies in the United States is that income and living standards are surprisingly volatile. In aggregate terms the long recognised cyclical pattern associated with life course stages is evident and, on average, most people's living standards do move in the anticipated direction. However, significant fluctuations in incomes and changes in family composition are commonplace irrespective of life stage and many individuals experience major changes in living standards.

Predictability of change

It is important to ask how predictable fluctuations are, both at the level of the individual and in aggregate. Predictability allows for the possibility of planning.

In the early years of the PSID survey a question was included asking respondents whether they thought that they would be better or worse off in the next few years. Eighty six per cent of those who experienced a sharp fall in living standards did not anticipate it. Even among respondents approaching retirement no more than 40 per cent of males and around 30 per cent of females predicted a fall in income (Burkhauser and Duncan (n.d.).

In addition to this direct evidence, attempts have been made to predict falls in living standards on the basis of the life course patterning described above. The results are dismal. Only two per cent of the variation in the chance of experiencing a 50 per cent fall in living standard and only seven per cent of the overall variation in family income is explicable in terms of age. Even when race, education, verbal ability and a host of attitudinal measures are added to age, less than ten per cent of the variation in the pattern of living standards over time can be explained (Duncan and Morgan, 1981). Duncan (1988, p. 134) concludes that:

'although varying systematically by age and other life-cycle demographic measures, income trends would not appear to be very predictable if forecast on the basis of these measured characteristics. These same characteristics also fail to explain much of the variance in the stability of family income. Sudden large drops in living standards are neither expected according to respondents' own prior reports, predictable based on respondents' demographic characteristics, nor explicable as the spurious result of measurement error'.

So, while in aggregate the patterning of incomes over time is clear, with the same movements in relative prosperity that Rowntree recognised almost a century ago, accurate prediction by, or on behalf of, individuals appears a long way off. These findings, albeit predominantly based on American data, are consistent with the use of public or private insurance as a funding mechanism for income maintenance provision. The actuarial risk can be readily calculated but individuals themselves are unable to predict whether they will ever need to have recourse to the system.

Redistribution

Each year the CSO publishes analyses of the redistributive effects of UK Government's tax and spending programmes which demonstrate the overwhelming importance of social security as a mechanism for reducing income inequalities. While redistribution per se may not be a primary objective of social security provision, the degree of impact can readily be understood in light of the size of the programme, the importance of income tested schemes and the phasing out of earnings related benefits.

Parts of the social security system, most obviously Child Benefit, are also aimed explicitly to achieve horizontal redistribution of income, that is transfers between individuals with similar incomes but different needs. Horizontal redistribution may also be interpreted as the transfers between the different stages of a person's life course which serve to even out the periods of relative want and prosperity documented in the previous section. Take, for example, the fully funded state pension scheme, outlined in the 1942 Beveridge Report. With flat rate contributions and flat rate pensions this aimed to ensure that individuals redistributed their 'own' income over the life course for each person would, on average, have received back what they had contributed to the scheme.

Acknowledging the importance of time has two sets of consequences when thinking about redistribution in the context of social security. The first appertains to the measurement and reduction of inequality. The second relates to the role of the social security systems in effecting income transfers over time.

Measurement and monitoring

The choice of accounting period affects measures of inequality in the same way as it affects the extent of recorded poverty. In essence, the longer the accounting period, the more egalitarian the income distribution appears to be. This effect results from the process of averaging out fluctuations in individuals' incomes and is demonstrated by Table 4.3 using Australian data. The table compares estimates of life time income constructed from a dynamic microsimulation model with a cohort of individual's annual income. The estimates were obtained by taking a cross-sectional survey and 'aging' it, year by year, simulating the occurrence of such events as marriage, divorce, birth, children leaving home. The events were randomly assigned to individuals in accord with the probability of these events occurring in the population as a whole. The Gini coefficient - a measure of inequality where zero indicates complete equality and one defines the situation where all resources are held by a single individual - falls very substantially in all cases (Harding, 1990). This is because the life-time pattern of alternating sequences of relative want and affluence, shown in Figure 4.1, is evened out.

Another set of issues arises when attempting to measure any change in inequality which may have occurred (or been achieved) over time. Measures

80

of relative inequality, such as the Gini coefficient, do not take account of rises in overall income. It may be, for example, that people who are in favour of increased income equality may nevertheless be prepared to accept an 'undesirable' increase in inequality if all incomes rise to a significant extent. Jenkins (1991) has shown that in Britain indices of social welfare which give high weight to inequality reduction relative to average income growth fell between 1976 and 1986 while indices with the opposite balance of priorities rose.

Table 4.3
Gini coefficients of annualised lifetime and annual income measures

Measure	Annualised Lifetime		Annual	
	Males	Females	Males	Females
Earnings	.286	.334	.542	.685
Original income	.320	.352	.510	.606
Gross income	.299	.296	.470	.507
Disposable income	.232	.246	.398	.447
Equivalent income	.200	.183	.356	.349

Source: Harding (1990)

People might also be willing to tolerate a growth in inequality if it were to coincide with an increased chance of an individual moving from the bottom to higher deciles between one year and the next. Unfortunately, it requires longitudinal information to operationalise measures of social welfare that overtly balance equality of outcome against equality of opportunity and, of course, this is currently unavailable in Britain (Jenkins, 1991).

Likewise, the process by which changes in income distribution is achieved must remain exceptionally murky until it is possible to track the experiences of particular individuals. For example, if the mean incomes of two groups of individuals A and B became more equal over time this could result from a number of different processes. The mean income in one group might have fallen. The mean income of the other may have risen. Both processes may have occurred. Within either group the dispersion of incomes may have fallen or increased. All incomes may have remained the same but individuals may have changed groups.

The consequences of this lack of clarity may be illustrated by reference to the analyses of low income included in the 1983 'Reform of Social Security' Green Paper (HMSO, 1985). This showed that between 1971 and 1982 the composition of the lowest quintile of the income distribution had changed markedly. In 1971 the lowest quintile comprised 52 per cent pensioners, 17 per cent couples with children and 19 per cent single persons of working age. By 1982 only 27 per cent of the quintile were pensioners, while the proportions comprising couples with children and single persons had risen to 23 per cent and 34 per cent respectively.

What is not clear is the extent to which the change in the relative position of pensioners reflected an increase in their incomes, or a decrease in the relative incomes of other groups which caused pensioners to be displaced from the lowest quintile. Nor is it apparent how far any increase in the average incomes of pensioners was due to the influx of younger pensioners with higher incomes, a higher death rate among poorer pensioners (due, perhaps, to the direct link between income and morbidity and mortality, or simply to the lower pension coverage of older cohorts). What is most unlikely, although of course theoretically possible, is that the incomes of individuals who were pensioners in both 1971 and 1982 increased; it is more likely that they were subject to attrition caused by inflation and other factors documented elsewhere (e.g. Walker and Hutton, 1988).

Effecting temporal redistribution

Social security benefits allied to the tax system effect both horizontal and vertical redistribution. Resources are transferred between individuals and over time. Social security provisions serve to even out the short and long term fluctuations in incomes and income needs ratios that have been the focus in earlier sections. Since, relatively small numbers of individuals are in receipt of benefits permanently, with the majority alternately paying into the corporate kitty and drawing from it, the social security system acts as an aid to individuals managing the fluctuating cash flows that seem to characterise modern life.

82

Few studies have assessed how effective existing policies are in this respect. Table 4.4 plots the value of benefits minus taxes for life course groups according to the level of original income (that is, income prior to receipt of benefit and before the levying of taxes). The original income is 'equivalised' to take account of differences in needs, but the net benefit/tax gain is not. The data are for 1982 and exclude benefits in kind and the

Table 4.4
Net benefit/tax gain, 1982 (£ per week)

| Life-cycle group | Quintiles of equivalent original income | | | | |
	Bottom (£ p.w.)	2nd (£ p.w.)	3rd (£ p.w.)	4th (£ p.w.)	Top (£ p.w.)
Young single	+ 30	+ 1	- 7	- 19	- 44
Young married	+ 51	(+ 9)	- 2	- 29	- 64
Family formation	+ 64	+ 1	- 16	- 32	- 62
Middle childrearing	+ 88	0	- 25	- 41	- 105
Complete family	+ 80	+ 2	- 23	- 43	- 97
Early dispersal	+ 90	+ 10	- 36	- 66	- 121
Two generations	+ 72	+ 30	- 21	- 58	- 102
Empty nest	+ 57	+ 34	- 11	- 28	- 64
Early retirement	+ 60	+ 49	+ 30	+ 18	- 22
Old and single	+ 42	+ 31	+ 22	+ 9	- 13
Lone parent	+ 63	+ 26	- 10	- 23	(- 46)

Bracketed numbers are based on 10 families or less.

Source: O'Higgins, Bradshaw and Walker (1988)

impact of indirect taxation. The table shows that, for most life course groups, the break between receiving a net gain and making a net loss through the tax-benefit system occurred between the second and third quintiles of original income, although the average benefit received by households in the second quintile was generally very small. The exception is pensioners who continued to receive a net gain up to the fourth quintile of net income reflecting the fact that the state pension is not means-tested.

The treatment of households in the bottom quintile of original income varied considerably between life course groups. (In 1982 the average weekly original income for this quintile - that is, income before state intervention - was equivalent to only £5 for a married couple.) Families, particularly those with older children, received substantially larger sums than did pensioners and other groups without children. However, a very different pattern emerges (not shown in table 4.4) if the net income from the state is converted to take account of household needs. Pensioner couples received 52 per cent more than a 'complete' family or one in the middle stages of child rearing while single young people received 25 per cent more. Families with younger children also appear to have gained substantially more than did families with older ones, and single pensioners 39 per cent more than single young people.

Similarly inequitable patterns are evident among higher income families who, on balance, pay more in taxes than they receive back in benefits. Families with children in the fourth and top quintile of the original income distribution pay markedly larger sums in tax and national insurance than do families at other stages in the life cycle. The reason is that at these levels of income Child Benefit payments are swamped by the effect of the tax system which is largely insensitive to variations in households' needs as opposed to differences in gross income. For example, the needs of single people and complete families are very different: the equivalence scale used implies that to be placed in the top quintile of equivalent net income a complete family would require a net income (i.e. not equivalenced) of £420 per week and a single person only £182. Yet, the average tax rate (net of benefits) for a complete family and a single person in the top quintile of equivalent net income is virtually identical (namely, 23 and 24 per cent respectively).

A much more sophisticated analysis taking account of service provision, indirect taxation and the impact of policies on individual behaviour is required before firm conclusions can be drawn. Nevertheless, an a priori case can be made that the state's activity is rather less in tune with variations in life cycle factors than it might be.

The analysis presented in Table 4.4 relates to transfers occurring in a single year and is essentially static in form. That presented for Australia, in Figures 4.4 and 4.5, also relates to the situation in a particular year but attempts to show what would happen to individuals who lived their entire lives in the conditions that appertained in a single year. A comparison between the two figures shows that individuals whose life time earnings place them in the top half of the income distribution receive less benefit and, with the exception of the sixth decile, pay more tax than would be apparent on the basis of annual income. In contrast, individuals with lower life time earnings receive higher benefit income. The degree of 'churning', paying taxes while receiving benefits, which is one measure of the administrative efficiency of the global system, is much reduced when adopting a life time perspective.

Finally, it is worth noting that the transfer of income over the life span which is facilitated by social security can create potential inefficiencies which are not apparent when a short-term view is taken. One example of this is the occupational pension trap. Walker et al (1989) show that because of the interaction between occupational pensions and means-tested social security provision, 21 per cent of pensioners gained no financial benefit whatsoever from their occupational pension - which served merely to offset entitlement to income support, - and a further 30 per cent did not enjoy the full financial benefit of their pension.

Similarly, Walker et al calculated that, in 1982, 32 per cent of pensioners faced a savings trap where savings did not contribute to higher living standards but served simply to debar them from Supplementary Benefit receipt. (This proportion may be lower under the regulations that apply to Income Support which replaced Supplementary Benefit in 1988.) From the viewpoint of the individual, people who will ultimately be confronted by savings and pension traps might do better to live for today and let tomorrow - retirement, unemployment, accident - look after itself. From the viewpoint of the Government, the traps have the effect of shifting responsibility for welfare from the State to the individual. The problem facing the individual, which on this occasion works to the advantage of Government, is that the future is inherently uncertain and that, in any case, calculating future pension entitlement is almost as impossible as predicting the structure of the benefit regime at the point when one comes to rely on it.

Reflections

What then have we learned from taking explicit account of time in thinking about the objectives of redistribution, compensation and the maintenance of incomes? First, as in the two preceding chapters, one must conclude that not to take account of time is foolhardy since it almost inevitably leads to error and misunderstanding. The raison d'être of policies is to respond to, and to

Figure 4.4
Difference between average annualised cash transfers received and average annualised adjusted income taxes paid, by decile of annualised lifetime equivalent income

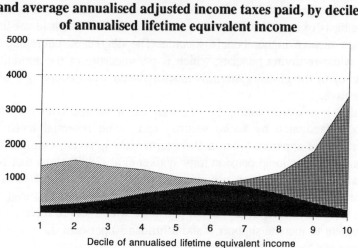

Figure 4.5
Difference between average annual cash transfers received and average annual adjusted income taxes paid, by decile of annual equivalent income

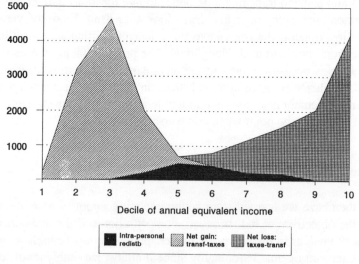

Source: Harding (1990)

bring about, change. But change, itself, is of course an element in a temporal process and the outcome of other processes that operate over time. What to do, when to act and what happens when action occurs can only be accurately determined by recording changes as they happen. Therefore, whether it was appropriate, for example, to try and redistribute social security expenditure away from the elderly towards families with children as occurred in Britain in the mid 1980s cannot be established on the basis of the cross-sectional information that is currently available.

Secondly, it is evident that people's economic circumstances change radically and frequently in ways that, though generally unpredictable at an individual level, often follow a clear pattern in aggregate. This would seem to confirm the suitability of social insurance as a mechanism for meeting definable financial risks and for managing resources over the life course. Moreover, the rather surprising lack of anticipation of the consequences of future events, revealed by the failure of well over half of older Americans to foresee the fall in living standards on retirement, suggests that voluntary insurance may not prove effective. Some measure of compulsion, or very active encouragement, would appear to be required. In this respect the British system seems well adapted to the realities of the situation.

Thirdly, one remembers the striking prevalence of sudden and substantial falls in income that are unrelated to the kind of events which contingency benefits might readily be designed to cover (Duncan, 1988). This again suggests that the British system, with its emphasis on general income maintenance schemes rather than contingency specific schemes, constitutes an appropriate approach. However, Britain's emphasis on poverty relief rather than the maintenance of living standards means that, on the basis of the evidence presented above, there are likely to be large numbers of individuals who suffer substantial falls in income but remain above the means-tested floor and hence receive no assistance from the state.

Fourthly, the longitudinal evidence, at one and the same time, underlines the need to maintain living standards and calls into question the appropriateness and feasibility of such a goal. While many individuals do suddenly experience a drop in income or change in needs which dramatically erodes living standards, the American evidence raises the possibility that relatively few people ever enjoy a stable standard of living, particularly those on higher and lower incomes. Whether the concept of permanent income holds at the level of the individual is certainly questionable and, in any case, it would be difficult to operationalise and use as a datum for social security purposes. Likewise, the uncertainty of individuals' long term income flows makes the assessment of income lost as a result of an accident, or through the onset of disability, next to impossible to assess.

Basing payments on a record of income linked contributions has the effect of averaging out income fluctuations and may be as good a method to adopt as any. However, unless payments are linked to recent income, which of course may not be representative of lifetime earnings, the effective replacement ratios, and therefore the extent to which benefits protect current living standards, are likely to vary markedly according, among other things, to stage in the life course.

Finally, it appears that the attempts of Governments to redistribute resources vertically are probably more effective when viewed from a lifetime perspective than when measured across units of time that politicians might consider relevant. Even so, the evidence reported suggests that attempts in Britain to match resources to life-course fluctuations in living standards leave much scope for improvement. However, the discussion here revolves full circle because the evidence reported relates to the period prior to the social security changes of the late 1980s and without longitudinal data the impact of those reforms cannot satisfactorily be assessed.

5 Targeting and administration of benefits

The previous two chapters sought to explore the consequences of explicitly considering time when thinking about the design of social security schemes. The focus of this chapter turns to the targeting and administration of benefits, but certain of the earlier findings inform the approach adopted here. First, it was evident that ignoring time, as has generally been necessary because of an absence of longitudinal information, can produce distortions when attempting to define the target population or the characteristics of those in receipt of benefit. It can also hinder attempts to formulate a clear idea of the problem to be addressed by benefit provisions. This, in turn, acts as a constraint on the achievement of current policy goals and poses a limit on the extent to which the performance of policies can be effectively monitored.

Secondly, and more radically, taking explicit account of time may help inform the choice of policy objective and raise the possibility of new ones. For example, the focus on long term reliance on welfare benefits which has dominated recent debates in the USA, and has been of more than passing concern in Britain, is predicated on assumptions about the desirability of short rather than long periods of benefit receipt (SSRC, 1988; Murray, 1984; 1990). It also requires appropriate data to determine the extent of long term reliance on social security. Again, a recognition that the circumstances associated with the beginning and end of spells of benefit receipt might be amenable to policy intervention can shift policy in the direction of proactivity and prevention.

The distinction between ignoring a temporal perspective, which operates as a constraint, and adopting one, which may result in new policy opportunities, is used to structure this chapter. The first three sections respectively cover targeting, promotion and other aspects of administration. The fourth briefly addresses the data requirements which follow from incorporating a temporal approach into the analysis of social security issues.

Targeting

Constraints on definition and measurement

By way of introduction it is worth reiterating the almost obvious. Individuals' financial and other needs are not constant over time. Rather they are inherently lumpy, last for varying durations and, at the level of the individual, are frequently unpredictable.

The probability of encountering needs that lead people to become eligible for categorical or income tested benefits is affected by numerous factors. Group memberships such as class, gender and ethnic status are important but so are considerations that are inherently time dependent. At the aggregate, societal level one thinks of the current position in the economic cycle and along secular trend lines, prevailing social attitudes and behaviour patterns, etc. For individuals, stage in the life course is of utmost importance, mediated by the balance between resources and needs at earlier points in their lives, and people's willingness and ability to manage resources over the life course by means of saving, investment in self development and the acquisition of consumable assets.

It follows that the populations requiring, receiving or potentially eligible for benefits are stable neither in terms of characteristics nor membership. To assume stability, as is sometimes forced upon policy makers by a lack of longitudinal data, may lead to error or, at least, to a lack of clarity. Some of the implications of this inherent instability in claimant populations are now illustrated with reference to targeting.

Targeting of benefits may be conceptualised in various ways. One is to think of it operating at different levels. At a strategic level resources are allocated between different categories of need or between different categories of needy people. The shift in resources from pensioners to families with children which was sought in the 1988 social security reforms in Britain illustrates this level of targeting (Cmnd 9691, 1985).

At a tactical level, that is relating to individual benefits, targeting has at least two meanings. The first concerns the degree to which administrative definitions of need accurately match those prescribed by Ministers, the

90

latter being a reflection of needs which are recognised socially and interpreted through the political process. The second meaning relates to the extent to which people with qualifying levels of need receive benefit (take up).

A third level of targeting occurs within particular benefit populations when attempts are made to direct resources to specific subgroups; in Britain this happens with the system of premiums under Income Support. At each of the three levels the effectiveness of targeting is constrained by the resources made available. An additional distinction may therefore be made between targeting efficiency, directing benefits to the most disadvantaged, and targeting effectiveness, the extent to which all needs are met.

Strategic targeting

Evidence presented by the UK Government to support the shift in resources from pensioners to families in the mid 1980s related to the change in the composition of the lowest quintile of the equivalised income distribution (Cmnd 9519, 1985). The income measure used was normal weekly income and no account was taken of variations in income flows because the information was obtained from the cross-sectional Family Expenditure Survey.

It is at least possible that different conclusions might have been reached if information had been available on the stability of peoples' circumstances. Many of the families appearing in the lowest income quintile in 1982 were affected by unemployment and most spells of unemployment are known to be short. Pensioners' circumstances, on the other hand, are much more stable (although probably less stable than is usually assumed, see Chapter 3 and Coe, 1988) and pensioners would generally be expected to remain in the lowest quintile while families affected by unemployment would not.

Restating the argument in more technical terms, the social security system in the mid 1980s was assumed to have low levels of vertical expenditure efficiency because relatively large sums of money were going to pensioners who were ostensibly better off. However, the vertical efficiency of the system might have been understated because the definition of need did not incorporate a measure of the duration of the shortfall in income in relation to needs. How great an understatement would depend on the relative weights assigned to duration and income shortfall.

A second consideration, again at a strategic level of targeting, is that cross-sectional data limits what can be learnt about the changes affecting target populations. As a consequence explanatory models are weaker and social security expenditure forecasts less accurate.

The problem is that, whenever more than one factor is changing, it is impossible to generate accurate predictions from aggregate cross-sectional data. For example, it was pointed out in Chapter 3 that it is hard to determine whether the rising incomes of the elderly are mostly a reflection of differential death rates, better inflation proofing of existing pensions or higher pensions and greater coverage among the recently retired. Likewise predicting the rise in income support expenditure resulting from an increase in unemployment is difficult. This is because the flow of new cases is affected by the national insurance contribution records of those becoming unemployed, since these determine entitlement to unemployment benefit, which are in turn dependent on previous work history.

Tactical targeting

The dynamic nature of peoples' circumstances is perhaps most evident in thinking about the targeting of a particular benefit. The target population with qualifying needs is constantly changing. Unless application is instantaneous this fact alone prevents universal take up, while differential turnover in the target populations of different benefits may go some way to explaining the variation in take up rates (see the section below for a discussion of attainable take up rates).

Flux in the target population causes other measurement problems. Cross sectional statistics tend to understate the throughput of individuals with short spells of entitlement. For example, annual statistics would not generally distinguish between two people, one of whom was eligible for benefit in the first six months of the year and the other for the last six months; they would be recorded as a single case. Equally many people whose period of entitlement occurred between the points of data collection would be omitted altogether. One effect of this is to emphasize the characteristics of long term recipients of a scheme relative to those with short periods of receipt. It may also result in a distorted understanding of the characteristics of those who have not taken up the benefit.

A second problem resulting from the dynamism of people's circumstances is the tendency to understate the total number of people falling within the scope of the scheme. Understatement is least when the eligible population is stable or composed primarily of the same individuals undergoing repeated periods of eligibility, and greatest when the population comprises a succession of different individuals. One consequence of this understatement is to risk inflating estimates of take up. Another is to distort perceptions of the relative effectiveness of different kinds of benefit. For example, a selective income supplement which is instituted in order to assist relatively small numbers of people on a continuing basis may be going to large numbers of people to tide them over a particular situation, say household formation. In such circumstances it might be more effective to introduce a universal benefit, restricted in amount or duration, to cover the contingency and thus avoid the problems associated with income testing.

A further measurement problem is that of 'benefit drag' which tends to inflate take up estimates (Walker, 1978). This problem principally affects benefits such as Family Credit in Britain which have a relatively long entitlement period. The numerator of the take up fraction is inflated by the inclusion of individuals who, though no longer eligible for benefit, continue to receive it throughout the period of entitlement, while the size of the denominator is understated by the exclusion of people who were once eligible for benefit and who could still be receiving it had they applied. Although official estimates of take up attempt to take account of the effects of benefit drag, accurate information is dependent on the availability of longitudinal data.

Take up measures are now usually presented in two forms. One gives the proportion of the eligible population in receipt, the other expresses the amount of benefit claimed as a percentage of that due. Both measures are subject to the problems mentioned above, while the relative effect of resolving, or controlling for them, is dependent on the nature of the relationship between the size of award (actual and potential) and the period for which it is (or could be) in payment. If the relationship is strongly positive, the measure based on benefit expenditure will be the more distorted by benefit dynamics. The opposite is true if the relationship is negative, that is, if the weekly benefit received by those who are only temporarily in receipt of benefit is much greater than those who are dependent on benefit for longer periods.

Within benefit targeting

Two time dependent considerations are pertinent here. The first consideration relates to the periodicity of needs and to the rapidity of peoples' changes in circumstances. Take, for instance, the UK Social Fund which aims to target assistance on those (primarily) Income Support recipients with special needs. Its design is premised on the assumption that certain needs are one-off and not generally repeated. At the time of its introduction there was no systematic evidence to the contrary. However, the reality of implementation reveals that substantial numbers of individuals make repeated applications to the social fund with the result that some applications have to be rejected and much administrative effort has to go into the re-scheduling of loans (Walker, Dix and Huby, 1991). Moreover, there is growing evidence that the needs faced by those who might ostensibly benefit from community care grants are frequently for continuing financial assistance which the social fund is not designed to meet (Becker and Silburn, 1990).

Earlier, the effectiveness of the 1982/3 Housing Benefit Scheme in Britain had been seriously undermined by the rapidity with which some individuals moved on and off supplementary benefit since the administrative procedures proved to be extremely sensitive to changes in circumstances (Walker, 1985).

The second consideration simply reiterates the potential for incorporating duration into assumptions about differential needs and the problems that may arise when this is not done. In the UK the structure of Income Support and associated benefits, such as Housing Benefit and Family Credit, makes distinctions between different kinds of need through the payment of premiums. There are premiums for the elderly and the disabled, groups that might be expected to spend relatively long periods on benefit. However, without longitudinal data, policies relating to the adequacy of benefits, and the appropriateness of paying different levels of benefit to different groups, cannot take systematic account of variations in the time that individuals are likely to spend on benefit. Indeed, if this were possible, a point to be developed in the next section, it might be appropriate not only to adjust the level of benefit to take account of duration but to instigate policies to affect durations.

New targeting objectives

Taking explicit account of time raises new opportunities when thinking about the targeting of benefits. Buhr and Leibfried (1994), for example, have focused on duration of benefit receipt and examined how different conceptualisations may be used to inform targeting decisions. They distinguish between the traditional measures of spell length, based on the duration of current spells, and contrast these with two 'life-course' measures. The first, a gross concept, records the length of the period between first receiving benefit to the present spell including periods when benefit was not received. The second, net concept, counts the total length of time spent in receipt of benefit.

Buhr and Leibfried point out that the 'current' or 'last spell' concept is most useful when attempting to assess the current financial burden of the system and the need for immediate intervention. Life course measures are better indicators of the impact of a scheme, in terms of its effect on people's ability to help themselves, in determining the nature of the problems faced by beneficiaries and the appropriate type and timing of interventions.

By establishing the characteristics of those who move on to benefit and monitoring the period of their receipt it might be possible to target proactive policies on selective groups of benefit recipients and preventive procedures on at risk groups.

These possibilities may usefully be explored by reference to work undertaken by David Ellwood on the targeting of AFDC in the United States. AFDC (Aid to Families with Dependent Children) is the scheme almost universally equated with 'Welfare' in America. It provides means-tested assistance for dependent children and their families but, in practice, is received mainly by lone parent families. There is no employment test and a substantial proportion of recipients work while in receipt of AFDC.

The first point to observe is the objective of the study:

> Recent work by several authors ... has emphasised the twofold role of the Aid to Families with Dependent Children (AFDC) programme for female family heads: to provide short-term relief to a large number of women, and to provide long-term income maintenance to a much smaller number. While the bulk of the individuals who ever use AFDC seem to be short-term recipients, the majority of the resources are devoted to providing benefits to long-term recipients. Thus, such studies have prescribed attempting to identify likely long-term recipients early on and to target employment and social services toward them in an effort to reduce their dependency, both for fiscal and humanitarian purposes (Ellwood, 1986, p.ix).

The objective, therefore, is a proactive one: to identify means of targeting extra, non social security resources, to enable individuals to reduce the length of time spent on benefit. The rationale is to achieve reductions in the welfare caseloads in the long run (Ellwood, 1986, p.35). In order to do this it is necessary to be able to identify in advance groups of individuals who are likely to experience long spells; it would make little sense to focus resources on those who have already been on benefit for a long period and may be about to leave of their own accord. Since those who are on benefit

for longer than average also consume a disproportionate share of programme resources (assuming that the level of their benefit is no less than average), focusing attention on them increases the scope for welfare savings.

Not surprisingly there are numerous technical difficulties in identifying applicants who are likely to remain on benefit for a long time. Leaving these aside, Table 5.1 presents some instructive results from Ellwood's work. He chose to explore the implications of targeting groups with a high probability of receiving benefit for 10 or more years, and in so doing, was mindful of the fact that, for practical administrative reasons, it would be necessary to identify reasonably large subgroups. The table shows, for example, that people aged under 22 constitute 30 per cent of first time applicants and 36 per cent of recipients at any one time. Without intervention 33 per cent would remain on benefit for at least ten years with an average duration of 8.2 years for the subgroup as a whole.

Being single and having a young child at the time of application emerge as important risk factors. Race and education are also important. The figures in Table 5.1 deliberately do not show the marginal impact which individual variables have on the likelihood of staying on benefit for a decade or more. (The reason for this is a pragmatic policy one: targeting additional help on the basis of a limited set of factors does not hold other factors constant.) When other factors are held constant the age of the mother and the youngest child appear only to have a negligible effect on the time spent on benefit. However, women who are very young when they first receive AFDC, or have young children, tend also to be single and this characteristic is highly correlated with long term receipt.

In the USA most schemes to provide training and employment do not target young mothers. This is because it had previously been thought that such schemes would be more effective in helping people with older children. There is also a reluctance to force mothers of young children into work. Ellwood questions the wisdom of this strategy. Seventy four per cent of women beginning a spell of AFDC have children under six and the majority of recipients have children aged under three. Such mothers have great difficulty escaping from benefit and current guidelines, which offer services only to those with a youngest child aged over five, mean a delay of five or more years before any help can be given.

Ellwood recognised that although single mothers were the most likely to remain on benefit for lengthy periods, 'political, practical and ethical problems may work against targeting on the basis of marital status'. Instead a programme for young mothers was proposed supplemented by schemes for older women with low levels of educational attainment and no recent work experience, a group also at risk of protracted benefit receipt.

The research also noted that while, as shown in Table 5.1, people with disabilities did not stay on benefit over long, attention should be given to whether current training and employment services should be expanded to cover this group. This was because disability, of itself, acted to lengthen spells but this was masked by the fact that the disabled in the sample were much more likely to be widows, to be older and to have fewer children which all served to reduce the length of spells on benefit. However, very few women with disabilities ever left AFDC for employment (the principal routes off benefit were through marriage and the growing up of their children which makes them ineligible for AFDC).

Previous work had indicated that the chances of moving off AFDC decline very rapidly after two years. This raises the possibility that interventions could be delayed for two years in order to avoid directing resources to large numbers of people who would rapidly move off benefit of their own accord. However, while a 'wait and see' strategy appeared to be justified when the focus was on individual spells of receipt (Bane and Ellwood, 1983) a different conclusion was reached when account was taken of multiple spells. People with very short spells, it seemed, were more likely to return to AFDC and far fewer people had short durations when repeat claims were taken into account. In practice, a policy of waiting before offering services succeeded in screening out relatively few cases and considerable amounts of benefit would have needed to have been paid out during the waiting period which would have offset the gains achieved from better targeting of supplementary services.

In 1993 Ellwood left Harvard University to become Assistant Secretary in the US Department of Health and Human Services where, at the time of writing, he is engaged in developing a policy response to President Clinton's pledge to impose a two year limit on AFDC payments. While Wisconsin and Florida have proposed simply to withdraw benefits after two years, the Clinton administration is committed to offering some form of training or work experience, 'a piece on the career ladder' (DeParle, 1993). In costing alternative strategies Ellwood's team has, of course, to predict the number of AFDC recipients who would still be on benefit after two years. Presumably using similar methodology to that which Ellwood (1986) had developed in his earlier work (and which is exploited in Chapter 8) the planning team estimates that roughly three-fifths of recipients could be affected by the two year time limit although half of these would be excluded under current rules, because of the young age of their children.

Table 5.1
Percentage of AFDC recipients with various characteristics and average total durations of AFDC receipt

Recipient characteristics at time of first spell Beginning	Percent of all first-time recipients (new beginnings)	Percent of recipients at any point in time*	Average No. of years of AFDC receipt	Percent who will have AFDC spells of 10 or more years
Age				
under 22	30.0	35.9	8.23	32.8
22-30	40.7	41.9	7.08	25.8
31-40	11.8	8.8	5.15	15.0
Over 40	17.6	13.4	5.23	15.8
Race/ethnicity				
white	55.2	47.7	5.95	19.6
black	40.1	47.4	8.14	32.0
other	4.8	4.8	6.94	25.5
Years of education				
under 9	9.7	9.6	6.81	24.5
9-11	37.6	41.9	7.65	29.2
over 11	52.7	48.5	6.33	21.8
Marital status				
single	29.5	40.0	9.33	39.3
divorced	28.1	20.2	4.94	13.7
separated	32.3	31.9	6.80	24.4
widowed	8.4	5.3	4.37	10.2
Number of children				
0-1	43.4	48.7	7.71	29.7
2-3	42.8	37.3	6.04	20.1
over 3	13.8	13.7	6.83	24.5
Age of youngest child				
under 3	51.3	60.4	8.09	31.9
3-5	22.5	22.3	6.79	24.2
6-10	19.7	12.9	4.51	11.3
over 10	6.5	4.4	4.71	12.4
Work experience				
worked in the last 2 years	65.8	59.6	6.53	23.0
did not work in the last 2 years	34.2	39.8	8.00	31.2
Disability status				
no disability	81.6	81.4	6.85	24.8
disability limits work	18.4	18.6	6.97	25.0

Source: *Simulation model estimates are based on the 15-year Panel Study of Income Dynamics. For each individual who began a first spell on or after the third sample year of the PSID, probabilities are predicted for exiting from first spell, for recidivism, and for exiting from later spells, based on logit modelling.*

* These figures assume that the AFDC caseload is in a 'steady state'.

The AFDC example illustrates how a knowledge of flows onto and out of benefit can present further options for targeting resources. In some respects the example is limited. It focuses primarily on the policy leverage gained from a knowledge of durations and linked characteristics. Longitudinal data which covered the period prior to receipt might make it possible to instigate preventive action. The kind of information required would need to cover the events that precipitate a benefit application and the nature of the circumstances which lead a person experiencing the event to make an application or, indeed, to need to. A knowledge of the factors that combine to take people out of benefit might yield insights into the kind of assistance packages that could be introduced to assist them.

To conclude, rather than simply accepting a demand led system of social security, thinking about the temporal processes involved, combined with access to the right kinds of data, creates potential for constructing packages of measures which provide a route out of benefit and a defence against ever having to use them at all. Clearly it is important not to overstate the potential. Much depends on the effectiveness of the proactive and preventive policies available - a mixture of training, employment and support services in the case of AFDC. Moreover, the efficiency of targeting is bound to be dependent on the characteristics of the benefit population since this determines the extent to which discrete target groups can be defined.

Promotion of benefits

Limitations on promotion

The problems of accurately targeting policies in the absence of explicitly temporal data also conspire to undermine the effectiveness of benefit promotions. The paucity of longitudinal data in relation to targeting applies equally to strategies for promoting the take up of benefits. This section first emphasises that understanding of the nature of the target population is necessarily distorted, or blurred, by the absence of time explicit data. Secondly, the principal models of benefit take up are discussed, drawing attention to their failure to take explicit account of time and an alternative approach is presented.

a)   Knowing the target population. Cross sectional data cannot capture the dynamics of a benefit's target population which is continually altering in form in response to the changing circumstances of individuals and the ebb and flow of socio-economic forces. Point in time statistics give excessive weight to the characteristics of long term recipients, blurring the image of new and prospective applicants who form the target of most promotion activity. Likewise, they offer few insights into who receives benefit, over what period of time and for what purpose; whether a particular benefit performs primarily as a one-off means of financial support or as a recurrent component of a household's income. Information which overcame these deficiencies might underwrite new promotional strategies (see below).

The Food Stamp Programme in the USA serves as a useful example of how longitudinal data can change perceptions of a benefit. The policy thrust in the USA in recent years has increasingly placed assistance programmes in a short-term remedial role: providing help for a family until it is able to become financially independent. Food Stamps was seen as a central component in this strategy (Burstein and Visher, 1989). What longitudinal research showed was that, because the Food Stamp Programme is the only US income maintenance scheme open to all low income people regardless of age, family structure and other characteristics, it was meeting a variety of different needs for a diverse population.

A change in household composition (usually the loss of a family head or new family formation) was found to be as important as a fall in earnings or other taxable income in precipitating claims. Most claims followed the trigger event quickly, usually within the same month. Turnover of the claimant population was high, the number of households receiving Food Stamps in any year is 70 per cent greater than the number in receipt in any given month and, in contrast with AFDC, an increase in earnings constituted the most important route off benefit (taken by 53 per cent of ex-recipients).

Food Stamps, it would appear therefore, do contribute to crisis management, tiding households over a short-lived difficulty. On the other hand, over a third of spells on Food Stamps last for more than two years and a fifth for over five years. Moreover, 'recidivism', repeat claiming, is common (32 per cent in a two-year period, Burstein and Visher, (1989)) such that when this is taken into account the average time that households spend on the Food Stamp Programme increases to between 4-6 years. A considerable proportion of Food Stamp users are therefore long-term poor or experience life as a process of lurching from one financial crisis to the next.

The longitudinal research also revealed that turnover among the households who were eligible for Food Stamps was far greater than for those who had actually claimed Food Stamps. (The probability that an eligible household became ineligible each month was about 17 per cent, and the probability that a previously ineligible household became eligible was 6.3 per cent (Carr, Doyle and Lubitz, 1984).) Therefore a very substantial proportion of those bridging a short spell of low income - the group on which the programme has traditionally been targeted - made no claim on the system. Why this should be, and how individuals fund the shortfall income, is not yet well understood. It may be that the periods of low income are planned, or that they are expected to be short-lived. Alternatively some people may prefer to rely on personal and informal sources of finance rather than experience the stigma of food stamp receipt.

In summary, therefore, time explicit research rewrote official perceptions of the function and achievements of the Food Stamp Programme in the USA. Further research is currently in train using the SIPP survey which generates monthly data about families' financial circumstances (Shea and Short, 1993).

b) *Process of application.* There are advantages to be gained from conceptualising the application for a benefit as a process rather than as an event. To take a simple example, the time taken between becoming eligible for a benefit and receiving it is likely to vary between one person and another and between one benefit and another. These variations have obvious implications for achieved take up levels. The classic models which have been developed to describe and explain take up, while recognising that they are dealing with a process, have nevertheless singularly failed to capitalise on the potential advantages.

The most influential model of take up to date is that proposed by Kerr (1983). Kerr (1983) suggests that someone applying for a means-tested benefit has to pass a determinant sequence of thresholds:

i)   Perceived need
ii)   Basic knowledge about a benefit
iii) Perceived eligibility for a benefit
iv)   Perceived utility of receiving the benefit
v)   Beliefs and feelings
vi)   Perceived stability of circumstances
vii) Make a claim

Each threshold implies the acquisition and evaluation of information. The model has been widely adopted, refined and evaluated (Ritchie and Matthews, 1982; Ritchie and England, 1988; Corden, 1983). As a result it has been suggested that the sequence of stages is not fixed and that, rather than a failure to pass one of the thresholds being sufficient to deter a claim, claimants may trade-off one consideration against another (Craig, 1989).

Most recently, it has been suggested that trigger events might influence decisions at any stage by affecting the weight which individuals give to the elements in any trade off. For example, a sudden drop in income could increase the relative weight given to perceived need in the overall trade-off, which could outweigh the negative attitudes. This could in turn trigger the search for information (van Oorschot, 1991).

Kerr's model is surprisingly static in form. It was designed to explain non take-up, ostensibly a state, rather than claiming behaviour per se. Indeed Davies and Ritchie (1988), in their evaluation of the Kerr model found that it was much better at predicting who would not claim (which it did correctly in 91 per cent of cases) than who would claim (for which it was only 44 per cent efficient). In the model, successful take up of benefit is presented as a stable end state, akin to non take-up and there are no recursive elements. The stages are not necessarily perceived to have durations and therefore no attempt was made to assess the length of the take up process. In later reformulations, as we have seen, the notion of a fixed progression through the stages has been substantially modified.

One threshold in Kerr's model, to do with stability of circumstances, has received relatively little attention partly because it was placed last in the hierarchy of thresholds. Whether this is the appropriate position is perhaps a moot point (McLaughlin, Walker and Ritchie, 1990). It might be, for example, that individuals' perception of need and receptivity to information about benefits is conditioned by the view that they take of the permanence or otherwise of their circumstances. Pensioners might be expected to consider their situation to be permanent, or at least long-term, whereas the evidence suggest that newly unemployed people see their circumstances as transitory (Heady and Smyth, 1989). As important, there is precious little information about the relationship between delays in claiming and non-take up. It is by no means certain that the reasons for delay are the same as those which generate permanent non-claiming (Craig, 1989) although Corden (1983), in Britain, found that applicants for Family Income Supplement, the precursor of Family Credit, had often been eligible for benefit for several months prior to claiming. This suggests that, at least in the case of Family Income Supplement, a proportion of the eligible non-claimant population eventually got round to claiming.

Another aspect of claiming which fits uneasily into the Kerr-type models is the prevalence of unsuccessful applications for some benefits (Corden, 1987). This can impose significant administrative costs and delay processing of successful claims. Finally, Kerr's model has been found to work better for some benefits than others and may describe the experiences of pensioners more accurately than those of other groups although the reasons for this remain mysterious.

An alternative model (Walker, 1980), which has never been tested empirically, draws more directly on the literature on information seeking and use (Rogers and Shoemaker, 1973; Donohew, Tipton and Honey, 1978) and attempts more accurately to capture the dynamics of information acquisition. The model is premised on a number of assumptions which include the notion that the information environment is not static, that disinformation is always present and that individuals' information needs are dynamic, varying according to context and circumstance. Six recursive stages are proposed during which different parts of the information environment may be sampled in different ways, for different purposes (Figure 5.1). During the pre awareness stage the individual may or may not be eligible for the benefit in question. They may or may not have accurate or inaccurate information about the benefit and they will almost certainly have some knowledge and views about the purpose and characteristics of the social security system. However, the crucial feature of this period is that any information about the benefit would not be considered relevant.

By the awareness stage the potential applicant will have become sensitized to the relevance of information. This may result, for example, from a change in circumstance, the onset of disability, a relapse, a financial crisis, or contact with people in similar circumstances in receipt of benefit. The search stage may involve active and passive search: the deliberate sampling of the information environment in search of a solution to a problem; or simply an openness to new ideas. It may be at this stage that mass promotions prove to be most effective.

Potential applicants will make choices about who to consult according to the perceived sensitivity of the issue and the difficulty of the decision. Formal and informal intermediaries may play a crucial role. The process of consultation and decision may be one and the same but, when separated analytically, questions are prompted about the rationality of the decision and the extent and accuracy of the information employed. The process of application may divide into support, application and further support. The support may be physical (completion of the application form, accompaniment to a medical assessment etc.) or moral and emotional. Again informal and formal intermediaries may be of critical significance.

The outcome of the application is unlikely to be an end state. Rather both successful and unsuccessful applicants may monitor their new situation, determine that it is unsatisfactory and return to earlier steps in the process. Changes in individual circumstances and in the benefit system will also act to make the situation unstable.

The potential advantage of models such as that presented in Figure 5.1 is not so much that they may better describe people's access into the benefit system (unproven to date) but rather that they use process as a means of structuring possible intervention strategies. In so doing they focus attention on the information environment, its structure and the content and availability of information, rather than placing the burden of responsibility overwhelmingly on the potential applicant. They emphasise the dynamics of information needs - the utility of information changes as decisions are taken and circumstances alter - and information supply - information becomes outdated and corrupted to the extent that it becomes disinformation. This latter consideration provides potential insight into unsuccessful claiming. Process models also allow for the possibility that different benefits, and varying target groups, exhibit characteristics - some of them inherently temporal - which may affect the claiming process and take up levels.

Promotion strategies

a)   Attainable take up rates. As already noted, the take up of benefits varies from one social security scheme to another and may reflect differences in the dynamics of the target populations. Developing this observation and linking it with insights from process models of information acquisition, points to the possibility of building diagnostic models of attainable take up levels. The value of such models would be to inform decisions about the most effective allocation of resources, as between promotion and general administration and between one benefit and another, in attempting to enhance overall take up.

This is not the place to specify the precise form that the models would take. Suffice to say that three sets of parameters are involved which could be further extended and revised as appropriate. The first relates to the dynamic characteristics of the target population, in particular the rate at which people become eligible for the benefit and the duration of eligibility. The second set of parameters concerns the time between becoming eligible and making a claim, while the final set relates to the time taken to process claims. Assigning values to these simple parameters would permit simulations of steady state take up levels which could be compared with estimates of actual take up. Where actual take up rates fell far short of the theoretically attainable ones the benefits might be selected for special promotion or for supplementary research in order to ascertain why take up was unusually low.

Attainable take up rates can be expected to vary between benefits. In Britain, for example, they might be expected to be lower for Income Support, which has a very volatile target population and relatively short durations of eligibility, than for Child Benefit where durations probably average in the order of sixteen years. Other things being equal, take up might be lower for Invalid Care Allowance because entitlement is dependent on payment of Attendance Allowance; not only are there waiting times for receipt of Attendance Allowance but the take up of one benefit is dependent on the (incomplete) take up of another. Lengthy processing times, perhaps characteristic of disability benefits because of the need for medical assessments, would hold down take up levels. Take up among first time applicants might well be relatively low because the application process could be longer than for other more experienced applicants.

Full calibration of the models would require longitudinal data that is probably only available through panel interview surveys. However, in the first instance it might be sufficient to insert approximations based on more readily available information and examine how sensitive the models were to variations in the constituent elements. This might, in itself, indicate whether it was preferable, as a means of increasing take up, to direct resources to promotion per se or to reducing processing times. More refined judgements would become possible with better data. For example, it might be evident that take up rates could be most effectively enhanced by targeting promotion on a group with above average durations of eligibility, or on one which seemed to delay application longer than the norm. Likewise, it might be possible to determine whether investing in general awareness information, rather than detailed eligibility material, was likely to have more impact on take up levels.

b)   *Promoting individual benefits.* The discussion so far has shown that a more explicit awareness of the temporal aspects of social security provisions can throw additional light on the use made of specific benefits and on the dynamic characteristics of target populations. Taking account of the temporal nature of different needs and the dynamics of benefit populations might also assist in the promotion strategies for individual benefits.

Table 5.2 offers a simple classification of benefits according to whether the financial need which is generally met is anticipated or unanticipated, and whether it is one off or recurrent. The classification relates to the actual use

Figure 5.1
A model of benefit information search (after Walker, 1980)

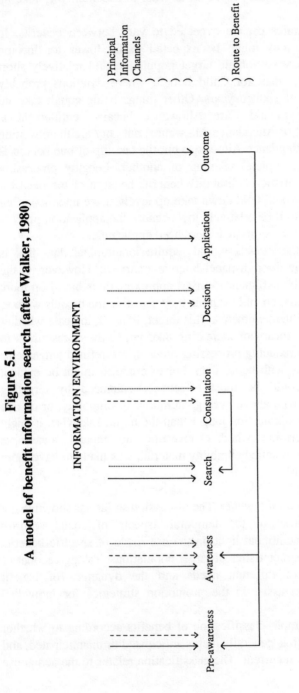

made of benefits which may or not relate to the purpose for which it was intended.

Table 5.2
Types of benefit need

	Predictable Needs	Unpredictable Needs
One off Need		
Repeated Need		

The most difficult promotional problems are likely to arise when the need is one off and unexpected. This might characterise some women affected by relationship breakdown who will previously have had little, if any, contact with the benefit system; it may go part way to explaining why in Britain the promotion strategies appear to be least effective among this group (Leeming and Unell, 1992). In these circumstances one might aim to raise general awareness of the system and to engender positive attitudes towards it. This is necessary if the potential applicant is to feel confident about making an application, to know how to go about it and is to receive lay support in doing so. The magnitude of this task is probably a partial explanation of why the level of take-up of some benefits is so low as to give cause for concern. It would also be appropriate to alert all the support agencies and professionals to whom the potential applicant might turn for resolution of non financial aspects of the precipitating problem.

In the three other situations defined in Table 5.2 it is possible to build promotion on prior contact. The repeated need to apply for benefit means that the efficient and effective delivery of benefit, which can contribute so much to the customer's experience, can itself become part of the promotion process engendering a willingness to reapply when the need arises. The flipside of this coin no doubt also applies: there is evidence that a bad initial experience can deter future applications (Craig, 1989).

The scope for building on prior contact is perhaps greatest when the need is repeated and predictable. Without longitudinal data it is unclear how many individuals fall into circumstances of this kind. One example, however, is individuals with periodic earnings who move on and off Income

107

Support. In situations of this kind it may well be appropriate to retain the possibility of contact with applicants when they move off benefit and to alert them of information and changes germane to future claims. An analogous situation already applies for those benefits in Britain which have a fixed eligibility period, such as Housing Benefit and Family Credit, which means that applicants are required to reapply. Notices sent out warning recipients that the time for renewals is nigh is akin to a personalised take up campaign which, on the evidence available, is usually very successful (Marsh and McKay, 1992).

In some circumstances the potentially high costs attached to such a strategy, particularly if the numbers involved are large or the benefit payments small, might point to changes in the structure of the benefit. A fixed period of entitlement might be applied, possibly to a sub-category of applicants, or earnings disregards could be spread over a longer period and exceptional short term earnings offset against them, thus obviating the need to move off benefit only to have to reapply almost immediately.

The predictability of needs, either at a group or individual level, also allows for the possibility of prevention. This is, of course, the premise on which the national insurance system is built (see Chapter 4).

Some other administrative aspects

The social security system is a collective response to the dynamism of individuals' circumstances and administration is driven by the requirement to respond to this dynamism. The dynamics may be long term. The obvious example is the build up of pensions when the state assists in the life time management of resources, facilitating transfers from the relatively prosperous periods of employment to the time of retirement. On other occasions the pressures are immediate as when staff in benefits offices work furiously in order to make a counter payment before closing time. The more that can be learned about the nature of the dynamics that provide the external driving force on the system, the better equipped the system is likely to be at devising effective and efficient schemes and procedures.

Changes in circumstances

Changes in circumstances which occur while people are in receipt of a benefit pose particular administrative dilemmas. A change is only important if it has a material affect on a person's entitlement: increasing it, reducing it or taking the person out of benefit altogether. The problem lies in the difficulty of distinguishing in advance those changes which will have such a substantive effect from those which will not. At the simplest level the administrative solution depends on deciding on a balance between the administrative savings that might result from ignoring changes and savings in the cost of benefit to be made from recognising them. However, because so little is known about the dynamics of individuals' circumstances the basic information necessary to inform the administrative solution is often unavailable. (In reality, of course, there are other considerations beyond savings such as the inequities which would creep into the system if, for example, reporting of a change in circumstance was made voluntary.)

Research has been commissioned in Britain to investigate the administrative consequences of changes in circumstances, but, as yet, the findings are unavailable. As noted above, in the context of the 1982/3 Housing Benefit system, when a scheme is unduly sensitive to changes, or when the administrative tasks set in train to respond to them are particularly complex, the consequences can make a scheme close to unworkable.

Stability of circumstances

Closely related are a set of issues appertaining to the assumptions which are made about the stability of individuals' circumstances. Assumptions are made about the variability of income when determining the time period over which income is to be assessed for benefit purposes. A single monthly salary slip may be accepted as proof of earnings whereas a weekly wage slip is unlikely to be (Walker, Hedges and Massey, 1987). Concern has been expressed about the possibility that some applicants for benefits may be able to adjust the flow of their income, particularly payments of overtime, to maximise entitlements to benefits. This issue has particular salience in the context of benefits with long periods of entitlement, itself in part a response to a desire to minimise the administrative costs of responding to frequent changes in circumstances.

Corresponding assumptions are made about the stability of employment. Collecting contributions through employers would be impossible if all spells of employment were short. The prevalence of self employment in the building industry is evidence of this. The short term nature of the employment, and the consequently fluctuating labour force, no doubt serve to reinforce the desire of some contractors to avoid having to pay employers' contributions. Whether some of the trends towards less secure forms of employment will develop to such an extent as to place an employer administered contribution system under severe strain, time alone will tell.

Individuals and households, budgeting for today and in the longer term, make assumptions about the stability, or the planned trajectory, of their financial circumstances. A new mortgage or hire-purchase agreement is premised on a particular flow of income. Pension plans, including those offered by the state, are based on assumptions about the likely number of years which will be spent in employment. It is often when the assumptions prove to be incorrect that individuals turn to the social security system. The evidence from the USA reported in Chapter 4 illustrates that people's circumstances are far from stable and the occurrence, nature and extent of the changes that people experience are largely unexpected.

Moreover, there are grounds for believing that financial instability is increasing although this cannot yet be confirmed empirically. Relationship breakdown has increased dramatically in Britain. Unemployment levels in the last ten years were two to three times those in earlier years, and there is some evidence that unemployment is reaching different and wider sections of the community than in earlier times. There is evidence of an increase in less secure jobs, disproportionately occupied by women (Lonsdale, 1987), while the skills and aptitudes required by employees are changing fast. As a result the experience of a single lifetime career may be becoming increasingly rare. If these trends continue, then life plans and social security systems based on assumptions of stability or steady progression may become increasingly anachronistic. The clientele of social security would similarly change, resulting in a need to reach a wider cross section of the public during periods in the life cycle that have traditionally been characterised by relative prosperity.

Benefit durations

The earlier discussion showed that the ability to predict the time that people are likely to spend on benefit from a knowledge of their circumstances introduces the possibility of a new policy goal, namely to influence the time for which individuals remain on benefit. This might be attractive financially if cost effective means could be found of helping people to move out of benefit. Equally it may be considered both personally and socially desirable for some groups of social security recipients to become financially self-sufficient.

Being able to predict durations has other advantages. It may allow more cost effective payment methods to be developed differentiating shorter and longer term recipients. It could inform decisions about the procedures to adopt in response to changes in circumstances: if most spells of receipt are likely to be short it might be possible to dispense with change of circumstances provisions altogether. Periods of entitlement could be set so as to coincide with modal spells of eligibility with possible savings in processing costs. As mentioned already, benefit levels could be set to take account of the likely duration on benefit and additional supportive services might be provided for potentially long term cases.

The extent of repeat claims for AFDC in America was sufficient to warrant adjustment of the targeting strategy. Certainly, this is important if a goal of policy is to be to reduce overall durations on benefit and short term cases are more likely than others to reapply. Some savings in time and administration might also be possible if decisions about filing and storage of case papers were based on analyses of benefit dynamics.

Multiple benefit receipt

Some benefits relate to others in complex ways. Receipt of one benefit may preclude receipt of another. Housing Benefit and Family Credit in Britain can be received simultaneously although each benefit affects entitlement for the other. Sickness Benefit is a step on a benefit career to Invalidity Benefit. Receipt of Invalid Care Allowance is dependent on the receipt of Attendance Allowance by the person receiving care. Family Credit is designed partly to facilitate people moving off Income Support and ultimately out of the benefit system altogether (see Chapters 8 and 9). As yet little is known about the packages of benefits and the standard of living that in practice they support. This clearly has implications for the targeting of benefits, both individually and in concert. It also places limitations on the extent to which the administration of benefits might be simplified or, in other respects, be made more efficient. Likewise there is much to be learnt about the way in which individual benefits support and frustrate the objectives of others (Thirlway, 1989, McLaughlin, 1987).

Unravelling the nature and extent of movements between benefits and combinations of benefits obviously requires detailed longitudinal data which has yet to be assembled. Two pairs of questions need answers. First, what were people doing prior to benefit receipt (specifically what were their sources of income, including benefits?) and what change in circumstances triggered receipt of benefit? Secondly, where did people go on leaving the benefit (specifically what were their sources of income, including benefits?) and what factors facilitated the move off benefit? These questions can be further refined by examining the characteristics of individuals who move on and off benefits and comparing with those who do not.

In the first instance, the questions to be addressed by analyses of this kind are probably best formulated with respect to individual benefits. As analyses are undertaken, however, it is likely that the thrust of the questions will shift from a benefit centred focus to a system-wide perspective (Lewis and Morrison, 1988). A study in the USA of the multiple receipt of Old Age Survivors and Disability Insurance, Unemployment Insurance, Supplemental Security Income, AFDC and Food Stamps (Doyle cited in Long, Beebout and Skidmore, 1986) found that a third of recipients reported some change in the package of benefits received during one year and that one-fifth experienced three or more transitions. Exhaustion of eligibility for unemployment insurance was an important precipitant of Food Stamp participation.

Conclusion

The aim in this chapter has been to begin thinking about the implications of taking greater account of time and process in the targeting and administration of social security.

The main thrust of the argument is that a failure to take more account of the dynamic nature of need acts to distort and obscure understanding of the effectiveness and use made of individual benefits, and hence to constrain policy development. Paying explicit attention to dynamics may result in improved targeting, promotion and administration and to policies which seek to alter the dynamics of benefit receipt.

The argument has been presented at a general level rather than in relation to specific benefits. This has been a necessary step in unpacking the potential of a new way of thinking.

A lack of data has meant that in the past understanding of some phenomena has been blurred or even distorted, while the potential for fine tuning and developing policy has remained untapped. By way of conclusion it may be worth spelling out the kinds of data that are required if a dynamic approach to policy formation and administration is to be adopted.

Repeated reference has been made to longitudinal data. Longitudinal data may be derived from surveys in which a sample is drawn from a population and the same people are interviewed on a number of occasions (waves) yielding measures which can then be compared for the same individuals over time (i.e. between waves). Longitudinal surveys are to be distinguished from repeated cross-sectional surveys where measures taken from a sample drawn from a population at one point in time are compared with measures from a second sample drawn from the same population at a different date.

Repeated cross sectional surveys are usually used to measure change at an aggregate level, that is 'net' change. Average income may have risen - a net change - but aggregate data derived from repeated cross sectional data cannot determine whether the average increase results from a rise in everybody's income or from a rise in some people's incomes outweighing the fall in other people's. This can only be determined by examining change at the individual level, 'gross' change, which is best achieved by means of a longitudinal survey.

It is possible to use a cross sectional survey to examine net change, but only by the use of retrospective questions. For example, respondents might be asked to report their income for each month over the last year. However, retrospective questions are notoriously subject to recall errors and therefore longitudinal surveys are to be preferred for measuring change at the individual level (Bailar, 1989; Dippo, 1989). Longitudinal surveys can also be used for measuring aggregate change although they can sometimes be affected by differential sample attrition (people with particular characteristics may be prone to refuse at later waves of the survey). This has to be 'corrected' by special weighting.

Longitudinal data can be constructed from administrative records provided each individual is assigned a unique identifier. This can be done in several ways producing data sets with different characteristics. One approach is the cohort method in which people on (or coming onto) benefit are included in the sample in one year (or occasion) and are followed up in every subsequent year until they leave the system. Once they leave the system they cannot rejoin the sample even if they return to the system by receiving benefit again. Cohort samples eventually wither away as people leave the system.

Another method is the standing sample which is the form increasingly being adopted by the UK Department of Social Security when generating analytic samples such as the Annual Statistical Enquiry. In this case individuals are included in the sample if their individual identifier is of a particular form (e.g. the person's national insurance number ends in particular digits). A person with the appropriate identifier will be included in the sample whenever they are on benefit at the time when the sample is drawn. Leaving aside the possibility of error, when a person does not appear in the sample he or she can be assumed not to be in receipt of benefit. Typically, however, it is not possible to tell whether a person who

113

is included on two consecutive occasions moved off benefit during the intervening period. (This latter problem may be addressed either by reducing the period between each wave of data collection or by retrospectively gathering information about the intervening period.)

Longitudinal data derived from administrative records have a number of advantages over survey based material. There are no problems of response or sample attrition and the information recorded should be highly accurate. Large samples of specific subgroups are normally relatively easy to compile. Studies based on administrative records are inexpensive whereas longitudinal surveys are the very opposite. The principal disadvantage is that information is not generally available about the circumstances of people prior to applying for benefit and the factors that precipitated application, or their circumstances after they have ceased to receive benefit. For information of this kind it is usually necessary to rely on information collected in longitudinal surveys and in this regard the British Household Panel Study is of particular importance.

The different characteristics of survey and record based data mean that the requirements for time sensitive information are unlikely to be met by a single monolithic study. Different policy questions will need to be addressed in varying ways, probably by different studies. One particularly fruitful possibility, however, is to combine approaches. The British Household Panel Study could be linked to a study of records. Analysis of standing sample data sets could be accompanied by postal or interview enquiries to ascertain information about periods when people were not in receipt of benefit.

This incremental, 'mix and match' strategy also means that there is no need to delay studies of benefit dynamics until some distant age when longitudinal data is readily available. Exploiting existing data will not only inform current policy developments, but also generate the experience and expertise necessary fully to utilise the potential of the main longitudinal series as soon as they become available.

TAKING ACCOUNT OF TIME:
EXAMPLES

6 Patterns of childhood poverty in the USA

The radical reappraisal of the nature of poverty that occurred in the USA during the 1980s was in no small measure attributable to the availability of information on families' financial and other circumstances derived from long running panel studies (George and Howards, 1991; Ruggles, 1990; Ellwood 1988; Danziger and Weinberg, 1986; Duncan, Coe and Hill, 1984).

Poverty is now less frequently viewed as a simple either/or state with the poor being contrasted with the non-poor. Rather, poverty is seen to be dynamic, occurring in spells each of which has a beginning and (most) an end that are in turn associated with a set of 'triggers' or precipitating factors (Bane and Ellwood, 1986; Burkhauser and Duncan, 1989).

Likewise, poverty is typically differentiated according to the length of spell. The large majority of spells have been shown to be short. How short depends on the length of accounting period over which needs and resources are assessed. However, it is the existence of long-term or persistent poverty which has perhaps attracted most comment and policy attention (see Chapter 3, and Murray, 1984; Duncan and Rodgers, 1990). There are numerous grounds for believing that the longer the spell of poverty, the lower the level of economic welfare and the greater the economic and social disadvantage. Persistent poverty also provides a necessary, if insufficient, condition for the development of an underclass or the manifestation of

---

[1] A variant of this Chapter was presented as a conference paper under the joint authorship of Karl Ashworth, Martha Hill and Robert Walker (1992). We are grateful to Dr Hill for letting us modify and reproduce it here.

underclass-like behaviour (Ruggles, 1989). Moreover, the very duration of persistent poverty means that it affects a disproportionate number of the individuals who are poor at any one time. Consequently a large portion of welfare expenditure is, in practice, directed towards the long-term poor.

However, the reappraisal of American poverty has neglected a number of considerations which are the focii of this chapter. First, relatively little attention has been paid to the temporal patterning of the poverty experienced by individuals and families. It is established below that many children encounter repeated spells of poverty which sometimes merge to form a type of poverty that may be as economically disadvantageous as permanent poverty.

Secondly, little account has been taken of the severity of the poverty suffered by the poor; that is the extent to which resources fall short of needs. The economic circumstances of families with incomes a few dollars short of the poverty standard have been treated as equivalent to those with resources equalling only a half or a third of requirements whereas in reality the level of their economic welfare is very different.

A third neglected issue relates to the way in which poverty might affect living standards in the longer term and the extent to which resources built up during periods of relative prosperity are, or might, be used to tide people over periods of want. This links with the way in which spells of poverty are distributed over time and the balance between resources and needs that is experienced during poverty and periods of relative affluence.

Fourthly, there is surprisingly little recent work on the distribution of poverty. This observation applies particularly to studies of poverty dynamics where rather greater attention is paid to the characteristics of spells than to the characteristics of the individuals who are affected.

The aim in this chapter is to map the social distribution of different types of poverty and to explore the associated pattern of living standards in the short and longer term. The focus is on childhood poverty. Children suffer disproportionately more poverty than adults, reflecting both the financial demands and limitations which they impose on family budgets, and it is becoming evident that some carry the scars of the experience into adulthood (Hernandez, 1993; Danziger and Stern, 1990; Bane and Ellwood, 1989).

The approach

There is not space to detail the developing debate about the nature of poverty or to elucidate the reasons for the particular focus that has come to be adopted (see Chapter 2). Suffice to say, that the long-standing disagreements about the causes of poverty remain with some commentators giving greater weight to personal characteristics (Elder, 1988; Murray, 1984; Mead, 1989) and others to structural considerations (George and Howards, 1990; Ellwood, 1988). Where there is perhaps consensus, however, is in the belief that the duration of poverty is an important determinant of individuals' economic welfare and that people who experience long spells of poverty may be placed at a longer term disadvantage.

One technical problem associated with attempting to assess the duration of poverty relates to spell censorship (see Chapter 2). This occurs when a spell of poverty begins before the observation period offered by a study (left-hand censorship) or ends after the completion of the study (right-hand censorship). Bane and Ellwood's (1986) innovative response to the problem of right hand censorship opened the way to the systematic study of duration and had a profound impact on the poverty debate (Burstein and Visher, 1989; Coe, 1988; Holden, Burkhauser and Feaster, 1988). What they did was to use the observed probability of leaving a spell after a given period to generate a distribution of spell lengths given the assumption of a no-growth steady state (see Annex A). However, in so doing the unit of analysis shifts from the individual to the spell which, in turn, diverts attention away from questions to do with distribution of poverty among different social groups.

A different response to the problem of spell censorship is adopted in this chapter which develops ideas from life-course analysis (Chapter 2 and Elder, 1988). In essence, this involves setting the observation period to coincide with a sociologically, socially or personally meaningful period of time such as a life-stage. In this way any spell censorship that occurs coincides with a socially meaningful event or transition. As a consequence it becomes possible to talk about the extent of poverty in childhood, working life or old age and hence to address distributional issues head-on.

Such a formulation also allows the temporal patterning of spells to be examined. This is important for three principal reasons. First, a single long spell of poverty is likely to be experienced differently from a series of shorter spells of the same total duration. Adaptive responses may be different as may any long term effects on personal well-being. Equally, the aetiology of the poverty is unlikely to be the same.

Secondly, different types of poverty are likely to require different policy responses and selective targeting. For example, a Government might want to bridge repeated short spells of poverty, perhaps by offering loans, but would probably think twice about such a strategy in relation to long spells (Ashworth, Hill and Walker, 1994).

Thirdly, as noted in Chapter 2, there is a direct link between the patterning of poverty spells over time and the prevalence of poverty within a population. The smallest number of people will be touched by poverty when individual spells of poverty are long and repeat spells are frequent.

The data were taken from the Panel Study of Income Dynamics (PSID), a longitudinal survey which commenced in 1968 and is still continuing. Five waves of children were selected from the PSID datatape: those aged one in 1969, 1970, 1971, 1972 or 1973. These five waves were then treated as a single cohort in order to maintain a sample size capable of producing robust statistics. Childhood was defined as the first fifteen years of life. The sixteenth year and above were avoided because the chances of children splitting from the parental household increase dramatically after the fifteenth year of life (Buck and Scott, 1991).

Poverty is defined by an income to needs ratio of less than one. Income and needs were first adjusted to a 1987 dollar value using the Consumer Price Index U-X1 weights. The PSID need measures were used in this study (but see below). They are based on the 'Low-Cost Plan' for individual weekly food expenditure requirements, a budget that is 25 per cent higher than the 'Thrifty Food Plan' forming the basis of official US poverty statistics. This latter budget is designed to meet nutritional requirements on a short-term, emergency basis and is, arguably, overly parsimonious for children in long-term poverty. No adjustment was made to the needs for farmers to reflect their lower food costs. Income refers to total family income including cash transfers but excluding Food Stamps (see Hill, Walker and Ashworth (1993) for a discussion of the impact of Food Stamps).

Over the period covered by the analysis (1968-1987) the annual rate of poverty among children first fell from about 12 per cent in 1968 to 11 per cent in 1974, rose to over 15 per cent in 1983 falling back to around 13 per cent in 1987.

Types of childhood poverty

Duration

Table 6.1 is quite familiar territory for those who have followed the developing debate on childhood poverty. It shows that 38 per cent of children experience some poverty during their first fifteen years which compares with an annual poverty rate of between 11 per cent (in 1974) and

15 per cent (in 1983). The largest group experiencing poverty do so for a relatively short period, one to three years, but a fifth, representing seven per cent of all children, spend much the greater part of their childhood in families with insufficient resources to meet basic needs.

Table 6.1
Prevalence and duration of poverty in childhood

| | \multicolumn{6}{c}{Years in Poverty} |
	0	1-3	4-6	7-10	11-15	ALL[a]
% of all children	62	18	8	5	7	99
% of children experiencing poverty	-	46	22	13	20	101
% of all childhood poverty[b]	0	14	20	19	48	101
Weighted sample	12932	3643	1710	1025	1547	20857
Unweighted sample	619	216	134	123	177	1269

a   All percentages are based on weighted sample.
b   Childhood poverty defined as the total number of years of poverty experienced by all children in the cohort (i.e. child years that were years of poverty).

While the figures may be familiar, it is hard to dismiss them as being unimportant. During the late 1960s about 3.5 million children were born each year in the USA so that the seven per cent who were destined to spend most of their first years in poverty translates into 245,000 children. If the proportion were to hold constant for successive cohorts (and some have suggested that the situation has worsened) that would mean that in any year one could find about 3.7 million children with similarly depressing prospects.

The table shows that the majority of those who are poor are not poor for long periods with the result that the proportion of children who ever experience poverty exceeds the proportion poor in any one year by a factor of almost three (38 per cent and 13.6 per cent respectively). However, this is not to say that poverty is evenly distributed. If it were, given the total sum of poverty experienced by children in the cohort (expressed in child-years), every single child could expect to spend two of their first fifteen years in poverty.

Patterns of poverty

Table 6.2 takes account of the frequency, duration and spacing of spells to define six patterns of poverty that might be argued, a priori, to constitute different experiences. The six patterns, or types of poverty, are defined as follows:

1. Transient poverty, a single spell of poverty lasting a single year;
2. Occasional poverty, more than one spell of poverty but none lasting more than one year; in practice, the duration of relative prosperity always exceeds the duration of poverty in this cohort;
3. Recurrent poverty, repeated spells of poverty, some separated by more than a year and some exceeding a year in length;
4. Persistent poverty, a single spell of poverty lasting between two and 13 years;
5. Chronic poverty, repeated spells of poverty never separated by more than a year of relative prosperity;
6. Permanent poverty, poverty lasting continuously for fifteen years.

All six kinds of poverty were found in the cohort. By far the most common is recurrent poverty which described the experience of 16 per cent of children, 41 per cent of those who were ever poor, and 53 per cent of those in poverty at any given time. This finding underlines the inappropriateness of ignoring multiple spells of poverty as has happened in the past and draws attention to the instability which seems to characterise many peoples' lives (Chapter 4, Duncan, 1988; Burkhauser and Duncan, n.d.). For the households in which these children reside - noting, though, that some children will move households - the experience is one of frustrated prospects, when spells of relative prosperity are followed by longish spells of poverty; circumstances in which plans are impossible or, else, are as likely as not to come to nought[2].

Table 6.2
Patterns of poverty

	% of all children	Pattern of Poverty[a]		Duration Means (SD) Years	Weighted sample	Unweighted sample
		% of children experiencing poverty	% of all childhood poverty[c]			
No poverty	62	-	-	0.0(0.0)	12932	619
Transient	10	27	5	1.0(0.0)	2162	113
Occasional	3	8	4	2.5(0.8)	637	44
Recurrent	16	41	53	6.9(2.9)	3240	294
Persistent	5	14	12	4.7(3.3)	1102	90
Chronic	2	5	13	13.5(0.7)	426	55
Permanent	2	5	13	15.0(1.0)	358	54
ALL[b]	100	100	100	5.4(4.4)	20857	1269

a See text for definition.
b All percentages are based on weighted sample.
c See Table 6.1 for definition.

---

[2] The recorded incidence of poverty is always a function of the definition used, a limitation that applies equally to the study of poverty types. Sensitivity analyses reported elsewhere (Ashworth, Hill and Walker, 1992; Hill, Walker and Ashworth, 1993) show that raising or lowering the poverty threshold does not change the rankings of the six types of poverty in terms of their relative frequency and involves few major shifts in the characteristics of children by poverty type.

Transient poverty, the second most common form, may be the least worrying from a policy viewpoint. First, it appears to be self rectifying. Secondly, it accounts for a very small proportion of total poverty and of the children who are poor at any one time (5 per cent). Occasional poverty, the other 'mild' form of poverty, where relatively lengthy periods of comparative prosperity are interspersed with short bouts of poverty, is even less common and only accounts for 3.5 per cent of total poverty.

Fourteen per cent of the children who are poor experience a single spell of persistent poverty. This particular form of poverty accounts for a similar proportion of total experienced in childhood (12 per cent). In marked contrast, the four per cent of children who are either permanently poor, or suffer chronic poverty with little respite, account for hugely disproportionate amounts of the total duration of poverty. As an inevitable corollary they form substantial proportions of the children who are poor at any given time (13 per cent in each case).

Duration remains central to this typology and is apparent in the fourth column of Table 6.2 which shows the average length of poverty associated with each poverty type. Durations for transient and permanent poverty are fixed. On average, children experiencing recurrent poverty spend more time in poverty than those who experience a single persistent spell.

Severity and living standards

Table 6.3 gives an indication of the severity of poverty associated with each type of poverty and a measure of childhood living standards. Severity is indexed (in the first column) by the average of the income to needs ratio experienced in each year when income fell short of needs, living standards (in the second column) by the income to needs ratio, averaged over the 15 years of childhood. Both add weight to the contention that the six poverty types index different experiences.

Income averages about 70 per cent of needs during spells of poverty irrespective of whether a child spends between one to three, four to six or seven to 10 years in poverty. There is also very little difference in the severity of poverty encountered by children experiencing transient, occasional, recurrent or persistent poverty (although, as comparison of the standard deviations indicates, experience is more varied among the first two types of poverty). However, it is evident that poverty among children who are permanently poor, or who suffer very brief spells of respite, is very severe even when account is taken of differences in household composition.

For the former group annual income amounts to only 46 per cent of need and for the latter group it averages 59 per cent during spells of poverty.

Table 6.3
Severity of poverty[a]

	Income to needs ratio during poverty spells[b] Mean (SD) $	Income to needs ratio during childhood[c] Mean (SD) $
Duration		
0	-	3.31 (1.60)
1-3	.71 (.23)	2.32 (1.13)
4-6	.69 (.15)	1.43 (0.37)
7-10	.67 (.14)	1.08 (0.18)
11-15	.57 (.13)	0.66 (1.60)
Experience		
Transient	.71 (.26)	2.63 (1.30)
Occasional	.69 (.21)	1.82 (0.49)
Recurrent	.67 (.15)	1.21 (0.45)
Persistent	.70 (.14)	1.66 (0.63)
Chronic	.59 (.09)	0.66 (0.08)
Permanent	.46 (.13)	0.46 (0.13)
TOTAL	.67 (.20)	2.68 (1.63)

a   Some of the distributions depart significantly from normal and the interpretation given in the text is informed by comparison of the full distributions.
b   Average of ratios of income to needs for individual years in poverty.
c   Ratio of income to needs for individual years averaged over the 15 years of childhood.

The second column in Table 6.3 takes account of the income received in years when income exceeded needs to give a measure of childhood living standards. As the duration of poverty increases, so the number of years in which to acquire income in excess of minimum needs falls. Not surprisingly, therefore, the income to needs ratio falls steadily with duration with the turnaround point occurring between eight and nine years: children who are in poverty for any longer are entrenched in a childhood of penury.

The figures suggest that transient poverty is typically a one off aberration from an accustomed way of life. Certainly, children who experience a single year of poverty generally do not spend the remainder of their childhood living on the margins of poverty. The ratio of income to needs for these children, when averaged over the fifteen years of childhood, is 2.63 compared with 3.31 for children who are never poor. Indeed, one in six of them has an income to needs ratio that exceeds the average for children who are never poor.

In terms of childhood living standards, the position of children who encounter occasional short spells of poverty is comparable with those who experience a single spell of persistent poverty. In both cases the income deficits incurred during years of poverty are generally more than offset by income received in the more prosperous years. Nevertheless, taking childhood as a whole, income levels are not high. At first sight the apparent similarity between these groups is a little surprising since 65 per cent of the first group are in poverty only twice and none for more than four years, whereas 32 per cent of the second group have spells lasting five or more years. What appears to be happening is that, for many children, the repeated spells of poverty simply represent small downward fluctuations in the financial circumstances of families living for long periods on very constrained budgets. The single spells of persistent poverty, on the other hand, frequently constitute major departures from normal living standards of the kind associated with relationship breakdown, redundancy and substantial loss of earning power occasioned by illness and disability (see Duncan, 1988).

Recurrent poverty appears qualitatively different again and is very homogeneous given the large size of the group. It is severe and lasting hardship and experienced by 16 per cent of all children. Only 30 per cent of the children in this group live in families which have incomes during their childhood years, that exceed needs by more than 30 per cent. Moreover, for another 31 per cent of children income falls short of need; this proportion represents 2.6 million children, by far the largest group to spend their childhood beyond the margins of the affluent society.

126

If recurrent poverty is the most common experience of harsh poverty, the very worst experience is reserved for the two per cent of children in permanent poverty. Family income falls short of needs by 54 per cent, the equivalent of $6,540 per annum for a two person household. No child in this group resided with a family which had an income that averaged more than 70 per cent of needs and for 24 per cent of children the income-needs ratio was less than 0.33. This is poverty of a third world order.

Chronic poverty is also severe. During spells of poverty the shortfall in family income averaged 43 per cent and exceeded 50 per cent for one child in seven. Moreover, income received during the years when the family was not poor was never sufficient to offset the long spells of poverty. However, it did locate many of the children in chronic poverty one rung up the ladder from those in permanent poverty. Over the fifteen years of childhood, needs exceeded income by an average of 33 per cent; this was true of just five per cent of children in permanent poverty.

Correlates with poverty type

The next task is to explore, from two different perspectives, whether the six poverty types are differentially associated with various social and economic indicators. The first perspective, which leads us to ask whether certain groups are more or less prone to different kinds of poverty, is concerned with distributional questions and matters of equity. The second focuses on the poverty types and asks whether they are distinctive in terms of the kinds of people affected. This question is important in thinking about the ease with which the different forms of poverty might be identified and targeted for policy purposes.

The intention in this chapter is not to attempt to construct an explanatory model to account for the existence of different kinds of poverty. This will be attempted later in the research when more is known about the temporal patterning of poverty at other stages in the life-course. Rather we are content to assert that the six different patterns of poverty probably constitute different experiences which, as is explained elsewhere (Ashworth, Hill and Walker, 1994), are likely to be responsive to different policy initiatives (Chapter 10).

Nevertheless, it is difficult (and inappropriate) to avoid some reference to explanatory models in the selection of variables for a descriptive analysis. George and Howards (1991) distinguish between theories to explain the incidence of poverty (that explain why there is poverty) and those concerned with distribution (that explain which individuals are likely to be poor). The latter, relevant here, normally contain individualistic and structural elements with the relative weight given to each varying considerably.

Individualistic elements that have tended to be emphasised in the recent literature include lone-parent families, the consequence of pre-marital births and relationship breakdown, school drop-outs and limited attachment to the labour market (work as an aspiration rather than an obligation (Mead, 1989)). Structural factors include class, race and gender played out against a backcloth of relatively high levels of unemployment and historically low rates of economic growth. Individual variables and social phenomena assume different meanings according to emphasis. Limited education may indicate limited adherence to accepted values (Murray, 1984), or be a mechanism through which class inequalities are perpetuated (Duncan, 1984), a culpable failure on the part of either the individual or society to invest in the development of human capital. Likewise, the significance and even the existence of the underclass is contested (Murray, 1984; Wilson 1991; Hughes, 1988; McLanahan and Garfinkel, 1988).

Univariate correlates

The lack of a generally accepted model to explain the distribution of poverty means that indicators such as those presented in Table 6.4 are open to interpretation.

But the difference in the prevalence of childhood poverty between the various sub groups is, nevertheless, striking and underlines the inequitable distribution of poverty among children reported elsewhere (Ellwood, n.d.). Some of the values are very high. Sixty three per cent of children who spend time with a lone parent experience poverty. So do 69 per cent of those in families with limited earning power and 72 per cent where the family head spends time outside the labour market. Seventy nine per cent of African Americans suffer poverty as children.

The kinds of poverty experienced also vary markedly between subgroups. As a rule the groups which are least likely to experience poverty tend not to encounter it in its most severe form. Thus, 46 per cent of the children from well educated homes who do experience poverty suffer only a single transient spell while another 14 per cent face repeated short spells. In contrast over a quarter of African American children are either in poverty permanently or only escape for a year at a time. The same is true of 17 per cent of those with parents who are sometimes out of the labour market.

Table 6.4

The incidence of different patterns of poverty among selected groups

Percentages

		Transient	Occasional	Recurrent	Persistent	Chronic	Permanent	ALL	Prevalence[a]	Sample Size (weighted)
1) Number of children in poverty	1-3	43	5	34	16	1	1	100	37	12864
	>3	13	11	47	12	9	7	100	53	7993
2) Sex of head	Male	30	8	42	15	8	2	100	34	6436
	Female	16	10	35	9	16	16	100	76	1489
3) Years spent in family	0-14 years	23	8	38	14	8	6	100	63	7189
	15 years	30	7	45	13	1	2	100	24	13668
4) Education of Head	Up to: 11th Grade	25	5	46	14	5	5	100	50	8917
	12th Grade+	46	14	24	15	0	0	100	14	6214
5) Race of Head	White Caucasian	36	9	38	15	1	2	100	21	2924
	African-American	5	7	48	12	15	12	100	79	17159
6) Mean Hourly Earnings of Head (1987)	< $10 per hour	20	9	47	12	7	6	101	69	9118
	> $10 per hour	54	6	18	23	0	0	101	14	11739
7) Labour Market Status	Always in	39	10	37	13	1	0	100	24	14845
	Some period/s out	17	6	44	15	9	8	100	72	6012
8) Region	North/Central/West	31	8	41	15	4	2	100	34	14219
	South	20	8	42	12	8	9	100	47	6551
9) Time in Urban Area (largest city 100,000)	0-7 years	10	4	18	6	2	2	100	43	10436
	8-15 years	10	2	13	4	2	1	100	33	10421

a Percentage of children experiencing poverty in the first 16 years.

129

Notes to Table 6.4

1) Number of children: maximum number of children ever present in family unit over childhood.
2) Sex of family head at birth.
3) Years spent in a two parent family.
4) Education level of head same for between 10 and 15 years. 26 per cent of children are excluded.
5) Race of family head at birth.
6) Heads average hourly earnings over all 15 years converted to 1987 prices.
7) Number of years head is out of the labour market.
8) Region of birth. Too few children changed region to have a significant effect on results.
9) Number of years spent in area where the largest city had population greater than 100,000.

However, there are some qualifications to this rule. For example, the highest incidence of persistent poverty among ever poor children occurs among those from typically high earning families. This is consistent with the view of persistent poverty as being, in some cases, a marked departure from normal circumstances contingent upon some economic or domestic shock.

Indeed, persistent poverty is more evenly distributed across each of the socio-demographic groups than any other type of poverty which may reflect the occurrence of unanticipated, perhaps unpredictable events.

Multivariate correlates

Constraints of cell size make it impossible to construct a model that explores all the interactions between the variables presented in Table 6.4. Instead a series of partial models were investigated using combinations of three independent variables (poverty type being interpreted as the dependent variable). The associations reported below are those which appear most germane in the context of current policy interest (see Annex B).

a)   Economic interactions. The first analysis focused on the economic dimensions of poverty using indices of earning power, attachment to the labour force and region of birth (see Figure 6.1 which represents the first two sets of relationship diagramatically).

Three general observations can be made. First, a child in a low waged family is highly likely to spend time in poverty even if the parent remains firmly attached to the labour market. Four out of five children did so and in sixty per cent of these cases the poverty experienced was recurrent. But in the North, employment at least meant that children avoided permanent or chronic poverty.

Secondly, to live in a family where the head is not only low paid but also spends time out of the labour market virtually guarantees poverty for a child. What kind of poverty depends on where a child lives. If born in the South, 39 per cent of these children will experience permanent poverty or manage to escape it for no more than a year at a time. If born in the North only 17 per cent will suffer permanent and chronic poverty. Instead most are exposed to recurrent bouts of financial hardship.

Gender is also important because women are disproportionately represented among the low paid. A third of the families with low earning power and detached from the labour market were headed by a woman at the birth of the sampled child, and 19 per cent of the children involved always lived with a lone parent. These values compare with 10 and three per cent for the sample as a whole.

Thirdly, the different prevalence of poverty between Southern States compared with those in the North, Centre and West that was revealed in Table 6.4 can be decomposed into three principal elements. First, and most important in numerical terms, is the shortfall in families with well paid, secure jobs in the South compared with the North. In the latter case, over two thirds of children lived in homes where the head was always in work and earned in excess of $10 per hour. Only 14 per cent of these children ever experienced poverty and in 68 per cent of cases the experience was transitory. However, in the South only 53 per cent of children lived with parents that had secure, well paid jobs.

Secondly, high earnings appear to offer more protection against the economic trauma of unemployment in the North than in the South. Half of the children living in generally prosperous families in the North escape poverty altogether even if their parents spend some time out of the labour market. In the South this is true of only 14 per cent of the corresponding group. Finally, secure, well paid employment in the South is marginally less likely than in the North to provide a complete defence against poverty.

Permanent and chronic poverty are associated exclusively with a combination of low wages and limited attachment to employment. Recurrent

Figure 6.1
**Poverty type, labour market participation (always 'in' versus
sometimes 'out') and high and low wages**

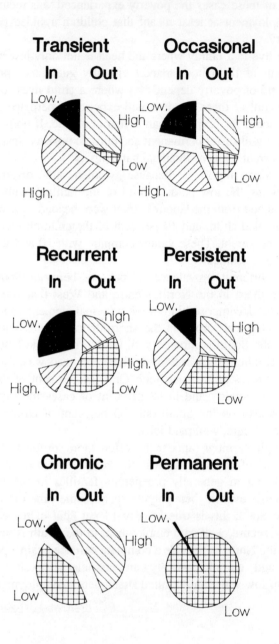

poverty, on the other hand, is common among all but two of the 16 groups included in the analysis. Both exceptions involve families with higher earning power. The risk of poverty for children of northern families with a head who is never out of the labour market is very low. When it occurs, however, it usually takes the form of a single spell. For 68 per cent the spell is transient; for another 19 per cent the spell is persistent. Only nine per cent encounter recurrent periods of poverty. The other exception, higher earning families in the South with some detachment from the labour market, presents a not dissimilar pattern. Once again a single spell is typical: for 43 per cent of children it lasts one year and for 25 per cent longer.

b)   *Social interactions.* The second analysis juxtaposes race[3] with family stability, and explores the interaction in the different economic and cultural contexts provided by the southern states compared with states in north, central and western USA. (Figure 6.2 omits the associations with geographic region.) The finding that childhood poverty is highest among black Americans living in the South will come as no surprise. The absolute figure (81 per cent) is nevertheless striking. So is the finding that the prevalence of poverty among black children living in the North is almost as great (77 per cent). The corresponding figures for white Americans are very much lower and show greater regional differentiation (28 per cent and 37 per cent for North and South respectively).

The higher levels of poverty in the South have different manifestations for black and white children. Caucasian children are more likely to experience repeated spells of poverty than their northern counterparts. The prevalence of recurrent poverty for example, is 16 per cent, compared with 10 per cent in the North. Two per cent also appear to be permanently poor. Among black children the prevalence of chronic (15 per cent), persistent and permanent poverty (both at 13 per cent) are all higher in the South but the prevalence of recurrent poverty correspondingly drops from 45 per cent to 31 per cent.

Black children are much more likely than their white counterparts to spend time in lone parent families and this is especially so in the South where 73 per cent of black children do so compared with just 27 per cent of white. (Corresponding figures for the North are 63 per cent and 37 per cent.)

---

[3] Data limitations only permit a distinction because Caucasian (white) and other children have been termed 'black'. Children of Hispanic origin are included as Black.

Figure 6.2
Variety type, race, 'one' and (always) 'two' parent family

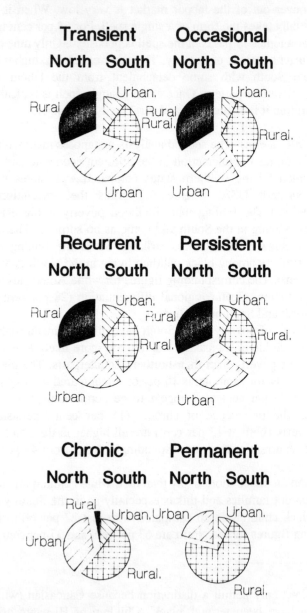

Figure 6.2
Variety type, race, 'one' and (always) 'two' parent family

Spending time with a lone parent dramatically increases the risk of poverty: from 23 per cent to 51 per cent for white children and from 49 per cent to 93 per cent for black. However, the type of poverty associated with a broken or incomplete home depends on the region of birth and race. In the North, 43 per cent of the white children who spend time without both parents and experience poverty suffer only transient spells. Virtually no white child born in the North suffers either chronic or permanent poverty associated with living with a lone parent but 11 per cent of those born in the South do so.

However, the extreme poverty associated with living for periods with a lone parent is most evident in the South where poverty is in any case endemic within the black community. Eighteen per cent are permanently poor and 23 per cent experience a single year's respite.

c) *Education as a class mediator.* The third model combined race, family stability and parental education to consider how far the observed relationships between poverty and the first two characteristics were affected by differences in education level.

Two conclusions emerge. First, while having a parent educated to twelfth grade or above noticeably reduces the risk of poverty faced by a white child (from 42 per cent to 11 per cent) it has no such straight-forward effect for black children (corresponding figures are 24 per cent and 26 per cent). Instead, the black child is better protected against the risk of experiencing the most severe forms of hardship. Less than one per cent of the black children with better educated parents are chronically or permanently poor compared with 19 per cent of other black children. More of those with better educated parents are likely to be poor only occasionally (24 per cent compared with 3 per cent) or to experience a single persistent spell (16 per cent contrasting with 8 per cent).

Secondly, the association between higher parental educational attainment and greater family stability among white children is reversed among black children: 80 per cent of black children with a family head who had completed twelfth grade spent time without one parent compared with 59 per cent where the head had not. This goes part way to explaining why the level of parental education does not reduce the risk of poverty among black children.

d) *Ecological associations.* The final model explored interactions between region, urbanism and race. (Figure 6.3 omits the associations with race.) Permanent, urban, childhood poverty, at least as portrayed in the

PSID data, is an exclusively black phenomenon affecting six per cent of the constituent black group or one per cent of predominantly urban dwellers. Seventy nine per cent of permanent poverty is located in the South and ninety per cent of this is rural with two thirds being borne by black children. Resources during childhood fall short of needs among this latter group by an average of 54 per cent. Sixteen per cent of black children living in rural areas of the South are continually poor and another 21 per cent escape for periods of no more than a year; only 11 per cent avoid poverty altogether.

Rural poverty in the North afflicts mainly white children (although black children are still disproportionately affected; indeed, 16 per cent suffer chronic poverty compared with only one per cent of their white counterparts). Sixty per cent of the white rural poverty is either recurrent or persistent. This differentiates it markedly from poverty suffered by urban white children. Over half (52 per cent) of the latter group experience transient poverty and only 40 per cent recurrent or persistent spells. The rural poverty experienced by white children is not noticeably more severe than urban poverty, either in terms of the ratio of income to needs when poor, or when averaged over childhood.

If the risk of poverty is greatest for black children in the rural South, at 77 per cent it is only marginally better for black children residing predominantly in the urban North. But the urban poverty typically takes a different form. It is much less likely to be chronic or permanent. Instead 61 per cent of ever poor, black urban children, that is 48 per cent of all black children living in urban areas, experience recurrent poverty. Typically family resources for this group exceed needs by about 22 per cent when measured over childhood.

Socio-demographic dimensions of poverty types

Having found that the incidence of different patterns of poverty varies markedly from one socio-demographic group to another, it remains to be asked whether the various types of poverty can be differentiated according to the characteristics of the children affected. Complex analyses reported elsewhere (Ashworth, Hill and Walker, 1992) confirm that they can.

To summarise, permanent poverty in childhood is overwhelmingly a problem of the rural South. Seventy one per cent of permanently poor children live there and, of these, 70 per cent are black, 70 per cent have spent time with lone parents and none of the families has access to wage

136

Figure 6.3
Poverty type, region and urban and rural location

Transient   Occasional

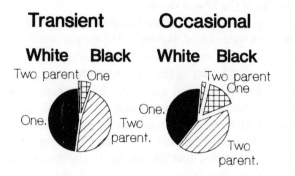

Recurrent   Persistent

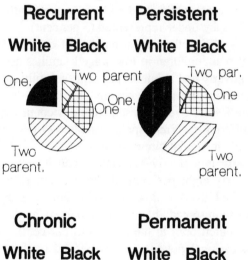

Chronic   Permanent

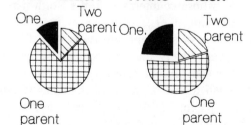

rates above $11 per hour. As noted already when chronic poverty occurs in the North, it is an exclusively urban phenomenon affecting black children. Fifty five per cent of the families are intact but in each case the family head has spent time out of the labour market.

Chronic poverty is also concentrated in the South though to a somewhat lesser extent than permanent poverty. (Sixty per cent of the children affected live in southern states.) The PSID results, which at this level of detail should be treated with caution, indicate that 53 per cent of chronic poverty may be located in rural areas and 89 per cent associated with a combination of low earnings and time spent out of the labour market.

Persistent spells of poverty are much more evenly distributed by region and racial group. As a consequence, 73 per cent of the children affected are white and 57 per cent live outside the South. A quarter of the children affected are white children living in urban areas in the North. Fifty nine per cent have lived for spells with lone parents, considerably higher than for the sample as a whole (35 per cent). Low wage families in the North are over represented (29 per cent) while children born in the South with parents in well paid secure jobs are under-represented (5 per cent).

Recurrent poverty afflicts the largest number of children and is relatively evenly spread. Even so, children in low waged families account for 70 per cent of recurrent poverty and about 42 per cent of family heads remained in employment throughout the period covered by the study. Black children from unstable families are over-represented and account for 36 per cent of all the children suffering recurrent spells. Another 24 per cent is accounted for by white children in similar circumstances.

Occasional poverty is similarly associated with lone parenthood among specific groups. Sixty eight per cent of the children suffering occasional bouts of poverty had lived with one parent; among these children two groups were over-represented: black children born in the South (20 per cent) and white children born in the North (18 per cent). Significantly, 38 per cent of all occasional poverty is experienced by generally well paid families in the South whose counterparts in the North may well have been able to escape poverty altogether.

Finally, the distribution of transient poverty is very different from that of the other poverty types. Ninety four per cent of the children affected are white. Forty two per cent live in generally prosperous homes where the head is firmly attached to the labour market. Virtually equal numbers of children live with two parent families (48 per cent) as spend time in families headed by a lone parent (52 per cent). In many respects the children affected have rather more in common with children who are never poor than they do with children suffering other types of poverty. A discriminant analysis not reported in detail in this chapter which included never poor children correctly allocated 71 per cent of them but misclassified 20 per cent of them to the 'transient poverty' group.

Brief discussion

This chapter is offered as a case-study in the differentiation of poverty made possible by taking explicit account of the patterning of poverty over time.

The approach that has been adopted derives from the simple, surely self-evident, propositions that first, a brief spell of poverty is not the same as a lifetime spent with resources outstripped by need and that secondly, neither is the same as repeated bouts of poverty separated by time that may allow for some financial and emotional repair. A six-fold typology was therefore constructed based on the number, duration and spacing of spells of poverty. By equating the observation period with a life-stage, in order partially to overcome the problems created by spell censorship, it was possible to explore the validity of this typology with reference to childhood poverty in the USA using data from the Panel Study of Income Dynamics.

While it is for the reader to judge the value of differentiating poverty in this way, as authors we are well pleased with this first attempt. Not only was each pattern found to occur among American children, each was distinguished by different levels of economic welfare measured over childhood, and associated with a unique set of socio-demographic characteristics. As such we feel that the study enriches previous accounts of childhood poverty in the USA and generates important new substantive and policy questions some of which are addressed in Chapter 10.

7 Patterns of single homelessness: The effects of closing a hostel

Alvaston Resettlement Unit, Derby, finally closed at the end of March 1992, the culmination of a policy that dates back to at least 1985. Resettlement units have a history that begins with the Poor Law and represents the last vestige of the once notorious system of indoor relief. In their current form it is often assumed that they provide temporary accommodation predominantly for men with an unsettled way of life. In fact it appears that Alvaston catered for men who were homeless for a range of different reasons, some of whom made their home at Alvaston for long periods of time.

Objectives and approach

This chapter draws on research funded by the Joseph Rowntree Foundation to establish the consequences of closing Alvaston. However, this is not the occasion to present a comprehensive account of the evaluation (for that, see Deacon, Vincent and Walker, 1993). Instead, information extracted from administrative records is used to explore three inter related issues. The first concerns the way in which Alvaston was used by the men who stayed there. Was it a regular port of call, a more or less permanent home or a crisis refuge? The second has to do with the lifestyle adopted by, or forced upon,

[1] This chapter draws upon research funded by the Joseph Rowntree Foundation and is adapted from Walker, Brittain, Deacon and Vincent (1993). The facts presented and views expressed are those of Walker and Ashworth and not necessarily those of the Foundation.

the men and whether it is possible to deduce this from their pattern of stays at Alvaston. The third bears more directly on the task of evaluation and asks what can be learned about the consequences of closure from a better understanding of hostel dynamics and the lifestyles of residents.

It was normal practice to keep records on each person staying at Alvaston. These typically comprised a wallet, which contained basic personal details and a record of previous stays at Alvaston; a more comprehensive booklet which was completed after a detailed interview with a senior member of staff held on a person's first visit - this was usually updated on subsequent visits; and an administrative medical form (not the residents' National Health records) which was completed by the visiting general practitioner. In addition, a registration book was available listing arrivals, departures and the men in residence on each night of the year, together with basic information about origins and destinations of the men who moved. These records are obviously confidential but, through the good offices of Alvaston staff, anonymised summary sheets were compiled from inspection of the unit records.

It is important to stress the limitations of administrative data. First and foremost, the information was not collected with the needs of research in mind. Residents were not asked fixed format questions and the answers were not necessarily recorded in a standardised way. Staff may not have completed the records accurately although the fact that this was the task of senior staff and that the records were in regular use should enhance the reliability of the information. The information collected was not comprehensive in research terms and the information that was recorded was not always available for all residents. There is also known (and unknown) bias in the records: for example, records were more comprehensive for long stay residents than for other men. On the other hand, if the records of long term residents had not been updated, the information available on their files may have been superseded by events.

While the inadequacies of the data should not be overlooked, administrative records do have enormous advantages. Some information was available about every person who stayed at Alvaston during the period in question. In particular, this meant that it was possible to record the movements of men who stayed for a single night and who were under-represented in surveys of residents conducted by the research team. Disproportionate numbers of residents had mental health and alcohol problems which adds to the difficulty of conducting research interviews. Because staff in the Unit had worked with many of the men over numerous years the records may in fact be more reliable than data gathered by research interview. Moreover, the information on medical conditions was completed by a general practitioner after an examination and was therefore much better than could have been obtained by a research worker. Also, while comprehensive information was not available for every resident, quite respectable 'response rates' were achieved for most topic areas.

From the records it is evident that Alvaston had a very diverse constituency of users. Over a quarter were aged 40-49 but four per cent were teenagers and three per cent aged over 70. Most were not local and between a quarter and a third had been on the road for more than a decade. Even more, however, had probably been homeless for less than twelve months. The largest number (21 per cent) cited the end of a marriage, or marital-like, relationship for their current predicament but unemployment was also particularly important among older men and especially those from Eire. Thirty one per cent of men had a serious drink problem according to medical records held by the Unit. Eleven per cent suffered from depression and six per cent had other mental health problems. Physical health was generally assessed to be good.

The chapter divides into three. The first explores the different ways in which Alvaston was used by the 514 of men who stayed there in 1991/92. The second identifies patterns of stays that may be indicative of varying life-styles while the third explores some of the effects of closing Alvaston.

Patterns of usage

Number and length of stays

All told some 804 stays were recorded in the admissions book between 1 April 1991 and the final closure of Alvaston (Table 7.1). A little over a third (36 per cent) of these stays lasted for a single night and half for three nights or less. At the other extreme, four per cent of spells lasted for nine months or more.

Over two-thirds of men (69 per cent) stayed only once at Alvaston during the final year[2]. For some of these their stay was long. Twenty men had lived at Alvaston for over a year by the time they left. One man made Alvaston his home for over ten years, and another six per cent had lived there for more than six months. However, most men stayed for less than four days and twenty four per cent stayed for a single night.

_____

[2] These figures relate to *men* rather than stays; see Table 7.6 for details.

Table 7.1

Length of stays 1991-1992

	All stays	Ended before 10.12.91	Started before 10.12.91	Started on or after 10.12.91
1 day	36	37	34	45
2 - 3 days	14			26
		26	24	
4 - 7 days	12			9
1 - 4 weeks	20	22	22	15
1 - 9 months	14	12	16	4
9 - 24 months	3	2	4	0
>2 years	1	1	1	0
Total %	100	100	100	100
Number	801	572	634	149

Thirty one per cent of men visited Alvaston on more than one occasion in 1991/92. Not surprisingly, second and subsequent stays were on average shorter than a single spell. This reflects the long spells of continuous residence which characterised some men's use of Alvaston. However, the modal spell length was a single night regardless of whether it was the first, second, or subsequent stay at Alvaston during that year. The median spell length was three or four days for the first three spells, and two for subsequent ones.

Weekend stays, beginning on a Friday or Saturday and ending on a Monday, were a notable feature of Alvaston life, comprising nearly nine per cent of all stays and 62 per cent of those lasting two or three days. Staff talked of men coming in for the weekend 'to get cleaned up' and it was also suggested that Friday and Saturdays were seen as a chance to 'have a night out' with their 'mates'. It would appear, therefore, that Alvaston users were not immune to the periodicity of twentieth century life imposed by the working week even if most had not worked for some considerable time (but see below).

The number of short stays which were recorded in the year before closure is slightly greater than would have been expected in a normal year. After the run down was formally announced on 10 December 1991, in principle, new arrivals were only allowed to register for a single night. However, the effects of this special regime were not great as is evident from the second and fourth columns of Table 7.1 which compares the duration of spells which ended before the 10 December with those which began after that date.

Even taking account of distortion introduced by the run down of Alvaston, it is clear that most residents stayed for very short periods with only a minority staying for more than a week. With men coming and going so quickly, one would anticipate that Alvaston presented a very unstable environment but this was not a feature immediately apparent when visiting the Unit. Instead one repeatedly recognised the same faces and encountered the same names.

The reason for this is evident from Table 7.2 which takes one day at random, 1 October 1991, and records how long each man resident in Alvaston on that night <u>eventually</u> spent in Alvaston on that particular visit. The image gained from this table is very different from that presented in Table 7.1. Rather than transience, the picture presented is one of almost permanence. Only two of the men present on that night stayed for less than a week, and 70 per cent stayed for over a month. A third of the residents lived in Alvaston for over nine months and, for them, Alvaston must have offered a semblance of home, rather than 'a bed for the night'. More than a fifth of residents (23 per cent) were aged over 60 and only 11 per cent were aged under 30 compared with 24 per cent of the men who stayed at Alvaston during the year.

The reason for the discrepancy between Tables 7.1 and 7.2 is that men who stayed for long periods gradually took over a large proportion of the bed places, whereas men using Alvaston for short periods followed each other into the same beds. To some extent these differences were institutionalised at Alvaston. A 'flat project' designed for long stay residents existed as part of a programme aimed at resettlement. Certain of the wings tended to be reserved for new arrivals who in time were transferred onto other wings as vacancies became available.

145

Table 7.2
Length of stays of men resident on 1 October 1991

	Percentages
2 days - 1 week	2
1 week - 4 weeks	21
1 - 3 months	23
6 months	17
6 - 9 months	7
> 9 months	30
Total %	100
Number	53

The accumulation of men who stayed for long periods was not only important in determining the atmosphere and social dynamics of Alvaston, it was also a major influence both on the use of resources and the functions performed by the unit. This is evident from Table 7.3 which shows that, although almost a quarter of the men who visited Alvaston in 1991/2 stayed for one night, they accounted for less than one per cent of the bed spaces that were occupied during the year. On the other hand, the six per cent of men who stayed for more than six months occupied 43 per cent of the bed spaces which were utilized. Even the 11 per cent of men who made repeated short visits to Alvaston - men who might traditionally, if erroneously, be considered to be the archetypical users of resettlement units - accounted for only six per cent of the bed spaces used.

Returning to the night of 1 October which, although chosen at random, might not be considered typical. No men booked into Alvaston on 1st October, a Tuesday, and quite a few men had left in the preceding week. As a result the proportion of men in Alvaston for a short stay may have been at a low ebb. But, as is discussed below, flows in and out of Alvaston were characterised by variety and uncertainty, and it is probable that no one night could be considered typical.

Routes to and from Alvaston

Figure 7.1 presents a graph of the number of men arriving at Alvaston on each day between 1 April 1991 and the effective closure on 20 March 1992. The numbers range between zero and eight with an average of

Table 7.3
Use of bed spaces

		Percentages
Patterns of Stays	Residents	Bed Spaces Used
Single stay		
1 day	24	(0.5)
2 - 7 days	17	1
8 days - 6 months	22	22
> 6 months	6	43
Multiple		
Short spells (less than one week)	16	6
Other	16	27
Total %	101	99
Number	514	23480*

* For simplicity of calculation, spells lasting over 12 months are truncated to 365 days. All other durations are treated as real even if they began before the 1 April 1991. The effect is that calendar time is partially replaced by 'spell time'.

between two and three. Slightly more men arrived on Fridays (2.8 on average) and comparatively few on Sundays (1.3). The number of arrivals was highest in the summer months and low in the period following the announcement of closure and over Christmas 1991 but with substantial day to day variation throughout the year. (It was usual for Alvaston to be heavily used over Christmas but staff reported that other resettlement units were also relatively little used at Christmas 1991, perhaps on account of the increasing availability of special accommodation over the festive period.)

It was possible from the registration book to get some idea of where men had slept the night before their stay at Alvaston and a much rougher impression of where they had left for. The records reveal many cases of men setting out on a long journey, only to return to Alvaston that night. Sometimes this was because plans were genuinely frustrated. On other occasions it was simply that men had not made up their minds what to do. Sometimes men simply lost the will to move when confronted by the reality of doing so.

Table 7.4 records the places where men said they had slept on the night before their arrival at Alvaston. (No record is available for 18 per cent of spells.) In just over half of the cases men said that they had slept rough on the night before their stay. This was typically in the local Derby/Nottingham area, although sizeable numbers had travelled considerable distances during the day. The number of men sleeping rough was highest among those on their first visit to Alvaston during 1991/2 (59 per cent) which will, of course, include men who were newly homeless. However, as many as 71 per cent of those who slept rough before their second visit had also done so before their first one which suggests that a group of men using Alvaston may have commonly slept rough. Those sleeping rough were just as likely to be young as old, and no other characteristic appears to differentiate between them.

While sleeping rough was an important part of the experience of Alvaston users, and may be part of the particular life style adopted by some of them, it is possible to exaggerate the proportion of nights that men slept out of doors. While the Alvaston records do not throw much light on this topic, it would appear likely that a common pattern was for men to sleep rough while in transit between two places where a bed was known to be available.

Fourteen per cent of stays at Alvaston were preceded by a night in a resettlement unit. This may underestimate the extent to which men were on a circuit of resettlement units since some of those sleeping rough may have been on their way to Alvaston from another resettlement unit. On the other hand, just over a third of these men had in fact slept at Alvaston the night before, leaving only to return the same evening.

It is sometimes suggested that some men travel on a circuit of resettlement units partly because they are denied access to other forms of hostels as a result of their stricter regimes. Certainly, men using resettlement units have been shown to have more significant mental and physical health problems than men in other types of hostels (O'Neill, 1989). In this regard it is probably significant that virtually twice as many spells at Alvaston were preceded by a night in a resettlement unit than in all other types of hostel combined. Indeed, it is remarkable just how few men did reach Alvaston directly from other hostels: more arrived there after being discharged from prison, police cells or hospital than came from other hostels (eight per cent and seven per cent respectively). This may also point to a shortage of other hostel accommodation within a day's journey of Alvaston. Forty five per cent of men moving to Alvaston from another resettlement unit came from either Leicester or Sheffield.

Figure 7.1
Number of arrivals at Alvaston: 1/4/91-24/3/92

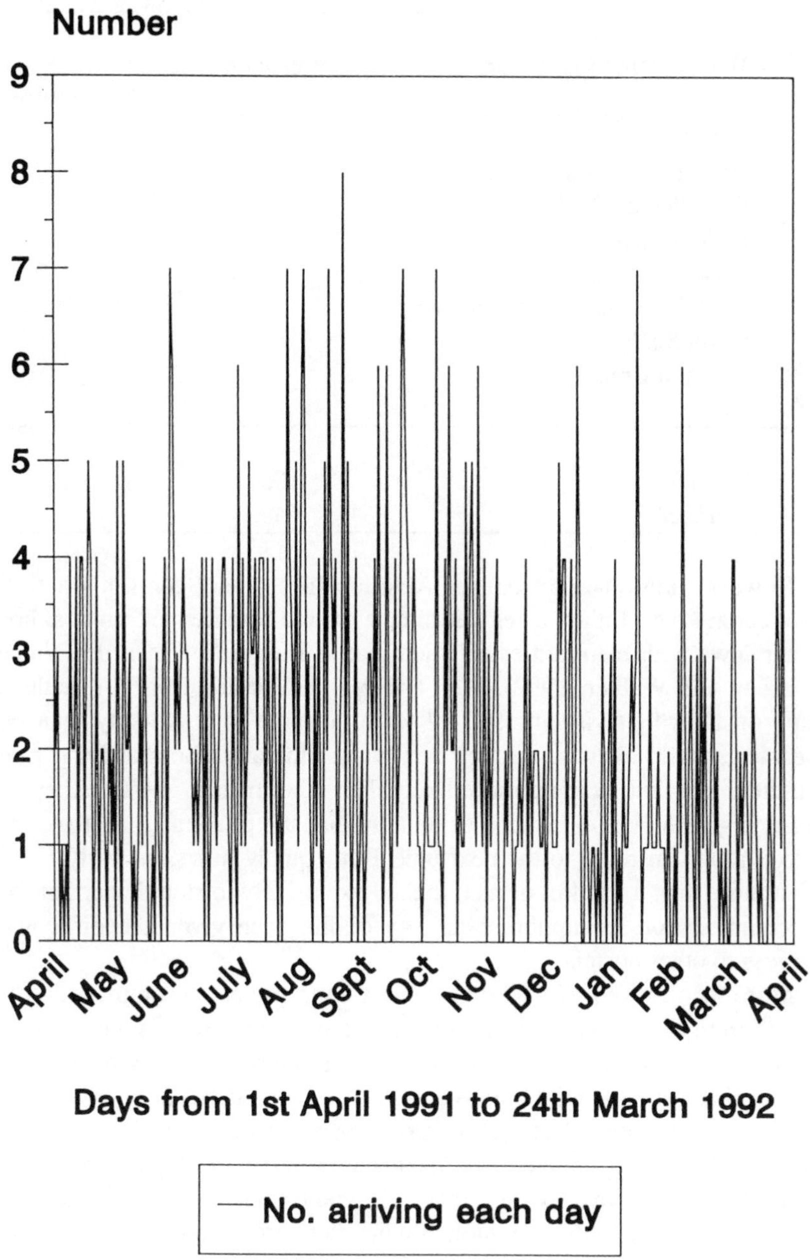
Number
9
8
7
6
5
4
3
2
1
0
April
May
June
July
Aug
Sept
Oct
Nov
Dec
Jan
Feb
March
April
Days from 1st April 1991 to 24th March 1992
No. arriving each day

Table 7.4
Places slept the night before arriving at Alvaston

Where slept night before	Percentages
Rough	52
Private accommodation	17
Resettlement Unit	14
Police/Prison	5
Hospital	3
Hostel (including Salvation Army)	3
Night Shelter	3
Bed and Breakfast	2
Other	1
Total %	100
Number	649

However, information from the Alvaston files cannot confirm whether or not certain men follow a regular circuit around resettlement units although interviews with men had established that at least a few men do (Vincent, Deacon and Walker, 1992). Men arriving at Alvaston from a resettlement unit on their first visit in 1991/92 were no more or less likely than other residents to do likewise on their next visit. Similarly, those arriving from a resettlement unit were no more likely than other men to say that they were planning to move on to another unit. Again, the problem is that men may sleep rough en route to the next unit. But, equally, it seems fairly unlikely that more than a handful of men looked exclusively to resettlement units for accommodation to support their way of life even given the difficulty of access to other hostels.

More men moved to Alvaston directly from private accommodation than came from other resettlement units and, if anything, rather more came from private accommodation on later visits. In a number of cases men reported having been staying with friends and relatives for various periods of time. In such circumstances these men might appropriately have been classified among the 'hidden homeless'. Then again, some of the relatively small number of long term Alvaston residents would book out to visit friends and return to Alvaston after having had what they termed 'a holiday'. Therefore, to assume that all of the men who repeatedly stayed at Alvaston had totally lost contact with people living a 'settled' way of life is drastically to oversimplify both the diversity of experience among men using Alvaston and the situation of individual users.

As noted above, the Alvaston register was of little value in establishing where men had left for. Leaving aside the 61 men who had been actively placed by staff, 43 after the closure announcement, a specific destination was recorded on only eight per cent of occasions with a broad location, sometimes as crude as 'the North', being noted for 57 per cent. The destinations recorded for these men are listed in Table 7.5 and show that the largest numbers were either taken away by the police or admitted to hospital. Small numbers also went to relatives, to other private accommodation, to hostels or to bed and breakfast establishments. But to reiterate, the vast majority of men left without any clear indication of their destination and not infrequently without telling staff that they were going.

Ways of living

Patterns of stays

An emergent theme in this chapter is that Alvaston catered in diverse ways for men living a diversity of lifestyles. This observation is neatly illustrated by Table 7.6 which categorises men according to the number and duration of their stays at Alvaston during its final year. Significant numbers of men with a wide range of characteristics fall into each of the 10 categories. Twenty four per cent of men stayed for a single night and another 17 per cent stayed on one occasion lasting for less than a week. Some men stayed longer, nine per cent for over a month and six per cent for more than twelve. Eleven per cent of men stayed for two or three short periods and five per cent visited Alvaston on four or more occasions during the final year. Some of the frequent visitors stayed for lengthy periods including seven per cent who stayed for more than a month on at least one occasion.

The taxonomy presented in Table 7.6 attempts to capture the degrees of experience spanning a single, short stay, a long period of residence and to the repeated usage that might be associated with a man of the road. To the extent that these distinctions point towards differences in lifestyle, it is appropriate to consider how stable they are from year to year. Unfortunately, it was only possible to obtain a detailed record of residence during Alvaston's final year although for those men staying in 1991/2 a check was made of stays in the preceding years (Table 7.7).

Table 7.5
Intended destinations of men* leaving Alvaston

	Percentages
Destination when not formally placed by Alvaston	
Police station	19
Hospital	16
Resettlement Unit	16
Hostel	15
Salvation Army Hostel	6
Relatives	8
Other private	6
Private lodging/bed and breakfast	2
Total %	88
Number	80
Location of destination (all men* leaving Alvaston)	
Derby/Nottinghamshire	65
Adjacent counties	10
Elsewhere	25
Total %	100
Number	460

*   Relates to spells at Alvaston; men may appear more than once in Table.

Table 7.6
Patterns of stays at Alvaston

		Percentages
Pattern	Duration	
	Single spells	
1	0 - 1 day	24
2	2 - 3 days	10
3	4 - 7 days	7
4	1 - 4 weeks	13
5	1 - 6 months	9
6	More than 6 months	6
	2 - 3 Spells	
7	All one week or less	11
8	At least one spell exceeding one week	9
9	At least one spell exceeding one month	7
10	4 - 5 spells	5
Total %		101
Number		514

In fact, 63 per cent of the men had not stayed in Alvaston at all in 1990/1. The proportion that had not done so was highest for men who had stayed for a single short spell (Patterns 1, 2 and 3). The experience was very different for men staying more than four times (Pattern 10), or for two or three times including one longer stay (Pattern 9): 70 per cent had visited Alvaston the previous year and over half of these had stayed more than once. Men staying over six months in 1991/92 (Pattern 6) were also more than likely to have been at Alvaston in the previous year, some of them without a break. Of the 70 per cent who were present in 1990/1, less than a quarter had more than one stay.

The above suggests a certain consistency across the two years for eight of the ten patterns identified in Table 7.6 although, of course, not every man in each group behaved according to the group norms. So, for example, two men staying a single night in 1991/2 had stayed on four or more occasions in 1990/1 and a fifth of men staying more than four times in 1991/2 had not visited in the previous year. For the other two groups (Patterns 5 and 8) a

Table 7.7
Patterns of stay, 1990/1 and 1991/2

Percentages

| Pattern of Stays 1991/92 | Number of Stays 1990/1 | | | | | Total |
	0	1	2-3	4+	%	Number
One Stay						
0 - 1 night	76	15	7	2	24	122
2 - 3 days	77	11	6	6	10	53
4 - 7 days	80	14	6	0	7	35
1 - 4 weeks	75	9	15	0	13	65
1 - 6 months	57	21	21	0	9	47
> 6 months	30	53	17	0	6	30
2 -3 Stays						
All one week or less	54	23	13	11	11	56
At least one spell 1 - 4 weeks	63	19	12	7	8	43
At least one spell exceeding one month	34	26	37	15	5	27
4 and 5 Spells	22	26	37	15	5	27
Percentage	63	19	14	4	100	
Total number	322	99	74	19		514

different overall pattern is evident. An unexpectedly high, sixty three per cent of men staying for two or three short spells (of less than a week, Pattern 8) in 1991/2 had not visited Alvaston in the preceding twelve months. The same was true of 57 per cent of those who had stayed for a period of between one and six months (Pattern 5). Why this should be so is unclear.

154

Given the enormous diversity evident among the men staying at Alvaston, and the rather tenuous argument that links the pattern of stays at Alvaston with the presumption of a particular lifestyle, one might not expect to find consistent differences between the characteristics of the men adopting one sequence of visits and another. In fact, some significant differences are evident (Figure 7.2). The men making four or more visits (Pattern 10), for example, were a relatively homogeneous group who might have described themselves as travelling men. Seventy three per cent had never married and sixty two per cent had been on the road for more than a decade. More than a fifth were aged over sixty and only four per cent were less than thirty. Fifty seven per cent had a drink problem, a figure in the top part of the range for Alvaston users although the proportion known to have a criminal record (37 per cent) was a little below average. The medical notes indicated that a very high proportion suffered from depression (35 per cent) and 17 per cent had other mental health problems.

The other group with a high incidence of depressional illnesses (28 per cent) were men who had stayed at Alvaston for two or three short spells in 1991/92 (Pattern 7). They tended to be rather younger with almost one in five being aged less than thirty and, although over a third had been on the road for a decade, one in ten had only just become homeless. The incidence of severe alcohol abuse and mental illness, other than depression, was lower than for other groups. It is tempting, but dangerous, given the imperfections of the information extracted from Alvaston files, to speculate on the direction of possible causation between depression and the apparently very unsettled existence of these two groups of men.

The group with the highest incidence of physical illness comprised men making a single stay lasting between one and four weeks (Pattern 4). A quarter were classified as being in only fair or poor health. In other respects the group differed little from the Alvaston average and it is tempting to think that, for at least a proportion of the men in this group, Alvaston provided a period of convalescence.

Perhaps not surprisingly, the most 'settled' group, those staying at Alvaston in excess of six months (Pattern 6), included almost a third of men who were aged over sixty and thirty seven per cent who had been on the road for ten years or more. The incidence of mental illness was similar to that of other groups, as was the extent of alcohol abuse, but the number with a known criminal record (20 per cent) was on the low side.

The other two groups of long term residents (Patterns 5 and 9), comprising men who stayed for at least one spell of over a month, were on average younger with a fifth aged under thirty. In each case at least half had criminal records. These two groups differed from each other, and from very long term residents, in terms of the pattern of known mental illness. While depression was relatively common among those staying for a single spell (Pattern 5) other mental illnesses were virtually unknown, whereas the incidence of both depression and other mental illness was about average for the men who stayed at Alvaston more than once in 1991/2 (Pattern 9). Those staying only once (Pattern 5) included an unusually large minority, 22 per cent, who moved into Alvaston directly after becoming homeless; they presumably used their relatively lengthy stay there as a haven to come to terms with their new status, to lay the foundations for a new life or to negotiate a return to their prior status.

Two other groups included sizeable minorities of newly homeless (Patterns 1 and 2). In both cases the men stayed only once and their stays at Alvaston were very short, three days or less. The groups are similar in that men involved tended to be young (in each case a third were in their teens or twenties), had comparatively low levels of alcohol abuse (that is one in three or four) and average levels of mental illness. They differ in two respects. First, 65 per cent of those who stayed for a single night (Pattern 1) were unmarried compared with only 43 per cent of those who stayed longer. Secondly, a surprising 39 per cent of the first group are known to have been on the road for a decade or more even though they only stayed at Alvaston for a single night in 1991/2.

The last finding suggests that men who stay a single night may subdivide into at least two distinct categories. This possibility is supported by the evidence presented in Table 7.8. This shows that the men who have been on the road for a decade were considerably older on average. Most had also visited Alvaston before and most were known to have a drink problem, neither of which was true for the other group, the majority of whom were newly homeless.

The final dimension of lifestyle to be investigated relates to weekend visits to Alvaston. It will be remembered that a disproportionate number of all visits to Alvaston lasted from a Friday or Saturday to a Monday. The question asked is whether particular sorts of men made a habit of visiting Alvaston at weekends and, on the basis of the evidence available from Unit records, the answer would appear to be a qualified 'no'.

156

Figure 7.2
Patterns of stays

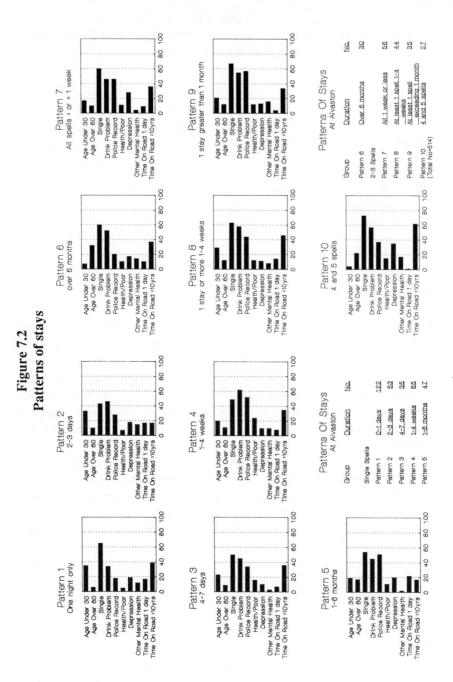

157

Table 7.8
**Characteristics of men who stayed a single night according to their
length of time on the road**

			Percentages
	Length of Time on the Road		
Characteristic	Unknown	Less than 10 years	More than 10 years
Aged under 40	64	77	11
Visited Alvaston in 1990/91	12	21	83
A drink problem	20	35	67
Number	40	17	18

Weekend visits

Altogether 63 men made weekend visits including five who made two. Just over half of weekend visits were made by the third of men who visited Alvaston more than once in 1991/92. A quarter of the men who made two or three short visits to Alvaston spent at least one weekend there, as did 40 per cent of those who were at Alvaston on four or more occasions. On the other hand, only one in six of the visits made by these two groups of travelling men occurred at weekends and one would expect a ratio of one in seven by chance alone.

Men visiting at weekends were twice as likely to suffer depression or some other illness than was the case among those who did not. It will be recalled, however, that depression was one of the characteristics found to be associated with men who visited Alvaston frequently.

So, it would appear that a disproportionate number of weekend visits were made by men who visited Alvaston frequently and weekend visitors were more likely to suffer from depression than other Alvaston users. This could create the impression of a particular kind of weekend visitor: the inveterate traveller perhaps in search of company. In reality, this phenomenon appears primarily to be an accident of mathematics. The frequent visitor, disproportionately prone to depression, had more chance of being at Alvaston at weekends simply because he visited there more often.

It is notable, however, that 54 per cent of men who made a single, two to three day visit in 1991/2 came at a weekend. While one might have expected a disproportionate number of these to involve experienced travelling men making an occasional visit, this does not appear to be the case.

To conclude, within the diversity that was Alvaston, it is nevertheless possible to discern patterning that suggests some of the experiences and life styles for which it catered. There were travelling men who visited Alvaston frequently for short spells, presumably on a circuit that often took in other resettlement units. Among this group were disproportionate numbers of men suffering depressive illnesses, many who had been on the road for many years and significant numbers aged in their sixties and even seventies. There were other men, also long time travellers, who visited Alvaston infrequently and sometimes for very short periods. Where they went in the interim is far from clear. They may have been the men, identified in the qualitative work, who followed seasonal work. However, the limited evidence available indicates that alcohol was an even greater problem for this group than for other Alvaston users.

Alvaston also provided a long term haven, a home, for some men; many, but by no means the majority, were quite elderly. For some, men who had been on the road for some time but were now physically ill, perhaps it offered a form of convalescence. For yet others Alvaston was a temporary sanctuary: many had criminal records and a noticeable minority were discharged into police custody.

But, as far as one can tell from the available evidence, for most users Alvaston provided temporary and never to be repeated shelter in the event of personal crisis. Sometimes this was for a single night. On other occasions men needed more time to tackle their problems and find some sort of solution that took them away from Alvaston.

Closing the hostel

The closure process

The number of men in Alvaston on any night naturally depended on the number staying on the preceding night and the numbers leaving and arriving on that day. It was clear from Figure 7.1 that there was considerable day to day variation in the number of newcomers and this variation is repeated in Figure 7.3 which shows the pattern of departures. Both series show a decline in the period following the formal announcement of closure on 10 December 1991 but it is more pronounced for arrivals than for departures.

The result is a very rapid, step-like decline in the number of residents from a secondary peak in mid December until final closure (Figure 7.4).

Earlier in the year the number of beds which had been occupied varied from a high of 74 in late September to a low of 40 in early July but generally ranged between the mid fifties and low sixties. Even the large swings resulted from quite small fluctuations in the flows into and out of Alvaston. The July low point was triggered by three closely spaced days when six or seven men left and four days later in the month when between four and five men departed. It was ended by a run of three days at the beginning of July when no men left Alvaston.

The sensitivity of occupancy rates to small variations enabled the run down of Alvaston to be managed effectively with relatively minor adjustments to procedures. As noted elsewhere (Deacon, Walker and Vincent, 1992), target occupancy was reduced to 35 from 12 December 1991 with individuals nominally being admitted only on an overnight basis. This strategy was not followed to the letter and many men were allowed to book in on successive days and to stay over a weekend. Even so, the proportion of men staying for a single night increased from 34 per cent to 45 per cent after the run-down began and the number staying for more than one week fell from 42 per cent to 19 per cent (see Table 7.1). The target occupancy rate was reached on 13 January 1992.

The closure was also accompanied by a programme of placements to accommodation opened to replace Alvaston and to other forms of provision. This process is documented elsewhere (Deacon, Vincent and Walker, 1992). Suffice to say, that the replacement accommodation in Nottingham comprised a direct access hostel for 17 older people and a special needs housing complex catering for 33 (although with priority given to women in the case of 18 of the units). In Derby a direct access hostel for 20 men and 10 women, a dry house for a total of 10 men and women and a care home for 12 people recovering from mental illness (which opened after Alvaston closed) were provided.

Strictly speaking, only men in residence on 10 December were eligible for the replacement programme although 10 of the 73 men arriving after this date were accommodated. Twenty placements took place before the formal closure announcement and 43 afterwards with two people being placed twice because the first attempt proved to be unsuccessful (Table 7.9). Altogether, 30 placements were made into replacement accommodation, six before the run down and 24 subsequently. Twenty two of the men placed after the run down began left on one of two Mondays in early February with five of them moving into the replacement hostel in Derby on the first date, and 12 on the second.

Effects of closure

Table 7.10 gives a partial indication of the kinds of men placed under the closure programme. As might be expected, the vast majority were long term residents: 82 per cent had been at Alvaston for more than a month and 33 per cent for over six months. Slightly more of those placed in the period before the run down had spent more than one spell at Alvaston during 1991/2 and one person had been placed after less than a week.

While it is to be expected that long term residents would need to be found accommodation, if for no other reason that it would be inhumane not to do so, this strategy nevertheless meant that the replacement provision served only a minority of the Alvaston constituency. Eighty two per cent of the men who were placed were drawn from groups with a pattern of usage that was shared by only 21 per cent of all Alvaston users. Two thirds of the men who spent more than six months at Alvaston in 1991/2 were found alternative accommodation as were 37 per of those who had stayed for more than a month. These are not inconsiderable achievements and represent a replacement of 46 per cent of the bed spaces offered and used by Alvaston in its final year. On the other hand, only five short stay residents were placed even though this group constituted 46 per cent of users and, as indicated above, will have included men with a range of severe psychological and behavioural conditions. These men received no compensation for the closure of Alvaston.

While a considerable amount of care went into the placement of Alvaston residents in new accommodation, especially during the period prior to the run down when staff had more time, there was still an element of chance in who was allocated a place. Whether a man was assisted depended on whether he was in Alvaston at all during the year and especially whether he was there during December 1991 and January 1992. Men who stayed in Alvaston for more than six months were, on statistical grounds alone, 339 times more likely to be 'eligible' for placement than men who stayed only one night. Likewise, they had a chance of selection between two and four times greater than men in the groups staying over six months and seven times greater than someone staying four or more times.

Figure 7.3
Number of departures from Alvaston: 1/4/91-24/3/92

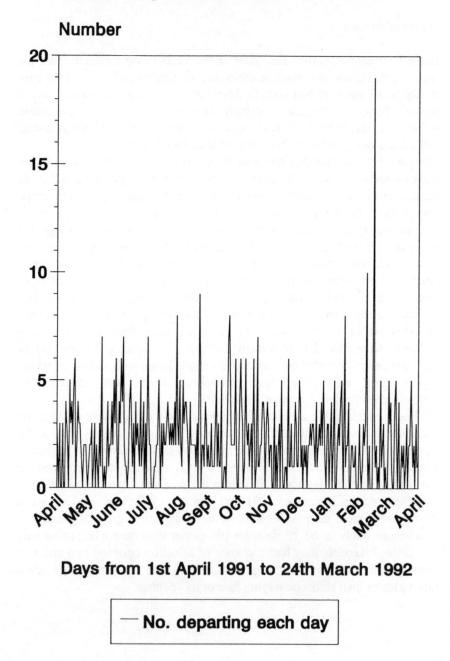

Days from 1st April 1991 to 24th March 1992

| — No. departing each day |

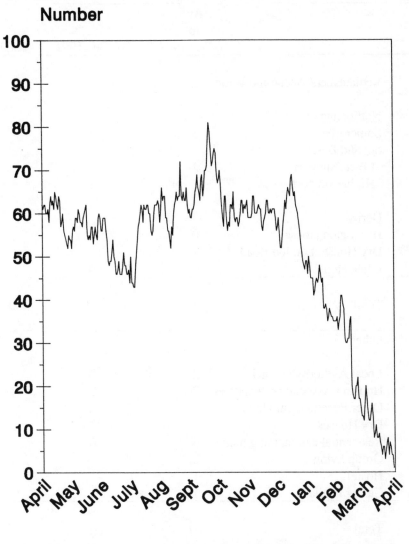

Figure 7.4
Number of beds in use at Alvaston: 1/4/91-24/3/92

Number

Days from 1st April 1991 to 24th March 1992

— No. of beds occupied

163

Table 7.9
Destinations of Alvaston residents who were actively placed

			Percentages
	1 April to 10 Dec 1991	10 Dec 1991	Total
Replacement Accommodation			
Nottingham			
Somerville	3	4	
Second Base			
Lower support	1		
Higher support		1	
Derby			
Hartington House	0	18	
Dry House, London Road	2	1	
Edale House[b]/	0	0	
Total	6	24	30
Other			
Local Authority tenancies	2	7	
Housing Association tenancies	2	2	
Other Resettlement Units		2	
Dry Houses		2	
Residential care/nursing homes	6	6	
Group living	2		
Hostel	1		
Caring landlady	1		
Total	20	43	63[a]

a   Includes two people who were placed twice after the first placement proved unsuccessful

b   Opened after Alvaston closed

Table 7.10
Pattern of stays of men placed and not placed

Pattern	Duration	Before 10 Dec 1991	Placed After 10 Dec 1991	Not Placed
				Percentages
Single spells				
1	0 - 1 day	0	0	27
2	2 - 3 days	0	0	12
3	4 - 7 days	5	0	8
4	1 - 4 weeks	5	5	14
5	1 - 6 months	16	24	8
6	>6 months	36	31	2
2 - 3 Spells				
7	All one week or less	0	2	12
8	At least one spell exceeding one week	0	7	9
9	At least one spell exceeding one month	32	26	4
10	4 - 5 Spells	5	5	5
	Total %	100	100	100
	Number	19	42	454

Table 7.11 compares the actual allocation with that which would have been expected by chance, given the time which men spent at Alvaston. The two distributions are strikingly similar though rather fewer of the longest stay residents were placed than might have been expected. However, this shortfall was largely made up from the other two groups of long term residents. Whether staff found it more difficult to place the men who had been at Alvaston for longest is an issue beyond the scope of this chapter. However, the accommodation included in the replacement package was typically not well matched with their needs (Deacon, Walker and Vincent,

1992). Frequent visitors to Alvaston fared as well as would have been expected given the total amount of time which they spent in residence.

The men who were placed in alternative accommodation differed little from those who were not, except that they included higher proportions of men aged in their sixties or seventies (Table 7.12). However, there is some suggestion that men placed before the formal run down of Alvaston began in December 1991 had less behavioural problems than those who were placed later. This is most evident with respect to alcohol abuse: strict no-drinking regimes operated in all the replacement accommodation. The men placed early may have been more prone to depression than other residents but equally they seem to have had marginally fewer other mental or physical health problems although the numbers involved are too small to reach categorical conclusions.

Table 7.11
Actual and 'chance' placements

Percentages

Pattern	Duration	Actually placed	Predicted to be placed according to chance*
	Single spells		
1	0 - 1 day	0	0
2	2 - 3 days	0	0
3	4 - 7 days	2	1
4	1 - 4 weeks	5	5
5	1 - 6 months	21	17
6	> 6 months	33	43
	2 - 3 Spells		
7	All one week or less	2	1
8	At least one spell exceeding one week	5	4
9	At least one spell exceeding one month	28	23
10	4 - 5 Spells	5	5
	Total	100	100

* Given the average duration of stay during 1991/92

Table 7.12
Characteristics of men

			Percentages
	Placed		Not
	Before	After	Placed
Characteristic	10 Dec 1991	10 Dec 1991	
Aged over 60	24	22	10
Drink problem	28	60	49
Depression	22	16	17
Other mental health problem	6	8	10
Health - not good/poor	6	12	11
Number	18	38	356

To summarise, chance probably played an important part in determining which residents 'benefited' from the closure of Alvaston in terms of securing places in the replacement provision. Longer term residents tended to fare best although those who had been at Alvaston for more than six months could have been expected to do a little better than they did. Short stay residents, who comprised most of the men who used Alvaston, simply lost somewhere that they could turn to for shelter, solace or temporary sanctuary.

Conclusion

Analysis of the information contained in administrative case papers provided a glimpse of the men who stayed at Alvaston during the last year of its existence and hinted at the different roles that Alvaston played in their lives. Uniquely, the information enabled some impression to be gained of the complex patterns of men's lives and the ways in which these determined the functions and affected the functioning of Alvaston.

However, before rehearsing conclusions it is important to reiterate the limitations of the analysis. Not only did the information available in the Unit records vary in its quality and comprehensiveness, it related only to the periods that men spent at Alvaston. While it is possible to speculate about the lives that men led away from Alvaston, the available data is akin to a sandwich without the filling (even Aero without the chocolate).

Nevertheless, the research makes some things very clear. First, Alvaston provided accommodation for men from many varied backgrounds who were brought together at different stages in their lives by the outwardly similar circumstance of requiring somewhere to sleep. To assume, as might the uninitiated, that Alvaston was used exclusively by men permanently travelling a circuit of hostels and resettlement units is very largely to misunderstand the way in which Alvaston operated. Men with this way of life probably constituted the minority of users.

Alvaston may well have differed from other resettlement units. Certainly the proportion of long stay residents appears to have been radically higher than in, for example, Leeds Resettlement Unit (Jones, 1987). (It is important to note, however, that no other study has established the total duration of residence rather than the time spent in residence at the point of survey, and the apparent difference is likely to be considerable for this reason alone (Vincent, Ashworth and Walker, 1991).) What this would seem to confirm is the wide differences between resettlement units reflecting policies adopted at individual units and the other provision in the area. In that Alvaston was almost the only direct access provision in Derby, it probably played a much broader role than perhaps the Leeds Resettlement Unit did.

Men who used Alvaston on a single occasion were far more numerous than the traditional man of the road. Moreover, the former included sizeable numbers who apparently used Alvaston as a first, and maybe only, port of call tiding them over a major crisis. At least one in six men arrived at Alvaston from some form of permanent accommodation and probably half had been homeless for less than a year before arriving at Alvaston.

Secondly, it is evident that men used Alvaston in different ways. There were men for whom Alvaston was a regular stop on a circuit. Sometimes the intervals between visits were short, in other cases they were mysteriously long. Some men, the largest group in 1991/2, stayed for a single night. Others seemingly used Alvaston to recuperate from both illness and personal crises. For yet others Alvaston was home.

In this regard the most interesting comparisons are with the recent survey by Elam (1992). This focused on admissions to London units but it also stressed the diversity of respondents. It found a similar juxtaposition of newly homeless and old-style men of the road. Half of the respondents were new to resettlement units, 40 per cent had been on the road for years. About a half had no medical problems, about a third had an abundance of them. A quarter had only just left a place they thought of as home, a third had been homeless for years. Of those who had stayed in the same unit before, 46 per cent had stayed for less than a week. When they left, 20 per cent had gone to friends, 18 per cent slept rough, 13 per cent had gone to another unit, 11 per cent to another hostel or project.

Thirdly, because of the varying lifestyles followed by the men who stayed at Alvaston and the different ways in which they used it, not everyone would have been affected similarly by its closure. Equally not all the men stood to benefit from the package of provision designed to replace Alvaston, even if they had had access to it which the majority of users did not. Those who stayed permanently at Alvaston lost a home; although most, but not all, were found alternative accommodation it was often not to their liking (Vincent, Deacon and Walker, 1992b). Men who travelled lost a staging post and very few were presented with any replacement. Those confronted with a crisis need for accommodation would simply have nowhere to turn. Indeed, the trend towards less direct access accommodation in the Derby and Nottingham areas that occurred in the late 1980s has continued since the closure of Alvaston. In total the replacement provision and other accommodation used to rehouse Alvaston residents was sufficient to cater for 46 per cent of the demand for bed spaces, but left 88 per cent of the users of Alvaston without housing.

A final insight gained from the analysis was a way of reconciling the to-ing and fro-ing that characterised the men's use of Alvaston with the continuity and stability that was also a feature of the hostel. While most men stayed for short periods, the majority of bed spaces over the final year were filled by permanent and semi-permanent residents. It was these men who forged the character of Alvaston just as much, and probably more so, than those who came and went. They were also the major beneficiaries of the resources that Alvaston represented and stood to gain most from the counselling and resettlement activities provided by staff. Ironically, however, they, as a group, apparently lost least as a result of the closure because they had the greatest chance of being included in the replacement package.

8 Benefit dynamics: The case of Family Credit

Introduction

Family Credit occupies a pivotal position in British social security provision even though it is received by only half a million families and accounts for just one per cent of overall Social Security expenditure (DSS, 1993). Introduced in April 1988, it replaced Family Income Supplement (FIS) as a scheme to provide financial assistance to low income employed and self-employed families with dependent children.

Its introduction was trailed in the 1985 Green Paper 'Reform of Social Security' where it was presented as an important new mechanism designed simultaneously to target financial help to low waged families, who were seen to suffer particular hardship, and to tackle the disincentive effects which are associated with means-tested benefits. The disincentives arise when benefit levels are set in relation to some measure of need, notably family size and structure, but wages are fixed according to different criteria that reflect the prevailing balance of power between labour and capital. In such circumstances families, especially those with children, may not readily be able to obtain more income when working than when in receipt of out of work benefits, the so called unemployment trap. By making Family Credit available on an income-related basis to families where at least one person is in paid employment, the worst features of this trap are likely to be avoided (see Marsh and McKay, 1993 for a full evaluation of Family Credit). As a consequence, unemployed families with children may find it to their financial advantage to seek and gain employment.

However, Family Credit is not restricted to people returning to work after a spell of unemployment. It can be claimed by any person with dependent children who is employed full time (more than 16 hours per week). Benefit is awarded for a fixed six month period and changes in circumstances during this period will not normally affect entitlement. Upon termination of a six month award individuals may renew their claim and continue in receipt of benefit provided they still meet the eligibility requirements.

It follows that Family Credit may be used in a variety of ways according to the social and economic circumstances of families. This will in turn influence the functions that Family Credit performs within the wider scheme of social security provision. A single six month claim, for example, would be consistent with Family Credit being used to negotiate the unemployment trap. Equally, though, single six months claims could also be related to movements down in the labour market - shorter hours or less well remunerated work - en route, perhaps, to unemployment or long term sickness. Similarly, when one of a working couple becomes unemployed it might generate a short-term difficulty resulting in a single claim for benefit. In each of these cases Family Credit operates as a transitional wage supplement to bridge families over a short lived set of circumstances. On the other hand, long periods of continuous receipt - entailing a series of renewed claims by families - point to the use of Family Credit as a long term wage subsidy for claimants who are employees and business subsidy for those who are self-employed. Repeat claims, where a period of time without benefit separates two claims, may indicate fluctuating or even cyclical economic or social circumstances.

The actual use made of Family Credit may or may not be in accord with the initial intentions and could signal a need to change the structure or mode of implementation of the benefit. For example, large numbers of repeated applications - 'churning' - might point to the need to lengthen the period of entitlement which would reduce administration and associated costs. A small amount of 'churning' means that the target group is either static or very dynamic with new families continually being introduced to the system such that promotional strategies might need to be tailored to newly eligible groups. Likewise, if it were possible to identify long term users at the point of initial application, and long term receipt was considered to be undesirable, it might be possible to initiate proactive policies to lessen durations.

Bearing these considerations in mind the aims of the exploratory analyses reported in this chapter were to establish the patterns of usage of Family Credit to assess the degree of churning and to identify the factors associated with the length of claims all with a view to better understanding its role as an income-related benefit.

The data and claimants' characteristics

The data analysed comprise a five per cent sample of successful applicants for Family Credit. They derive from monthly administrative records and include information taken from the application forms received by the Department of Social Security (DSS) and the former Department of Health and Social Security (DHSS).

The data run from the inception of the scheme, in April 1988, until December 1991 and thus include individuals transferring from Family Income Supplement (FIS) and claims terminating in July 1992. Family Credit was treated strictly separately from FIS and no attempt was made to include periods on FIS in the analysis of time on Family Credit. This strategy avoids problems associated with spells that start before the observation period begins. One other simplification was adopted in the analysis. When the scheme was introduced, in order to stagger the administrative load, initial awards of Family Credit were of variable length - between 14 and 39 weeks. These awards were dropped from the data file in order to maintain the six-monthly association with each award and avoid confusion when extrapolating to months spent in receipt of Family Credit. A small number of other awards of less than six months, the result of claimants reporting changes in circumstances, which lifted them out of the Family Credit threshold or coding errors, were also omitted from the analysis.

The study was inevitably constrained by the type and detail of information recorded on administrative records. Families in receipt of Family Credit were categorised according to family type and occupation as follows:

‒   **Family Type:** four groups were defined according to the number of parents (one or two) and the sex of the main earner;

‒   **Occupational Type:** six groups were formed based on whether employment status was self-employed, public sector or private sector, the latter group was divided into four groups by various occupations - professional, catering, manual, and miscellaneous;

173

A number of continuous variables were also available: weekly amount of Child Benefit, weekly amount of Family Credit, average hourly earnings, total weekly pre-Family Credit income, number of hours worked a week, gross earnings, age of the claimant, number of reckonable children aged under 18, and age of the youngest child.

Table 8.1 shows the relationships between each of the grouped variables and the continuous variables taken from a family's first claim. Couples with a male breadwinner constitute just over half (53 per cent) of those who received Family Credit during the first three and a half years. Lone parents, the vast majority of whom are women, constitute another 36 per cent. Families where 'traditional' roles have been reversed account for the remaining 11 per cent.

Two-parent families with a male earner appear to be at an earlier stage of child-rearing than do other family types; this is shown by the average lower age of the youngest child. They also have more children and therefore receive larger amounts of child benefit. Their hourly earnings average about the same as for other groups but they tend to work longer hours (not shown in Table 8.1) and have higher incomes before payment of Family Credit, which is reflected in smaller awards of Family Credit. To summarise, two-parent families with a male breadwinner have larger and younger families to support but, because they have higher earnings, they on average receive less Family Credit than other groups.

Families headed by a lone male parent account for a very small proportion of the Family Credit population. On average, they receive less Family Credit than lone parent families supported by a female earner. This is primarily because male lone parents work longer hours and have higher pre-Family Credit incomes. They appear to be at a later stage in the child-rearing process than other groups: the youngest child is, on average, just under ten years old and the claimants themselves are five to six years older than other recipients.

'Reverse role' couples, where the woman is in paid employment and the man is not, average the largest amounts of Family Credit. This results from a combination of above average family size and below average hours worked (wage rates are not very dissimilar from those of other groups). Such families tend to be at an intermediate stage in the process of child-rearing. The youngest child is, on average, aged around seven years.

Lone mothers have the lowest earnings of the four family types and work marginally fewer hours than women in reversed role families at somewhat lower rates of pay. Family Credit levels are consequently relatively high,

though not as high as for reverse role couples because on average they have
fewer children.

Table 8.1
Characteristics of Family Credit families, 1988-1991*

	Couples		Lone Parents	
	Male earner £	Female earner £	Male earner £	Female earner £
Average Weekly Family Credit	24.05	31.73	25.56	29.40
Average Weekly earnings	111.51	95.44	108.31	89.75
Total weekly income (Pre Family Credit)	131.75	121.52	123.34	110.22
Number of children	2.3	2.0	1.7	1.6
Age of youngest child (Years)	3.5	7.0	9.5	7.5
Per cent of families	53.3	11.3	1.5	33.9
Number	23,229	4,930	664	14,790

* The total sample size is 43,613

Table 8.2 reveals the way in which earnings and levels of Family Credit
relate to occupation. On average, the self-employed receive by far the

largest amounts of Family Credit: they work more hours than all other groups except miscellaneous workers, but incomes before Family Credit are low despite longer working hours. Public sector employees average the highest hourly earnings but tend to work fewer hours than other groups which lowers their weekly earnings and income prior to receipt of Family Credit.

Table 8.2
Further characteristics of Family Credit families 1988-1991

	Average Weekly Family Credit £	Average* Weekly Total Income £	Average Weekly Earnings £	Average Hourly Earnings £	Average Weekly Hours Worked**
Occupational Group:					
Self-employed	37.53	92.70	66.05	1.96	40.05
Public sector	21.52	133.46	112.98	3.22	35.00
Private sector					
- Professional	26.02	123.03	102.58	2.92	34.08
- Catering	29.73	118.94	98.34	2.81	34.07
- Manual	22.70	135.26	116.20	3.00	38.04
- Farming and Misc.	22.74	135.26	115.90	2.88	40.05

* includes Child Benefit and Family Credit
** omits erroneous records in the data

Duration of Family Credit receipt

When thinking about the length of time families spend on benefit, two distributions have important implications for policy. The first concerns the length of time new applicants are likely to spend on benefit. It indicates, for example, whether most of the people who ever receive benefit do so for short or long periods. The second distribution relates to the current case-load and indicates how long each person will have spent in receipt of Family Credit when they finish their current spell.

These two distributions will only be equivalent if all benefit recipients spend the same amount of time on benefit. If some individuals are, for some reason, destined to remain on benefit for longer than others then the longer term users will accumulate in the system over time. For example, consider the situation where a new benefit scheme is introduced and 100 people immediately apply successfully. It is assumed that 10 will leave after one month, 10 after two months and so on. One month after the scheme is introduced, another 100 people join with the same characteristics as those who initially applied. At this point, the claimant population comprises 190 people since 10 of the original claimants have already left. Of these 190, only 10 (5.3 per cent) will be in receipt for one month compared with 10 per cent of the initial 100. After two months, with another 100 successful applicants joining, the proportion destined to be on benefit for one month has fallen to 3.3 per cent, and those on for two months, to 6.6 per cent. As time goes by the proportion of cases with short durations continues to fall, whilst the proportion destined to have longer durations increases.

A result of this accumulation is that a small group of long term users consume a large proportion of the total available resources (see also Chapter 5). This assumes that long and short term users receive the same weekly benefit. If long term users have higher entitlements, then the concentration of resources could be even greater. This pattern of concentration may be undesirable for both fiscal and humanitarian reasons. It could be, therefore, advantageous to identify potential long-term users either before they enter the system (pre-benefit intervention) or upon entering the system, and not after they have achieved the long-term status by actual use.

A further corollary of the accumulation of long-term users in the system is that analyses based on point in time estimates will over-emphasise the characteristics of long-term users relative to short-term users. (See Chapters 2, 3 and 5 for further elucidation on this point.)

Analysing duration: spells and individuals

Reference was made in Chapter 5 to Bane and Ellwood's (1986) pioneering study of Aid to Families of Dependent Children (AFDC) in the United

States which involved the analysis of *spells*, i.e. uninterrupted periods of receipt. On the basis of their findings they recommended a number of targeting strategies. However, the problem with that study was that no distinction was made between single and repeat spells of benefit use (Ellwood (1986)). All spells were combined into a single data set, with spells rather than individuals treated as the unit of analysis, and analysed as if repeat spells were independent of prior spells. This approach means that the total amount of time spent on benefit by an *individual* is always under-estimated unless everybody experiences a single un-repeated spell.

To overcome this problem the length of the first spell of Family Credit, the probability of repeat spells, the time between spells, and the duration of further spells are estimated separately and then used together to gauge the total time spent in receipt of Family Credit during a given period (Ellwood, 1986). While a distinct improvement on earlier strategies, this approach necessarily assumes that repeat spells are independent of earlier ones. This may or may not be the case (see Annex B).

Therefore, to recap, in order to ascertain the total length of time spent on Family Credit, it is necessary to take account of the length of each continuous spell, comprising an application and subsequent renewals, and the extent of repeat applications.

Repeat applications

The number of repeat (as opposed to renewal) applications and, hence, the rate of churning through the system, appears to be relatively low. Eighty per cent of individuals who had received Family Credit in the period until December 1991 experienced only one spell on benefit, and less than one per cent had had more than three separate spells (Table 8.3). Thus, to date, the bulk of Family Credit applications have resulted in a single, unbroken period on benefit.

The corollary of this is that the vast majority of recipients do not appear to be prone to fluctuating socio-economic circumstances that repeatedly move them into and out of eligibility for Family Credit. Rather the majority of new applications (as opposed to renewals) come from people with no previous experience of Family Credit. This means that promotional strategies cannot assume detailed experiential knowledge of the benefit and the DSS in their advertising campaigns did not do so.

As time progresses this pattern may change. There will be more ex-recipients around and a longer time will have elapsed during which circumstances may have changed. Continual monitoring is required but if the pattern changes at all, it is likely to do so only slowly.

Table 8.3
Observed frequency of spells of Family Credit receipt

Number of Spells*	Frequency	Percentage
1	35028	80.3
2	7191	16.5
3	1247	2.9
4	133	0.3
5	12	0.0
6	2	0.0
	43613	100

* Period of unbroken Family Credit receipt

Observed spell lengths

Table 8.4 shows the length of time that families in the sample had spent on Family Credit. It should be remembered that those claiming Family Credit most recently had had less opportunity to experience long spells on benefit and a substantial number of people (38 per cent of the sample) had not finished their spell at the end of the observation period. Therefore, these figures have to be taken as underestimates of total duration and the number of long-term claimants is likely to rise.

It is apparent that well over half of all spells had lasted for six months: a single claim period without any renewal. Moreover, three-quarters of first spells, and over four-fifths of the second and third spells, appear to last for no more than a year (Table 8.4). Even when one adds repeated spells together, 65 per cent of families still receive Family Credit for a total period of less than a year. For the vast majority of families, therefore, Family Credit appears to be providing transitional support.

There are, though, a very small minority of families who are reliant on Family Credit for long periods: 14 per cent of families in the sample had already spent more than two years on benefit and three per cent more than three years. These are the families that accumulate over time and come to constitute a large proportion of the live caseload.

Estimated duration

Table 8.5 presents estimates of the length of time that families are likely to have spent on Family Credit when their current spell finally ends. These estimates are derived from a statistical model, the details of which are presented at Annex C. The modelling procedure is briefly described in the next paragraph which some readers may wish to skip.

The exit probability (p(e)t) - the proportion of those whose spell ends at time t, relative to those who are eligible to end at the same time point, is estimated for each given time point. When calculating the exit probability, families whose spell of receipt continues past the end of the observation period - right hand censored - are not counted as exiting but are treated as being eligible (at risk) to exit the system. Using the exit probability and the fact that all individuals are at risk of exiting after the first claim (RS_1), the risk set for time 2 can be calculated from $(1-(P(e)_1*RS_1))$, which is the right hand side of the equation giving the proportion exiting at time 1. By continuing this procedure over t time points the proportion of families exiting can be estimated at each time. This is the probability density function for those completing a spell of Family Credit. The complete formula is given in Annex C along with the formula for calculating the distribution of those receiving Family Credit at any point in time. The latter is a weighted and renormalized function of the former distribution, given certain assumptions.

Table 8.5 shows the predicted duration of Family Credit receipt for families at the beginning of a spell on benefit. As such it provides the best impression of how Family Credit has been 'used' by (or served) those families who received it during the 42 months after its introduction. Since spells are no longer truncated by the observation period, the average duration of a claim is considerably longer than evidenced in Table 8.4: 18

months as opposed to 12 months. Even so, about half of first spells lasted for a single claim period (six months) as did 42 per cent of second spells. About two-thirds of all spells lasted for twelve months or less.

Table 8.4
Observed length of spells 1-3 and total durations of
Family Credit receipt

Length (months)	Spell 1 Frequency	%	Spell 2 Frequency	%	Spell 3 Frequency	%	Total Frequency	%
6	24763	56.8	5202	60.8	914	65.8	19141	43.9
12	8198	18.8	1828	21.4	315	22.7	9283	21.3
18	4165	9.5	832	9.7	114	8.2	5490	12.6
24	2311	5.3	416	4.9	35	2.5	3511	8.1
30	1563	3.6	198	2.3	12	0.9	2518	5.8
36	1619	3.7	65	0.8	0	0	2373	5.4
42	811	1.9	11	0.1	-	-	10.85	2.5
48	183	0.4	-	-	-	-	212	0.5
TOTAL	43613	100	8512	100	1770	100	43613	100

The chances of moving off Family Credit decrease with the length of spell, falling from 47 per cent after the first period of entitlement to 15 per cent after the sixth continuous period (Table 8.5). Moreover, the probability of leaving a second spell is almost always lower than the probability of leaving a first. It follows that second spells are on average longer than first spells (24 months as opposed to 18 months).

Of course, the fact that the probability of moving off Family Credit declines over time does not necessarily mean that families are being seduced into a benefit culture. Rather, it may simply reflect the relative stability of the families' circumstances. The model predicts that about 15 per cent of first spells and 26 per cent of second spells will last for three or more years. It further predicts that eight per cent of first spells and 20 per cent of second spells will last for six years. Family Credit received by these families obviously provides long term support and may be viewed as a form of almost permanent wage subsidy.

As noted a number of times above, long term users tend to accumulate in the system. This is demonstrated by Table 8.6, which provides a snapshot of the user population at a given point in time. Over a six year period, the eight per cent who start a spell and whose spell lasts six years or more builds up to constitute about 30 per cent of the liveload. At that point the average duration of cases in the liveload is about three years. Fifty four per cent of those in the liveload who are in the midst of their first spell will have received Family Credit for more than two years by the time they leave. For those in their second spell, the corresponding figure is 70 per cent.

According to the model, therefore, the Family Credit system rapidly becomes one which predominantly provides a subsidy to wages despite the fact that the vast majority of families who ever use the system do so only for short periods.

Duration and claimant characteristics

Both for understanding, and from the view point of targeting, it is important to determine whether the amount of time which families spend on Family Credit is in any way related to their other characteristics.

The analysis required to achieve this is complex and only selected results are presented here (for a more complete treatment see Ashworth and Walker, 1992b). Estimates of the average durations derived for the liveload are consistently approximately twice those for families beginning a spell and only the latter are reported. Also for ease of presentation, variables that were treated as continuous in the model have been categorised.

Simple relationships

a)   First spells. The average length of a first spell on Family Credit is most closely related to the amount of benefit that a family receives (Table 8.7). Families in the lowest band make an average of one renewal and

Table 8.5
Predicted benefit durations for families beginning a spell

Claim Length (months)	Spell 1		Spell 2	
	Exit Rate[a]	Percentage of completed spells for those starting a spell[b]	Exit Rate[a]	Percentage of completed spells for those starting a spell[b]
6	.47	47	.42	42
12	.40	18	.38	16
18	.38	10	.34	10
24	.33	6	.23	5
30	.36	5	.18	3
36	.27	2	.06	1
42	.15	1	.06*	1
48	.15*	1	.06*	1
54	.15*	1	.06*	1
60	.15*	1	.06*	1
66	.15*	1	.06*	1
72	.15*	8**	.06*	20**
Mean length (months)	36.18	38.16	24.54	51.06

[a] The first exit probability was obtained by averaging across the sample, the remaining exit probabilities were derived from coefficients indexing the time period.

[b] The percentages exiting are derived from averaging across the sample as a whole, and do not relate directly to the exit probabilities because they include differences in exit rates related to individual differences as well.

* Assumed to remain constant from the last observed value
** Do not sum to one hundred because of rounding error

Table 8.6
Predicted benefit durations for Family Credit recipients at a point in time

Claim Length (months)	Spell 1		Spell 2	
	Exit Rate	Percentage of completed spells for those starting a spell	Exit Rate	Percentage of completed spells for those starting a spell
6	.47	15	.42	10
12	.40	12	.38	8
18	.38	10	.34	7
24	.33	8	.23	5
30	.36	8	.18	4
36	.27	5	.06	1
42	.15	2	.06*	1
48	.15*	2	.06*	1
54	.15*	2	.06*	2
60	.15*	2	.06*	2
66	.15*	3	.06*	2
72	.15*	30**	.06*	57**
Mean length	3.03	6.36	4.09	8.51

* Assumed to remain constant from the last observed value
** Do not sum to one hundred because of rounding error

therefore spend a year on benefit. Those in the top band average three renewals and stay on benefit for two years. As one might predict from this the level of income before receipt of Family Credit - composed mainly of the claimant's earnings and child benefit - is inversely related to duration: the lower the income, the longer families spend on Family Credit. Likewise, overall earnings - the product of hourly earnings and the number of hours worked - are also inversely related to duration: low earning families are likely to receive benefit for two years and high earners for only one year. The difference in spell length associated with average hourly earnings is less marked - those in the top band spend six months less in the system than those at the bottom band, but this may be because of the arbitrary nature of the groupings.

Table 8.7
Correlates with duration

	Average duration for those starting a spell (months)		number	
	1st Spell	2nd Spell	1st Spell	2nd Spell
Amount of Family Credit:				
£ 0 - 15	12	17	13037	2923
£16 - 30	17	23	12603	2245
£31 - 45	22	30	9506	1506
£46+	28	37	9094	1426
Work Status:				
Part time	21	28	17375	3083
Full time	16	22	23865	5026
Occupation:				
Self employed	20	30	4937	949
Public sector	17	21	3462	600
Private				
- Professional	19	25	10470	1744
- Catering	20	27	7031	1606
- Manual	16	22	12908	2660
- Miscellaneous	17	23	2384	550

More unexpected is the lack of any association between the duration of spells and the number of children or the age of the youngest child at the time of the first claim. The number of children affects the level of benefit which is known to increase duration: the lack of association results from a counteracting tendency for families with few children to spend less time on benefit; precisely why is unclear. The presence of a young child might be anticipated to restrict employment opportunities which might have been expected to lead to longer durations on benefit for lone mothers with young children. This is not the case for reasons which will become apparent later.

The time spent on Family Credit is related to the number of hours which are worked. Those working 37 hours a week or more (here labelled full-time) can expect to spend an average 15 months on their first spell, compared with 21 months for those working a shorter week. As would be expected, female earners are over-represented among those employed part-time. Women in reversed role couples and lone mothers work 35 and 32 hours per week respectively. These figures compare with 40 and 39 hours for couples with male breadwinners and lone fathers.

Rather strangely the self-employed appear not to spend longer on benefit than other groups even though they average much higher awards of Family Credit. One possible explanation is that the self-employed are more heterogeneous than other groups in terms of their incomes before receipt of Family Credit. Those whose businesses are prospering leave the system well before those that are doing badly and thus lower the average duration. Also, some self-employed may use Family Credit much like a start up grant, whereas others may need Family Credit to keep the business afloat. It is also worth noting that the pattern for second spells is somewhat different (see below).

Table 8.8 shows that the first spell of benefit experienced by lone mothers averages approximately six months longer than for other kinds of family: the mean duration is a year and three-quarters. Somewhat surprisingly, couples with a female breadwinner - reversed role couples - have shorter first spells than other families; the average is about 15 months. This is despite the fact that they average the highest amounts of Family Credit which, in general, is associated with longer spells of benefit receipt.

Briefly, to summarise, the families at greatest risk of suffering a long first spell on Family Credit are lone mothers and those receiving greater amounts of benefit.

b) *Second spells.* The pattern of associations described above is largely

186

Table 8.8
Family type and duration

		Average duration for those starting a spell (months)		number	
		1st Spell	2nd Spell	1st Spell	2nd Spell
Family Type:					
Couples -	male earner	17	23	21684	4825
	female earner	15	25	4678	598
Lone -	male earner	17	20	618	143
	female earner	22	28	14260	2543

repeated for second spells except that the spells are usually longer, and the differences between particular types of family are greater. Thus, the amount of Family Credit is still the most striking predictor of duration: the average length of the second spell ranges from just under 18 months, for families receiving £15 or less Family Credit, to over three years for families receiving more than £45. Moreover, those families receiving large amounts of Family Credit are in a sense doubly disadvantaged since the increase in average duration between spells one and two is greater than for those receiving less Family Credit. As with first spells, the relationship between duration and total earnings, income before Family Credit and hourly earnings is in the opposite direction.

Lone parents can again expect to experience longer spells of receipt than other families: they average twenty-eight months, or six months longer than the first spell. Relatively few reverse role couples proceed to a second spell (13 per cent) but those that do so are likely to find themselves on benefit for an average of ten months longer than on the first occasion. The shortest second spells are experienced by couples with a male breadwinner.

The differential between part time and full time workers is maintained for the second spell. Reflecting this, both groups can expect to spend six months longer in their second spell than in their first spell of Family Credit. Full time workers average a second spell length of twenty-two months, and part time workers, one of twenty-eight months.

The differences between occupational group are greater for second than for first spells. Self-employed families typically spend an average of nine months longer than the public sector employees on the second spell. This compares with a three month difference for the first spell.

Overall, it appears that the same kinds of family who experience long initial spells of Family Credit also experience long second spells. Moreover, second spells are generally longer than the first. Thus repeat claimants appear to be more than doubly disadvantaged. They are generally more likely to spend longer in the system not only because they come from groups with longer average first spells, but also because second spells are longer in general for these groups. The families that are most likely to be affected tend to have particularly low earnings and receive rather high amounts of benefit. Disproportionate numbers are headed by mothers.

Multivariate relationships

There are a priori reasons to suppose that the precise relationship between the length of a spell on Family Credit and the size of the award might vary for different types of family. To take one example, one might expect the presence of young children to restrict the potential earnings of lone mothers more than couples and hence increase the time spent on benefit. If this were the case, this could explain why the age of child appears not to be associated with time on benefit when all types of Family Credit recipient are considered together. The findings presented in this section suggest that this is so.

The results discussed below are restricted to those which are of practical value in understanding differences in spell durations. In fact, because of the large sample size, many more combinations of variables appear to have a statistically significant effect on duration. Also the relationships identified in the modelling are those which would occur if other things were held constant. In the real world other things are not constant and certain relationships may be concealed or exaggerated by inconsequential co-occurrence.

The duration of the first spell on Family Credit increases with the size of award for all types of family but not to the same extent (Table 8.9). For male earners, both as partners and as lone parents, the spell length increases by an average of 18 months as the Family Credit award rises from less than £15 to more than £45. The corresponding figure for women earners is about 12 months. One consequence is that the difference reported earlier, with families headed by a lone woman typically experiencing longer spells than

188

other groups, is only maintained among families receiving smaller awards; when awards exceed £45, the period of receipt is virtually identical for lone mothers, lone fathers and couples with a male earner.

a)   *Reverse role couples.* A second consequence of the differential relationship between size of award and duration is that the position of reverse role couples becomes increasingly anomalous as the size of award increases. The special circumstances of these couples have already been noted above: they tend to receive higher awards which should mean longer spells on benefit but, in fact, they experience spells that are, if anything, shorter than for other groups. Table 8.9 shows that, for awards in excess of £45, spells are as much as six months less than for other families.

The unusual experiences of reverse role couples are evident again in Table 8.10. Whereas, for other types of family, duration falls with earnings and total income, net of Family Credit, this is not so for reverse role couples. What must be happening is that variations in the amount of Family Credit received by these couples is determined less by differences in earnings than by other factors such as the number and age of children.

There are a number of possible explanations for the short spells of receipt experienced by reverse role couples. Marsh and McKay (1992) have suggested that Family Credit may act as a 'parachute' in the short term protecting families from the worst consequences of male unemployment. The female partner retains her job and claims Family Credit until her partner either finds another job, or exhausts his entitlement to unemployment benefit when it may become financially impractical for her to continue in employment (regardless of other reasons why she may want to hold onto her job). Another possibility, is that, in similar circumstances, the woman is able to increase her hours while the man cares for the children. Certainly a substantial proportion of the men in those families did receive unemployment benefit (16 per cent). Moreover, the time which reverse role couples spend on benefit is more closely associated with the number of children than for other family types (it increases with the number). For second spells duration was also positively related to the age of the youngest child.

b)   *Lone parents.* It was noted earlier that lone mothers are likely to spend longer on Family Credit than other groups including lone fathers. The latter earn slightly more per hour and work for longer perhaps because they have more flexible employment opportunities and easier access to child care. Within the Family Credit population, family structure also appears to

189

favour males insofar as their children tend to be older: half of male lone parents had a youngest child aged over nine, whereas half of lone mothers had a child under seven.

The association between spell length and family structure was concealed in the univariate analyses because the association was not simply a consequence of more children resulting in more benefit. In fact, as Table 8.11 shows, when one controls for family type, those families with three or more children tend to remain on benefit for between three and five months longer than families with one child. The pattern holds for both first and second spells. Even so, lone mothers with a single child can expect to spend the same time on Family Credit as other families with three children.

Table 8.9
Spell length, family type and amount of Family Credit

| | Length of spell in months | | | |
	£ 1-15	£16-30	£31-45	£46+
FIRST SPELL				
Family Type:				
Couples - male earner	11	16	22	28
female earner	10	13	16	22
Lone - male earner	11	15	22	29
female earner	14	19	25	29
SECOND SPELL				
Family Type:				
Couples - male earner	17	22	29	36
female earner	17	22	27	31
Lone - male earner	14	17	25	37
female earner	19	25	32	39

Table 8.10
Spell length, family type and amount of family income

| | First Spell | | | | Second Spell | | | |
| | Couples | | Lone | | Couples | | Lone | |
Length of Spell in Months	Male earner	Female earner	Male earner	Female earner	Male earner	Female earner	Male earner	Female earner
Earnings:								
Less than £65	24	15	25	26	32	21	38	34
£66 - £95	21	16	22	23	30	25	32	31
£96 - £150	16	15	16	19	23	25	16	24
More than £150	14	15	12	16	20	26	16	23
Average hourly Earnings:								
Less than £2	22	14	23	24	31	22	34	32
£2 - £3	17	15	17	22	25	24	23	29
£3 - £3.50	14	16	13	20	20	24	15	26
More than £3.50	14	16	13	18	21	27	16	25
Family income net of Family Credit:								
Less than £100	23	16	23	25	32	25	36	34
£101 - £125	17	15	17	20	26	25	21	27
£126 - £150	14	14	13	18	20	22	16	24
More than £150	14	15	13	17	20	26	16	24

Table 8.11
Spell length and family characteristics

| | First Spell | | | | Second Spell | | | |
| | Couples | | Lone | | Couples | | Lone | |
	Male earner	Female earner	Male earner	Female earner	Male earner	Female earner	Male earner	Female earner
Length of Spell in Months								
Number of Children:								
1	15	12	15	20	22	22	24	26
2	16	16	17	23	22	25	19	28
3+	19	19	20	25	24	27	15	32
Age of youngest child:								
0 - 4	16	14	18	20	23	22	12	28
5 - 11	17	16	17	23	23	25	21	28
12 - 18	17	16	15	20	23	27	22	26

As might be expected the time that lone parents spend on Family Credit is related to the age of their youngest child. For men the average duration falls to fifteen months when all children are aged over ten. This may reflect the greater independence of children, or simply the increased probability that children will age the family out of eligibility for Family Credit. Lone mothers, on the other hand, appear to spend the longest time on benefit when their youngest child is at primary school. This may be because they have established a durable employment pattern consistent with the requirements of childcare, although there does not seem to be a simple relationship between age of child and the number of hours worked.

Summary

To summarise, size of award is the factor most closely associated with the time that families spend on Family Credit. The larger the award, the longer the first and second spells. The strength of this relationship differs between different kinds of families. It is strong for lone parents headed by a woman but these families are more likely to experience longer periods on benefit than other groups irrespective of the size of the award. In their case, and that of male lone parents too, the number and age of children also appears to be associated with differences in the time spent on Family Credit although the precise pattern of relationships varies between the two kinds of lone parent.

Couples where the woman works, but not the man, appear to be very different from other families. Although, on average, they receive large awards, the time spent on benefit is typically short. Moreover, variations in the amount of benefit which they receive seem to be more closely related to differences in household size than to differences in income.

There are many reasons, technical and substantive, why the time spent on Family Credit might be associated with the size of the award. Those receiving small amounts may feel that it is not worth the hassle involved in reapplying. They may already be in relatively well paid jobs with a career structure that lifts them out of eligibility for benefit. Then again, it may take only a small change in their circumstances to make them ineligible for benefit. (The change introduced in October 1993, whereby small awards of £4.00 or less a week are paid in a lump sum at the start of a claim may affect the propensity of a claim).

Turning to people with large awards, the opposite arguments could apply. The principal wage earner may be in a low paid job and have few prospects.

In such cases Family Credit serves as an all but permanent wage subsidy. Equally, Family Credit represents a large contribution to family income which it may be impractical to do without. Then again it will take a substantial change in fortune to make such a family ineligible for benefit.

Churning

This section focuses on the kinds of family who return for a second spell of Family Credit and on the time it takes them to return. Such families are exceptional for, as has been reported above, the majority of Family Credit users so far have experienced a single spell. They are nevertheless of considerable interest both because they are likely to spend long periods on benefit and because there may be more of them in future.

There are a number of different reasons why families might return to Family Credit. Some families may experience cyclical fluctuations in income. Others, who perhaps used Family Credit as a 'parachute' cushioning the effects of unemployment, may have found employment once more, perhaps on lower wages than before. Yet others may previously have used Family Credit on an 'up escalator' into better paid work, only to experience disappointment and a fall in wages or working hours. Life course events may also be important: the arrival of a new child or the breakdown of a relationship and the consequent generation of a lone parent family. Then again, people early in their careers may be more likely to earn their way off benefit than older workers who have reached an income plateau.

There is a danger that the short period since the introduction of Family Credit may cause one to understate the number of families that, in the long term, will receive Family Credit on more than one occasion. But this is not the only problem facing the analyst studying repeat spells. People who have claimed Family Credit recently have less opportunity to make a repeat claim than those who first received Family Credit in 1988. An associated problem could arise if the kinds of family receiving Family Credit for the first time has changed over time.

Two techniques are used which, interpreted together, help to minimise the impact of these problems[1]. The results are summarised in Tables 8.12 and

---

[1] The first involves the use of a logistic regression model in which the odds of making a second successful application against not doing so are regressed on family characteristics. This approach is relatively straightforward but does not overcome the problems noted above. The

8.13. It is evident that the longer a person is off benefit, the less likely they are to return. (This is indicated by the hazard rate derived from the model.) It is also apparent (Table 8.13) that the average period between claims is long and exceeds the period over which data is available. This reflects the influence of the large number of Family Credit families who have never made a second application. Many of these families will in any case have ceased to be eligible for Family Credit simply because of the aging of their family.

Families receiving large awards during their first spell are less likely to experience a second spell on Family Credit but, if they do reapply, they are likely to do so relatively quickly. What appears to be the case, therefore, is that it requires a major change in circumstances to lift a family off Family Credit for the first time if they have been receiving large sums for long periods. Typically changes of this kind, such as a child leaving home, may for all practical purposes be irreversible. Where the change is not of this order, the family may rapidly come to need Family Credit again. Indeed, they may simply have forgotten to renew their claim.

Although families receiving larger amounts of Family Credit have longer first and second spells than families receiving smaller amounts, it is not generally the case that those families with longer first spells return sooner for a second spell. In fact, though not shown, families with longer first spells are likely to return later than do families with shorter first spells. This suggests that claimants whose circumstances have remained relatively stable for a long period do not, after eventually moving off Family Credit, experience fluctuating circumstances which move them repeatedly in and out of benefit. What cannot be established is whether their circumstances after leaving Family Credit improved or deteriorated.

---

second approach employs a hazard model and treats families who are not observed to make a second application as right-hand censored observations. The probability of making a second claim at time t is then estimated conditional upon not making a second claim until time t. This attempts to cope with the different opportunities that people have to make a second claim but only by assuming that all families will eventually do so.

This section deals with the unconditional probability of returning analysed with a binomial logistic model utilising the same model as was used in the analysis of spell lengths. The characteristics of individuals that were used were those taken at the start of the first spell. The logic underlying this choice is that the earliest chance to identify those individuals who are at risk of returning is at time of the first claim.

The probability of a second spell is also related to the type of family involved (Table 8.12). Couples with a male earner are the group most likely to experience another spell and they do so more quickly than other families. Such families are typically at a slightly earlier stage in the life course and so have more opportunity to reapply before the ages of their children exclude them from benefit. Certainly the probability of making a second claim and doing so relatively quickly falls as the age of the youngest child increases (Table 8.13).

Reverse role couples are the least likely to make a second claim despite experiencing the shortest first spells and therefore having more time in which to return to the system. One could surmise that this is because the events that brought these families into eligibility were more likely to constitute a major departure from their normal circumstances than was the case for other groups. This would be consistent with the fact that they receive benefit for relatively short periods. For example, it might be that some of these families usually have two earners which, on the basis of the recent PSI study (Marsh and McKay, 1992), would effectively exclude them from Family Credit. Family Credit, therefore, is used to tide them over a short spell when the husband is out of work. Alternatively - and a grimmer scenario - in some families the man may become unemployed and be unable to find employment for some considerable time. In this case the family first moves on to Family Credit and then on to Income Support (the safety net provided for out of work families) when the loss of Unemployment Benefit may reduce the financial incentive for the woman to remain in work. Interestingly, among those families supported by women, those with the youngest and oldest children were the least likely to make a second claim. In the former case, this may point to the use of Family Credit to facilitate parental childcare of pre-school aged children.

Also of interest, families who first claimed Family Credit later in the study period were likely to return for a second spell more quickly than families that applied earlier. This apparent increase in the volatility of the caseload, with more families experiencing fluctuating circumstances, may reflect the deepening economic recession or a secular trend towards increasing vulnerability of people in low income jobs that is often supposed to characterise the 'new poverty' (Cross, 1993).

Finally, it is worth reiterating that the likelihood that a family will receive Family Credit on more than one occasion is associated with life cycle factors, even though these are less important than the size of the first award. Families with older children are less likely to reclaim, presumably because children leave home and the needs element of the family benefit formula is reduced. In contrast, claimants aged 25-34 often reapply (possibly because they have young children) as do older parents when they have younger children (Table 8.13).

Table 8.12
Second spells on Family Credit

	Probability of Second Spell[a] %	Mean[b]	Duration between spells (yrs) Standard Deviation[b]
Family type:			
Couples - male earner	23	5.7	3.7
female earner	13	7.8	3.8
Lone - male earner	19	6.8	5.0
female earner	18	6.4	4.4
Size of first award:			
£0 - 15	22	6.7	3.9
£16 - 30	22	6.0	4.1
£31 - 45	18	6.0	4.1
£46+	14	5.5	3.7
Age of youngest child:			
0 - 4 years	22	5.5	3.3
5 - 11 years	19	5.9	3.6
12 - 18 years	14	9.2	5.7

[a] Estimated probabilities derived from logistic regression modelling averaged across population subgroups
[b] Average median estimates derived from a hazard model with the assumption that time follows a Weibull distribution

Table 8.13
Second claims: interaction between age of claimant and age of child

	Probability of second spell			
	Age of youngest child			
	0-4	5-11	12-18	Total
Age of claimant:				
16 - 24 years	.19	.19	.16	.19
25 - 34 years	.22	.21	.17	.22
35 - 44 years	.23	.19	.15	.19
45+ years	.23	.18	.13	.16
	—	—	—	—
Total	.22	.19	.04	

	Duration between spells (years)			
Age of claimant:				
16 -24 years	6.4	6.5	7.6	6.4
25 - 34 years	5.5	5.8	7.0	5.6
35 - 44 years	4.5	5.9	9.1	6.5
45+ years	4.2	6.6	10.3	7.7
Total	5.5	5.9	9.2	

Discussion and conclusion

The results presented in this chapter should be regarded as suggestive rather than definitive. They derive from information accumulated during the first 45 months of Family Credit administration. It takes time for a benefit to settle in and to become part of the landscape of social security provision. Likewise, the use made of a benefit, and the broader functions which it performs, may change rapidly during the early months of implementation (a possibility to be addressed in the next chapter). Equally important, 45 months is a relatively short period of time over which to observe families' use of a social security scheme. Finally, the variables which can be derived from administrative data seldom accord to the needs of analysis. Nevertheless, certain important findings have been presented that in turn serve to demonstrate the value of applying longitudinal analysis to administrative records.

On the basis of the evidence available it is evident that the largest number of families receive Family Credit for a single six months' claim period and repeated spells on benefit have so far proved to be the exception. Even when account is taken of the claims that were still in payment at the end of the study period, the <u>average</u> duration of a claim only rises from 12 to 18 months. This suggests that, for most claimants, Family Credit functions as a transitional benefit, bridging families across a short-lived set of circumstances, not as a form of long term wage subsidy. Only further work will indicate the extent to which Family Credit provides a bridge in or out of the labour market.

The relative infrequency of repeated spells of Family Credit receipt also suggests that the period of entitlement is not too short and does not generate considerable churning which could be administratively inefficient. Indeed, it may be that the entitlement periods for the recipients who make a single claim is too short, although no information is available on the profile of resources available to recipients during the six month period over which they receive Family Credit. Moreover, any move to reduce the period of entitlement from six months would entail extra administrative expense associated with processing 'unnecessary' applications from the 53 per cent of applicants who now receive Family Credit for periods of over six months.

The combination of short periods of receipt and few repeat awards means that a large proportion of applications come from families who have never previously received Family Credit. Therefore, strategies to promote take-up cannot rely on a detailed experiential knowledge of the benefit. However, this pattern of claims means that large numbers of families have at some time had recourse to Family Credit. As a consequence the newly eligible family potentially has access to a substantial pool or network of lay advice. This network may be supportive in terms of reinforcing the legitimacy of making a claim. Unfortunately, the knowledge of Family Credit held by most members of the network will probably be historic (since most periods of receipt are short) and hence inaccurate in detail unless they have followed the national advertising campaigns (see chapter 9) or studied the details printed in their child benefit order book.

Although applicants receive Family Credit for short periods, the modelling illustrates that long-term claimants accumulate in the system very rapidly. Assuming that there are no changes in the global function of Family Credit, one would expect 56 per cent of the current caseload to receive Family Credit continuously for over two years and 36 per cent to remain on benefit for six years or more. Given that long-term recipients average larger awards, this means that even greater proportions of the total benefit expenditure are directed to long-term users and, hence, towards long-term wage subsidy.

Predicting which applicants are likely to rely on Family Credit for long periods is very difficult on the basis of the information available on the administrative file. Indeed, it may never prove to be possible at the level of the individual although the analysis presented in this chapter is far from being the last word. Even so it is clear that, as a group, families receiving large awards are likely to remain on benefit for twice as long as those in receipt of small ones.

There are many possible reasons for this which require to be investigated by means of repeated interviews with Family Credit recipients. Nevertheless, it would seem that the size of the award is determined more by low family income than by the needs component of the eligibility formula (Ashworth and Walker, 1992b). Low wage rates, in particular, but also the number of hours worked are key factors. The logical response to these observations, if supported by further analysis, is to suggest that proactive policies designed to enhance earning power - perhaps skills training and childcare - may be needed to reduce spells spent on benefit. The childcare disregard to be introduced in October 1994 for certain families on Family Credit, accord with this logic and may affect the length of spells. Certainly actions which serve to reduce durations reverse the accumulation of long stay recipients within the system and initiate a reverse multiplier effect which serve disproportionately to reduce the proportion of benefit expenditure directed towards long-term wage subsidy.

In conclusion, it is appropriate to underline that analyses reported in this chapter were designed primarily to explore the potential value of longitudinal analyses of administrative records. The substantial difficulties encountered in such work are discussed elsewhere (Ashworth, 1993). However, while it was never the intention to provide definitive results for policy development or evaluation, to the extent that this chapter has cast new light on the role and functioning of Family Credit, it has demonstrated the utility of longitudinal analysis.

9 Family Credit: Aspects of a changing caseload

From Chapter 8 it is clear that most of the families who ever receive Family Credit do so for relatively short periods. It will be recalled that Family Credit is an income-tested benefit, introduced in Britain in 1988, which is aimed at low income families with children, having at least one person employed for 16 hours or more per week. Benefit awards last for six months after which they have to be renewed. Most families only renew their award once or twice and so most spells on benefit last for considerably less than 18 months. Moreover, relatively few applicants make a second or third claim once they have finished a spell on benefit. Family Credit appears typically to be used to bridge an unusual, short-lived set of circumstances.

However, a minority of families do receive Family Credit for much longer periods and some rely on Family Credit on repeated occasions. As a general rule, the larger the award the longer the time which families spend in receipt. Lone mothers are over-represented among families receiving a large award and their spells on benefit average about six months longer than those of other groups. On the other hand, although couples where the woman is in paid employment tend to receive large awards of Family Credit, their time on benefit is comparatively short. Families experiencing long spells on benefit tend to accumulate in the system while others come and go. As a consequence of this, it was predicted that by 1994 over 30 per cent of the caseload will be in the middle of a spell of receipt lasting six years or more.

The accumulation of long term recipients is likely to bring about a gradual change in the characteristics of the liveload until stability is reached. However, this process may well be disturbed by changes in the numbers and characteristics of families joining and leaving the system so that the claimant population remains in continuous flux. It is these aspects of benefit dynamics which constitute the focus of this chapter.

The analysis covers the 45 months from the introduction of the scheme in April 1988 until December 1991 and employs a longitudinal data set derived from a five per cent sample of administrative records. By the end of this period 346,000 families were in receipt of Family Credit, an increase of around 60 per cent on the numbers that used to receive Family Income Supplement, the benefit it replaced (Figure 9.1).

Family credit caseload 1988-91

Inertia and the build-up of caseload

Any change in the aggregate characteristics of a claimant population occurs as a mismatch between the characteristics of new applicants and those moving out of benefit receipt. Because Family Credit is generally payable unaltered for periods of six months, any change which occurs does so only very slowly. The characteristics of the population at a point in time are largely the result of applications and decisions taken sometime beforehand. The importance of this inertia is evident in Figures 9.2a and 9.2b which divide the Family Credit caseload according to the type of application made by recipients. Thus, it can be seen that, towards the end of 1991, well over eighty per cent of the Family Credit recipients were in the middle of a six month claim, only about 10 per cent had renewed a claim during the month with between five and eight per cent were beginning a new, or their first, spell on benefit.

The information presented in Figure 9.2 differs from that in Figure 9.1 in that it does not include claims made for Family Income Supplement which were automatically converted into Family Credit at the introduction of the new scheme. Once these claims came to an end, however, and the families had to reapply for Family Credit, they are recorded in Figure 9.2. In effect, therefore, Figure 9.2 relates entirely to awards made specifically for Family Credit.

About 200,000 families were transferred directly from Family Income Supplement to Family Credit and almost two-thirds of these went on to renew their claim. Therefore about 15 per cent of all the 875,000 families covered by the study moved into Family Credit directly from Family Income

204

Figure 9.1
Current awards of FIS and Family Credit

Thousands

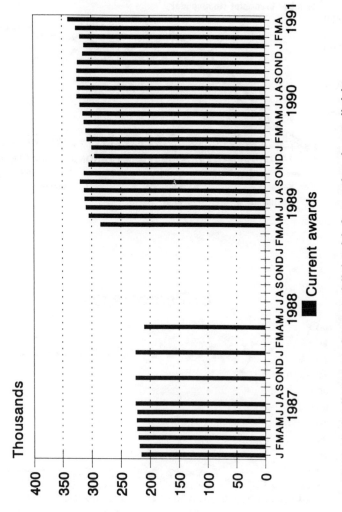

■ Current awards

January 1987 to April 1991 where published information is available
Source: Social Security Statistics

205

Figure 9.2
Family Credit caseload

a) Numbers

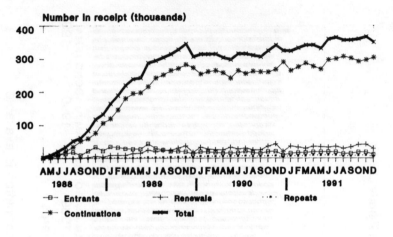

b) Percentages

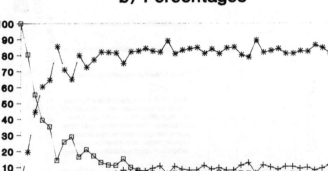

206

Supplement. The continuation from Family Income Supplement is even more striking when the focus is on total benefit months: 22 per cent of all the benefit months of Family Credit receipt are attributable to movements directly off Family Income Supplement.

Returning to Figure 9.2, this shows the rapidity with which continuing claims (in their second or subsequent month) came to dominate the characteristics of the Family Credit liveload. Three months after the introduction of the scheme claims continuing in payment outstripped new ones in the first month of payment and reached 80 per cent of the liveload by the end of the year. (After the first 12 months we reserve the term 'new' applicants for people who have not claimed Family Credit before although they may include some families that received Family Income Supplement in earlier periods.)

Unfortunately the administrative data for the first few months of the new scheme are rather unreliable. Nevertheless, there appears to be a gradual increase in successful applications. This trend continues to April 1989, only a little beyond the time when applicants who moved directly from Family Income Supplement onto Family Credit are no longer included as 'new' claims. There is a slight decline in the number of successful applications from families new to the scheme after June 1989, but little discernible change from November 1989 through to the end of the observation period over two years later. While the number of new claims stabilised at around 18,000 per month, there is, as might be expected, a gradual increase in the number of successful applications from people coming back into the system for a second or third period of receipt. By the end of 1991 these repeat awards accounted for about a third of families entering the system.

The relatively small, month to month variation in the number of new and repeat claims apparent in Figure 9.2 has a magnified effect on the size of the total caseload. This is again a simple mathematical consequence of the six month period of each claim. Thus, by the end of 1989, the steady rise in the number of new awards granted each month, reaching a peak of 44,400 in June 1989, translates into a total of 206,800 recipients in the midst of their first six month award that are carried forward from one month to the next. Moreover, the gradual growth in the Family Credit caseload that occurs from early 1990 - an increase from 314,500 in January 1990 to 350,120 in December 1991 - can be largely attributed to the growth in the number of

207

repeat claims from families who return to Family Credit after a spell out of the system.[1]

This is even more remarkable given that the monthly number of such repeat claims never exceeds 10,000.

Changing caseload composition

While inertia is a very strong feature of the development of the Family Credit caseload, certain changes in the composition of the caseload did occur over the first 45 months of the scheme. Figures 9.3, 9.4 and 9.5 summarise the changing composition according to the type of family, size of award and occupation respectively. Each figure relates exclusively to families who have applied for Family Credit rather than Family Income Supplement.

Couples with a male breadwinner constituted the largest group of recipients throughout the study period, generally comprising between 50 per cent and 56 per cent of the caseload (Figure 9.3). Lone mothers were the second largest group with lone fathers and couples with a female breadwinner some considerable way behind. However, the rise in the proportion of claims made by couples with a female breadwinner was inexorable. At the introduction of the scheme they accounted for only three per cent of the caseload; by the end of 1991 they comprised about 11 per cent of all families receiving Family Credit. The growth in the relative size of this group was largely at the expense of couples with a male breadwinner.

Figure 9.4 reveals a build up of recipients receiving large awards during the first 45 months of Family Credit. For the purposes of presentation, all awards made over the study period have been deflated to take account of movements in benefit and wage rates and divided into quartiles. Figure 9.4 shows the proportion of awards in payment in each month which fall into each quartile. Families receiving awards in the top quartile constituted about 18 per cent of all recipients at the commencement of the scheme and over 30 per cent by the end of 1991. Moreover, a substantial component of this

---

[1] The official published caseload figures, adjusted to take account of belatedly assessed claims, are slightly lower: End of January 1990: 300,000; End of December 1991: 347,000. These are point in time figures whereas the study estimates relate to all persons in receipt at any time during the month.

Figure 9.3
Family Credit caseload - Family type

a) Family Type: Thousands

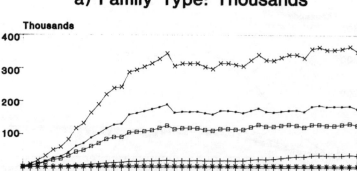

April 1988 - December 1991

b) Family Type: Percentage

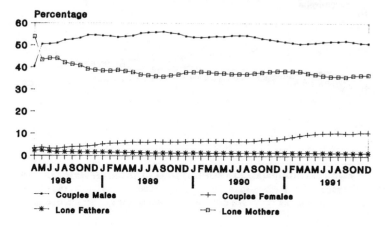

April 1988 - December 1991

209

Figure 9.4
Family Credit caseload - amount of Family Credit

a) Amount of Family Credit (thousands)

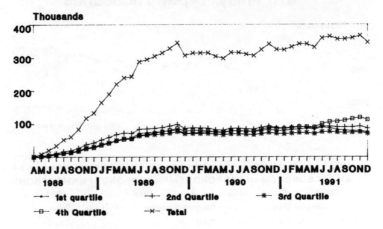

April 1988 - December 1991

b) Amount of Family Credit (percentage)

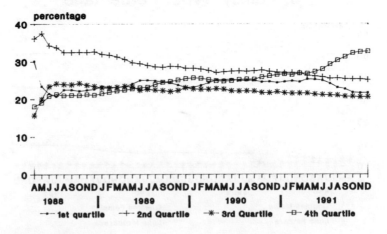

April 1988 - December 1991

Figure 9.5
Caseload

a) Occupational Type - thousands

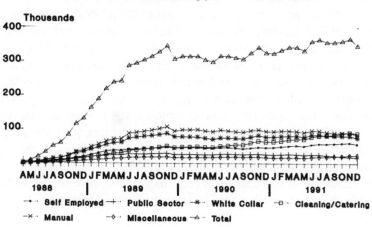

b) Occupational Type - percentage

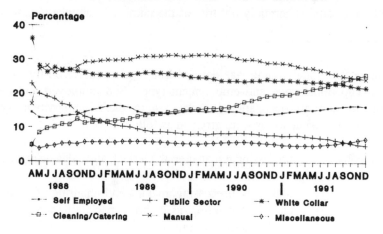

increase occurred after the scheme stabilised and when the statistical series is known to be more reliable. The proportion of families with the smallest awards varied over time but does not reveal any clear secular trend. On the other hand, the proportion of families with medium range awards has steadily fallen over the life of the scheme.

Figure 9.5 shows some substantial changes in the occupations from which Family Credit recipients are drawn[2]. The most significant changes relate to public sector employees. These fell from almost a quarter of the caseload to less than five per cent. At the same time, the numbers in catering and cleaning occupations rose from five per cent to almost thirty per cent. There was some fall in the proportion of applicants classified as being in manual occupations: the high point was in October 1989 when manual workers comprised 31 per cent of the caseload; by December 1991 the proportion had fallen to 24 per cent. In each case the trend continues through the period over which the statistics are most reliable.

The remainder of this Chapter is concerned with uncovering, in so far as is possible, the processes that have brought these changes about.

Applications for Family Credit 1988-91

Renewals and new applications

While the composition of the caseload is relatively stable from month to month, the same is certainly not true of the number of applications that are

---

2 The occupational coding was derived from two variables on the analytic file, occupational code and employment type. Self employed and public sector include all occupational codes within these employment types. Private sector occupations were grouped as follows:

White collar: professional managerial, clerical, and sales occupations

Manual: materials, processing, making and repairing of metal and electrical, painting, assembling, packaging, construction, mining, security, transport

Miscellaneous: Miscellaneous, unclassified and farming, catering and cleaning.

processed (Figure 9.6). Applications show a distinct seasonal patterning, with the number processed in December being only around half that in the peak months during the summer and autumn. Applications are also low in August. This broad seasonal patterning would appear to be largely driven by administrative considerations rather than the actual flow of applications received by the Family Credit Unit. The December trough reflects a three week month while the August low is linked to staff holidays.

The fluctuations in the overall number of applications are, to a degree, mirrored in the individual constituents: the lows in August and December are evident among renewals as well as among new and repeat applications. There are some differences however. The trend line for new applications is horizontal, or steadily downwards when expressed as a percentage of the applications processed each month, whereas, as might have been expected, the number and proportion of renewals increases over time. As a result, despite the relatively short duration of continuous periods of receipt documented in Ashworth and Walker (1992), the bulk of the applications processed each month are now renewals. However, it is the very brevity of spells that has caused the proportion of renewals to stabilise at around 55-60 per cent of successful applications. On the other hand, there are no grounds to believe that the penetration of Family Credit is increasing among new applicants. Indeed, the evidence in Figure 9.6 points in the opposite direction with repeat awards and renewals constituting an increasing proportion of applications at the expense of totally new claims. The significance to be attached to this finding depends on the rate of change of the population eligible for Family Credit (see below).

As might be expected, renewals follow a six monthly cycle with peaks and troughs repeated six months later but with a lower amplitude as a result of the proportion of applicants who fail to renew.

Advertising campaigns

Figure 9.7 records the timing of the main national advertising campaigns which, together with the pattern of applications, provides a basis for assessing the broad impact of the campaigns. The most striking campaign was that conducted between 17th April and 29th June 1989: the total number of applications received in June, 72,000, was 14,180 above the trend line (three-month moving average) and, unlike any subsequent campaign, this increase was largely attributable to a rise in new applications rather than in renewals.

The short campaigns in 1991 - one in February and March, ahead of the April uprating of benefits, the other in September - had their greatest effect on renewals. However, while the smaller proportional increase in applications associated with the earlier campaign continued for four months, the impact of the September campaign may have been more short-lived (although the end of the data series in the traditionally low processing month of December may be a distortion).

The campaign that ran from 24 May to 19 July 1990 may also have boosted total applications. The impact, though, appears to have been delayed until October and November, very probably because of the difficulty of processing the surge of applications coinciding with the staff holiday season. Assessing the magnitude of the impact is also made difficult by the substantial month to month variation in applications at this time and, particularly, by the small number of claims processed in December. Noting these limitations, it seems probable that the impact was less than in earlier years with perhaps three-quarters of the additional applications being due to renewals.

While there is clear evidence of the effect of advertising in the pattern of applications it is difficult to recognise the impact of these promotions in the gross caseload statistics (see Figure 9.2). This is undoubtedly partly a consequence of the lags built into the statistical series. A campaign may generate new applications in one month but because of the time taken to process these claims, which may actually be increased if the campaign is particularly successful, the impact may take some time to feed through into the caseload statistics. Additionally an unknown proportion of the applications will prove to be unsuccessful while the number that are successful and additional to the normal monthly workload is small in relation to the total caseload. Even so, the number of new applicants remained surprisingly constant during 1990 and 1991.

Likelihood of renewal

The six-monthly pattern of renewals, noted above, is likely to be a particularly important motor driving the administration of Family Credit and the characteristics of the caseload. Although, most recipients only renew their application once or twice (Chapter 8), renewals constitute almost 60 per cent of the successful applications processed each month. Families who renew their claims constitute the vehicle by which the characteristics of the current caseload are mapped onto future ones. The families who do not renew their applications and hence leave the system, and those who apply

214

Figure 9.6
Applications for Family Credit

a) Numbers

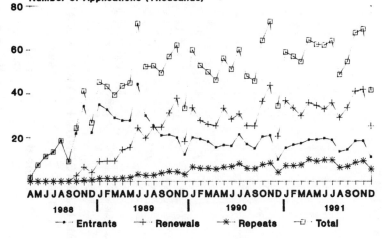

b) Proportions

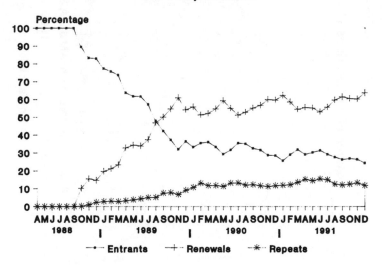

April 1988 - December 1991

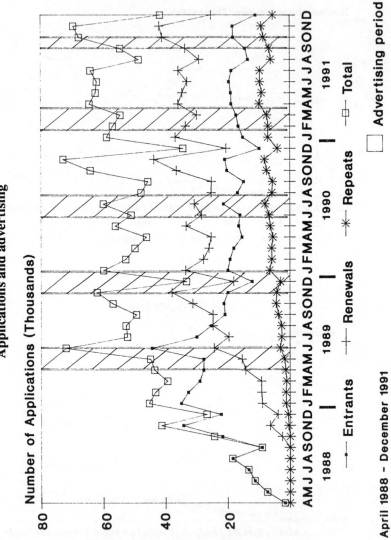

Figure 9.7
Applications and advertising

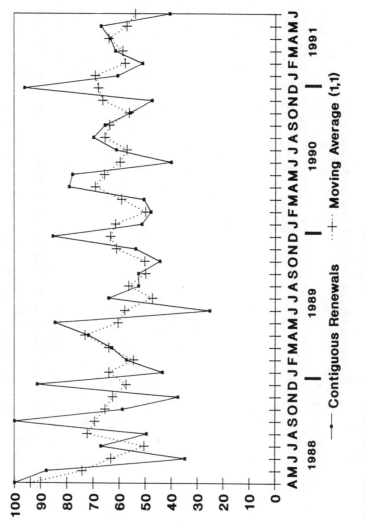

Figure 9.8

Proportion of applicants renewing claim

—■— Contiguous Renewals   ···+··· Moving Average (1,1)

April 1988 – June 1991

217

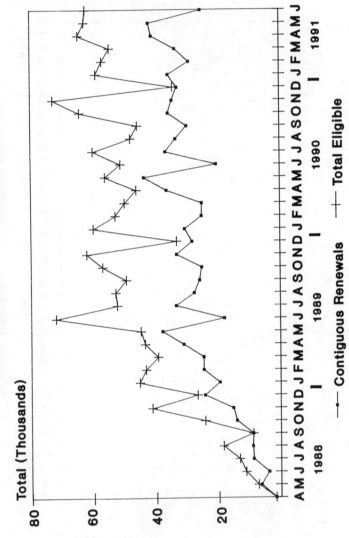

Figure 9.9
Numbers eligible to renew and renewing

Total (Thousands)

—■— Contiguous Renewals   —+— Total Eligible

April 1988 – June 1991

218

for a first or subsequent time determine the way in which the characteristics of the caseload change.

Figure 9.8 shows just how dramatically the proportion of applicants who renew their claims six months later varies from month to month. The variation, from around 40 per cent to over 95 per cent of a particular monthly cohort, is so extreme that it was decided to adopt different algorithms to check the results, but they were repeated. Even when a moving average (covering three months) is applied there is a wave like pattern typically traversing five or so months with the apogee around fifteen per cent above the nadir.

There is no clear basis for determining the reason for the substantial variation in the rate of renewal. Figure 9.9, which plots the renewal rate against the size of the monthly cohort of applications, offers some evidence to suggest that the renewal rate is lower among large cohorts and this is supported by modelling (Ashworth and Walker, 1992). Even so the relationship is not a strong one and varies for different types of applicant.

One hypothesis considered was that the renewal rate would be low where a large number of applications was the result of an exceptional intake of people new to Family Credit, say as the result of a special promotion. Two elements may be involved. The first is a simple 'swamping' mechanism. The additional applicants have the same characteristics as at other times with a preponderance of families that are not destined to remain on benefit for long. The subsequent failure of these 'short-stay' families to renew their claims lowers the renewal rate. The second possibility is that the advertising stimulates a disproportionate number of 'short stay' families to apply for Family Credit. Such people might be supposed to have only minimal entitlement to benefit or, perhaps, to experience a particularly short-lived set of circumstances. This latter possibility may hold for the wave of successful applications processed in June 1989 when less than a quarter of recipients renewed their claim; a disproportionate number of families successfully applying during this period received small awards. The same is true of applications at the time of the summer 1990 campaigns. However, even if this hypothesis does have some validity, it by no means explains all the variation.

It has not been possible adequately to test this or other hypotheses relating to differential renewal rates over time. Also, it has to be admitted that there seems to be no cogent reason why different types of applicant should behave differently, or be treated differentially, in the context of a large monthly cohort, something that the modelling reported in Ashworth and Walker (1992) indicates is the case. What is clear is that the rate at which applications are renewed is a crucial determinant of the size of the caseload and that advertising acts as an important stimulant to renewal.

Components of change

Family type

As was reported in Chapter 8, the length of Family Credit receipt varies noticeably according to the type of family. The average length of the first spell experienced by lone mothers is 22 months compared with 17 months for families headed by a man and only 15 months for couples where the woman is the main breadwinner.

These differences, which are larger for the second spell on benefit, are reflected in Figure 9.10. This shows that the proportion of lone mothers who renew their claim is higher than for other groups; the average is just below 70 per cent (although with considerable monthly variation) which compares with 60 per cent of couples with an employed father. As might be expected the figure is even lower for couples where the mother is the main earner (about 40 per cent).

The pattern of month to month variation is generally very similar for all types of family but there are some differences. Take, for example, couples who entered the system between late 1988 and August 1989, irrespective of whether they are headed by a man or a women. While there is substantial month to month variation, a downward trend is evident in the proportion of recipients in each successive cohort who successfully renew their claim. This trend is then reversed until the end of 1990. After that there is a fall in the number of renewals which is particularly marked for female headed families. While it is speculation, this pattern may reflect developments in the labour market. During the early period real wages were moving ahead quickly and employment growth was buoyant. Families may have been floated off benefit by rising wages, achieved either by moving jobs or simply as a result of wage inflation. Such opportunities would have lessened in the subsequent period as the recession strengthened its grip on the economy. The final fall in renewals may reflect redundancies and a movement onto unemployment benefit and income support.

The above pattern is not so evident among lone parent families, particularly those headed by a woman. Lone mothers tend to work fewer hours than other families on Family Credit and may, as a consequence, be less sensitive to the state of the wider economy.

220

There is another exception to the broadly similar pattern of renewals. This relates to a three month period just after the introduction of the scheme when the proportion of the couples with a woman breadwinner who renewed their award was very low. No reason for this is evident and it may simply reflect the lower reliability of the sample estimates at this time when the population of Family Credit recipients was still small.

The way in which the different rates of renewal affects the constituents of the Family Credit caseload can be seen in Figure 9.11. This shows the proportion of successful applicants who are new to the system, renew their claim, or return to benefit after a spell outside the system. This breakdown is presented for each family type for each month from April 1988 to December 1991.

While, as would be expected, the proportion of new claims generally falls over time as the number of renewals and repeat claims rises, the differences between each type of family are quite as striking as the similarities. Couples where the mother is the main breadwinner tend to experience shorter spells on benefit and hence fewer renew their claim. As a result, the number of new applicants continued to exceed renewals right to the end of the study period in December 1991. This situation did not exist for lone mothers or couples headed by a man at any time after September 1989.

While a very sizeable proportion of the couples that are headed by a woman are new to the scheme, the reverse is true of lone mothers: from the end of 1989 over 65 per cent of applications from lone mothers were from families seeking to renew their claim. A broadly similar pattern applies to couples with a male breadwinner but there are significant differences. First, and perhaps most noticeably, the proportion of couples with a male breadwinner making repeat claims rose more quickly and reached about 20 per cent in the middle of 1991 (although the number fell towards the end of the year). Secondly, there is rather more variation in the monthly ratio of renewals to new claims. In fact, there is a broad six monthly cycle, which is first evident as a peak in renewals during November 1989, but probably has its origins in the large number of applications in June of that year. Traces of this sequence can be detected among lone mothers but it would appear that the male headed couples who entered the system in this cohort contained an unusually high proportion of long term recipients.

As regards applications from lone fathers, the most striking feature is the enormous month to month variation in the number of successful awards. However, this variation is probably attributable to the small size of the group. Perhaps more notable is the high proportion of repeat claims, a feature that is also characteristic of couples where the man is the principal

Figure 9.10
Renewals by family type

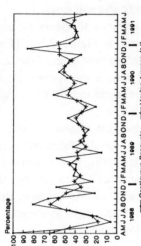

a) Couples with male breadwinners

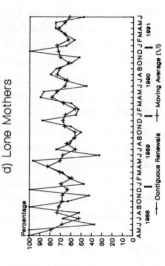

b) Couples with female Breadwinners

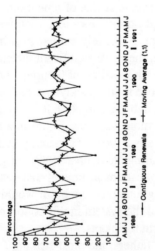

c) Lone Fathers

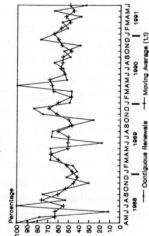

d) Lone Mothers

222

Figure 9.11
Type of application by family type

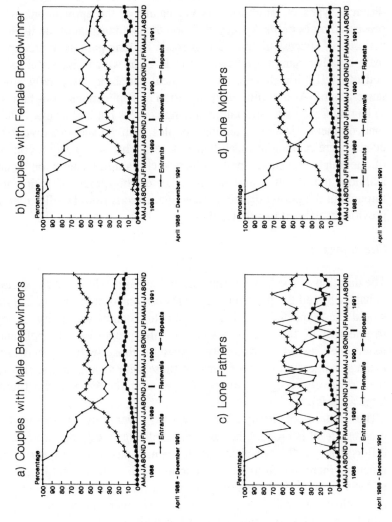

earner. Both these observations point to the possibility of greater instability in the employment experiences of men receiving Family Credit than is the case for women. This may be because gender-linked wage differentials mean that the men who fall within the scope of Family Credit are closer to the precarious periphery of the labour market than is the case for women.

Briefly, to summarise. The differential use made of Family Credit by different types of family affects the nature of the applications which are processed by Benefits Agency staff and the composition of the liveload. The majority of successful applications made by lone parents and couples with male breadwinners are renewals, the level of which had stabilised by the end of 1991 (though with some cyclical variability especially among the latter group). At that time the proportion of applications from families new to Family Credit was still falling among couples but had levelled out among lone mothers. However, among couples with female breadwinners, new claims were running at much higher levels. This was partly a consequence of the relatively short spells which such families spend on benefit. In addition, the absolute and relative size of this group of recipients grew throughout the period driven by new applications from families that had not previously claimed Family Credit.

Size of award

The duration of spells on Family Credit increases with the size of the award (Chapter 8) and the pattern of renewals presented in Figure 9.12 is much as would be expected. A high month to month variability is evident, irrespective of the size of award, but the proportion of applicants who renew their award is noticeably greater for those with larger awards. The average ranges from 46 per cent for those with awards in the first quartile (i.e., relatively small awards) to 67 per cent for those in the fourth (i.e., large awards).

The pattern of applications awarded over time is somewhat less predictable. It is broadly the same for applicants receiving large awards but differs for the 25 per cent granted small payments. In the first case, renewals increased from the introduction of the scheme and by the summer of 1989 constituted the majority of successful applications. Thereafter there is no clear discernible trend. Instead, a six monthly cycle is apparent in which a growth in the proportion of renewals is associated with a fall in the proportion of new awards and vice-versa. The origins of this pattern can be traced to a large influx of new claims in late 1988, many coming into the study sample when they successfully applied to renew a claim that had resulted from the automatic conversion of an award for Family Income Supplement. This initial wave was reinforced by a further influx in the early summer of 1989, which was coincident with the major national advertising campaign run between 17 April and 29 June. The subsequent peaks in applications appear to result from renewals associated with this large cohort rather than from fluctuations in the number of applications from families new to Family Credit (Figure 9.13). Indeed, from late 1989 onwards there was a steady, if haphazard fall, in the number of new applications that result in medium sized awards, although the number being awarded large awards was maintained.

An altogether different profile is apparent for families receiving the smallest awards. Rather than a six monthly cycle, a marked annual pattern is evident with the proportion of renewals peaking around year-end and falling relative to both new and repeat awards during the summer months. In the summers of 1990 and 1991 totally new awards exceeded renewals.

This pattern again seems to have its origins in the influx of new claims in late 1988 and, especially, the advertising campaign in the early summer of 1989. A third of the claims awarded in the peak month of June 1989 fell in the quartile of smallest awards (and almost two thirds were smaller than the median award). The renewal rate among this cohort appears to have been lower than among earlier and later cohorts and among those applicants receiving larger initial awards (in the region of 45 per cent rather than 60 per cent or more). As a result there is no sizeable increase in the number of renewals six months after the initial influx.

The increased number of renewals twelve months after the initial surge is not easy to explain. However, it seems possible that the relatively small number of applicants who came into the system as a result of the summer 1989 promotions and renewed their application were more than likely to renew a second time. This, combined with a high rate of first renewals among families applying during the summer of 1990, produces the large rise in the number of renewals during the following winter.

Another unusual feature of the behaviour of recipients receiving small awards is that significant numbers move off benefit only to reapply successfully later. During the early part of 1991, reapplications constituted around a quarter of all awards. The implication is that, while the financial circumstances of applicants receiving small awards may not be as severe as those of other groups, a significant number have resources that fluctuate around Family Credit levels. It is possible that their circumstances are particularly unstable: certainly they include disproportionate numbers of applicants in manual and miscellaneous occupations that might be

225

Figure 9.12
Renewals by size of award

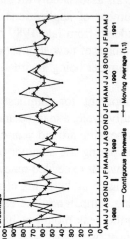

Family Credit Amount: First Quartile

April 1988 – June 1991

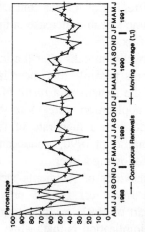

Family Credit Amount: Second Quartile

April 1988 – June 1991

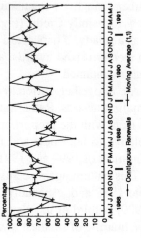

Family Credit Amount: Third Quartile

April 1988 – June 1991

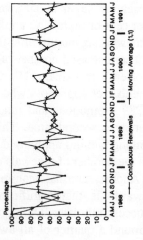

Family Credit Amount: Fourth Quartile

April 1988 – June 1991

Figure 9.13
Type of application by size of award

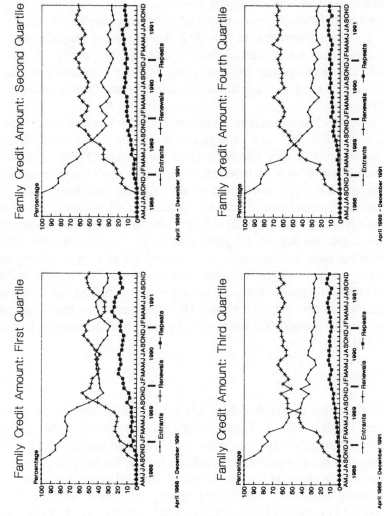

Family Credit Amount: First Quartile

Percentage

AMJJASONDJFMAMJJASONDJFMAMJJASONDJFMAMJJASOND

1988   1989   1990   1991

— Entrants   —†— Renewals   —■— Repeats

April 1988 – December 1991

Family Credit Amount: Second Quartile

Percentage

AMJJASONDJFMAMJJASONDJFMAMJJASONDJFMAMJJASOND

1988   1989   1990   1991

— Entrants   —†— Renewals   —■— Repeats

April 1988 – December 1991

Family Credit Amount: Third Quartile

Percentage

AMJJASONDJFMAMJJASONDJFMAMJJASONDJFMAMJJASOND

1988   1989   1990   1991

— Entrants   —†— Renewals   —■— Repeats

April 1988 – December 1991

Family Credit Amount: Fourth Quartile

Percentage

AMJJASONDJFMAMJJASONDJFMAMJJASONDJFMAMJJASOND

1988   1989   1990   1991

— Entrants   —†— Renewals   —■— Repeats

April 1988 – December 1991

associated with more precarious forms of employment, but also greater numbers of public sector employees where more stability is to be expected. Alternatively, it might simply be that the fluctuations in the resources-to-needs ratio, which they experience in common with other groups, straddle the eligibility threshold for Family Credit. Unfortunately, it is impossible to determine which possibility is more likely since there is no information relating to families' circumstances while not receiving Family Credit.

It is also interesting to note that the pattern of reapplications closely follows that for successful new claims. To the extent, therefore, that advertising campaigns are successful, or other circumstances conspire to produce a surge in applications, ex-claimants are also drawn back into the system.

One conclusion that may be drawn from this analysis, interpreted in the context of findings from Chapter 8, is that there is a steady build up of 'experienced' Family Credit users in the system. Those receiving larger awards tend to stay on benefit for longer consecutive periods, quite rapidly become the major constituent of the caseload and finally, dominate the monthly processing of successful applications. (The Family Credit data-file does not cover unsuccessful claims so that it is not clear whether renewals constitute the bulk of the total workload.) Applicants who receive the smallest awards do not stay in the system for as long as other groups but return to the system in substantial numbers. Finally, the build-up of experienced applicants has coincided with a sustained fall in the absolute number of new entrants: in mid 1989 the number of new applicants was running at about 7,000 per month; by late 1991 the number had fallen to 4,400.

Occupation

It was noted earlier that there has been some change in the occupations from which Family Credit recipients are drawn. The occupational classifications which it is possible to derive from administrative records are generally not comparable with other schemes, but there does seem to have been an increase in the proportion of recipients working in catering and cleaning (industries traditionally relying on female staff), a fall in the number of manual workers (predominantly male) and a fall in the number of public sector workers.

Figure 9.14 presents the composition of applications received between 1988 and 1991 for each of the occupational groups. They are generally rather similar with each showing the now familiar growth in the relative importance of renewals and repeat claims at the expense of new ones. The proportion of applications that are renewals appears to be a little lower for manual workers and those in miscellaneous occupations, compared with other groups, but generally any differences seem to be idiosyncratic. For example, there are pronounced peaks in the proportion of new applications made by public sector employees in August 1990 and September 1991. These coincide with specific advertising campaigns, but are not evident to any marked degree among other groups.

Another idiosyncratic feature, this time relating to successful claims from families working in miscellaneous occupations in the private sector, is the exceptional rise in the proportion of renewals, and a corresponding fall in the number of new claims, during the winter of 1990/91. This reflects on unparalleled increase in the proportion of applications of each monthly cohort that successfully renewed their applications (Figure 9.15).

The differing propensity of the various occupational groups to renew their applications is also shown in Figure 9.15. It can be seen that applicants in catering and cleaning occupations are considerably more likely than other groups to renew their claim and that this, more than anything else, explains the growth in the relative size of this group. Whereas in 1990 an average of 5,300 renewed their claim each month, by 1991 the number had risen to 8,220.

The pattern for public sector employees is rather different. The level of renewals is markedly lower and, additionally, there is a marked fall in the proportion of recipients renewing their applications from August 1991 onwards. This fall is evident among some other occupational groups, including white collar and self-employed workers, but it happens earlier and is much more significant for public sector employees. Thus, whereas 61 per cent of public servants who applied between July and December 1990 went on to renew their claim, this was true of only 40 per cent of those who applied in the first six months of 1991. This resulted in a noticeable fall in the average number of successful renewals received from public sector employees throughout 1991, at the same time as, to take one example, renewals from catering staff increased substantially. Moreover, the fall in the number of renewals from public sector employees was accompanied by a decline in the absolute number of new applicants. From a peak of 2,500 at the end of the transitional phase in June 1989, the number of new applications fell to an average of 1,260 each month in 1990, and to a monthly average of 960 in 1991.

The steady fall in the proportion of Family Credit recipients who are manual workers is largely explained by the disproportionate growth in the

Figure 9.14
Type of application by occupation

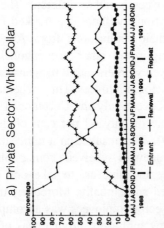

a) Private Sector: White Collar

b) Private Sector: Catering/Cleaning

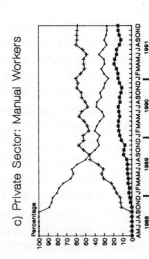

c) Private Sector: Manual Workers

d) Private Sector:Security/Miscellaneous

Figure 9.14 continued

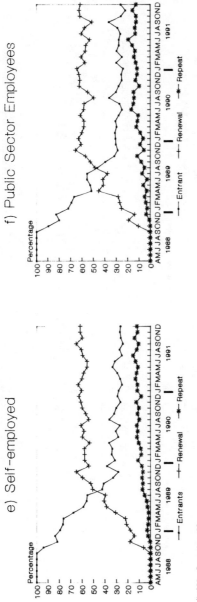

e) Self-employed

f) Public Sector Employees

April 1988 – December 1991

231

Figure 9.15
Renewals by type of occupation

a) Private Sector: White Collar

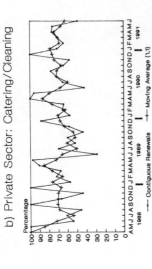

b) Private Sector: Catering/Cleaning

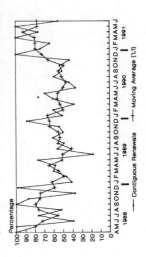

c) Private Sector: Manual Workers

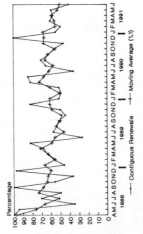

d) Private Sector:Security/Miscellaneous

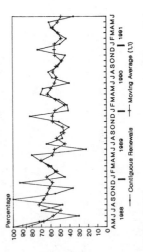

232

Figure 9.15 continued

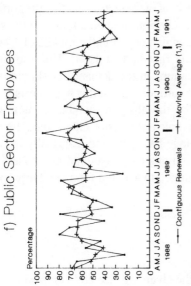

e) Self Employed

April 1988 – June 1991

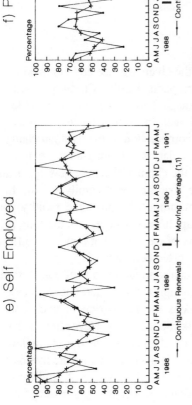

f) Public Sector Employees

April 1988 – June 1991

233

number of successful applications received from other groups. However, after June 1991 a steady fall in the absolute number of applications also occurred. This was the consequence of a reduction in the proportion of families renewing their applications, superimposed on a return to the secular decline in the number of new claims which began in the middle of 1989, but had temporarily been reversed in the first half of 1991. This sequence of events could be explained by fluctuations in the demand for skilled manual labour but it has not proved possible formally to test this hypothesis.

Finally, it is worth mentioning that the absolute number of new claims received each month from the self-employed has not fallen since the end of 1989, and indeed the smoothed average has increased marginally over time. This sets the self-employed apart from other occupational groups and is the principal reason why they have continued to account for a similar proportion of a growing caseload.

Discussion

This Chapter has begun to explore the changing size and composition of the Family Credit liveload. In some respects Family Credit is not the ideal benefit to study in this way. Because Family Credit is payable for six months, largely irrespective of changes in circumstances, a great deal of inertia is built into the system. The composition of the liveload changes only slowly in response to the accumulation of long-term recipients and variations in the mismatch between the characteristics of new applicants and those leaving the system. Despite the fact that Family Credit functions primarily as a means of short-term support to meet the rapidly changing needs of successive generations of applicants (Chapter 8), the long period of benefit entitlement creates a stability of caseload that may well differentiate Family Credit from all other means-tested benefits.

This stability is unlikely to be instantly apparent to staff administering the scheme. The number of successful applications that are processed each month varies markedly. So, too, does the proportion of each cohort that successfully reapplies for benefit six months later. Nevertheless, the month to month variation in the number of claims, and in the characteristics of applicants, has only a small and much delayed impact on the liveload.

But significant changes there have been. The number of families receiving large awards has increased substantially, principally as a result of the longer periods that such families spend on benefit rather than an increase in the number of large awards made to new applicants that might be anticipated as a result of the recession. As a consequence, the average size of awards payable to the current caseload will have moved ahead of the level of uprating. On the other hand, there has been little change in the number of small awards in payment. Families receiving small sums in Family Credit are less likely than other groups to renew their claims and tend not to accumulate in the system. But significant numbers return to the system - in some months a quarter of applicants receiving small awards have applied before - and this has prevented a decline in the relative importance of small awards.

One group which has declined, in both absolute and relative terms, is applicants who receive below average awards in the range £15-£30 (second quartile). It is noteworthy that families headed by a male are disproportionately represented among applicants receiving small awards and, moreover, that significant numbers make repeat claims. It is perhaps unlikely that the domestic circumstances of male-headed families are more unstable than those headed by women. This suggests greater instability in the workplace - which may be real, in the sense that men with earnings around Family Credit levels occupy precarious positions close to the bottom of the male earnings distribution - or simply a consequence of normal variations in income straddling the benefit threshold.

Another change in the composition of the caseload has been the steady rise in the number of two parent families where the wife is the principal breadwinner. The unusual behaviour of this group, which typically receives rather large awards for short periods, has been highlighted by other research (Marsh and McKay, 1992; see also Chapter 8) where there has been some speculation as to the reason for the emergence of this group of applicants. One possibility is that it is the result of permanent shifts in the pattern of family organisation. Alternatively it could be a response to particular economic circumstances; for example, the impact of male unemployment which turns two-earner into one-earner households. What this analysis has shown is that the growth has been driven primarily by applications from families who have never before been in receipt of Family Credit. Repeat claims are less frequent than for families with a male breadwinner and renewals are comparatively rare (although they were increasing until the end of 1990). This evidence, the rapidity of the increase, and especially the shortness of the awards, points to an economic rather than a sociodemographic basis for the growth in the number of 'reverse-role' couples receiving Family Credit. Work that is underway which links Family Credit records with other benefits may throw further light on this phenomenon.

Other notable changes in the composition of the caseload include the fall in public sector and manual employees - reflecting a reduction in the time spent on benefit and a decline in the absolute number of new applications - and the sustained growth in applicants working in catering and cleaning occupations.

The latter trend is perhaps exaggerated by the data available which shows the proportion of Family Credit recipients employed in catering and cleaning increasing fivefold, to about 30 per cent of the caseload. Perhaps half of this growth is attributable to long-term Family Income Supplement recipients being transferred directly onto Family Credit. Certainly much of the subsequent growth - itself far from inconsequential - is due to the accumulation of long-term recipients rather than to new applications (which fell) or repeat ones (which, nevertheless, did increase). The prevalence of women employed in catering and cleaning is clearly an important factor in the growth of this group. Most of the applicants employed in the sector are lone mothers who typically spend long spells on Family Credit. Wages are lower than any of the other industrial sectors used in the research and the level of awards is correspondingly higher. Large awards are associated with long spells on benefit which leads to an accumulation within the caseload. However, this is not the total story. For example, while lone mothers and couples headed by a woman are equally likely to work in catering or cleaning, the former group has grown as a proportion of the total caseload while the latter has not. Likewise, 55 per cent of applicants employed in catering and cleaning are male, and over 75 per cent of female applicants work in other industries.

The analysis has also considered the impact of advertising campaigns and revealed that certain campaigns were apparently more effective than others and that, in some cases, the effect was sustained over longer periods of time. The research team is not privy to the precise details and strategies of the various campaigns and no attempt has been made to explain the differences. However, it would appear that, with the exception of the advertising between April and June 1989, the campaigns have - in terms of numbers of applications - served mainly to encourage current applicants to renew their awards rather than to stimulate eligible non-claimants.

This interpretation requires qualification since effectiveness needs to be judged in relation to the size of the target group. As the take-up rate rises, an increasing proportion of the population with potential entitlement in a given period are already in the system. If the recent high estimates of take-up are correct (Marsh and McKay, 1992; Fry and Stark, 1992) one would expect to draw the bulk of future applicants from the existing caseload which appears to be happening with Family Credit irrespective of whether an advertising campaign is underway. However, advertising does seem to increase the proportion of recipients that renew their claims which suggests that, at other times, families with entitlement to Family Credit are failing to do so with adverse effects on the overall level of take-up[3]. It is also worth noting that there is no evidence that advertising simply makes potential applicants apply earlier than they otherwise would. If this were the case one would expect to find applications in the months following a campaign to be below the trend line, and this does not appear to happen.

[3] No information is available on the extent to which advertising stimulates unsuccessful attempts to renew Family Credit awards.

10 Time past and future

To answer the simple question 'how long do spells of poverty last?' requires a fundamental reappraisal of the nature, causes and consequences of poverty. Poverty can no longer be conceptualised as a static state with an immutable distinction between the 'poor' and the 'non-poor'. Rather it has to be seen as a dynamic process in which spells of poverty have definable beginnings and ends. This opens the way to thinking about the specific causes of poverty and creates a new research agenda concerned with the factors or triggers associated with the beginning of spells.

This dynamic view of poverty also points to the possibility of creating a united theoretical framework that links micro and macro analyses and reconciles structural and personal models of causation (Chapter 3). The factual basis to inform this framework requires identification of the different kinds of events that trigger spells of poverty; specification of the distribution of these events within the population as a whole; and measurement of the differing risk that the events will result in poverty. Poverty is understood not simply as a shortfall in resources, or even in terms of the occurrence of events that produce shortfalls in resources, but more in relation to the circumstances that mean that the occurrence of a particular sequence of events results in poverty.

Recognising the dynamic nature of poverty, with relatively large numbers of families and individuals making transitions in and out of poverty, may also predicate a new policy agenda; one that is proactive rather than reactive, stresses prevention rather than alleviation, and aims explicitly to bring spells of poverty to an early end.

In the opening chapter we stressed that we would only begin to sketch out these new agendas, that we would pose questions rather than provide answers and that, for the most part, we would be presenting aspirations rather, than achievements. We acknowledged, too, that taking a small step forward rather than leaping a yard, was a consequence of our own inadequacies, faced with the multifarious implications that attach to a process view of poverty. This book is an invitation to others to help define and prioritise the issues that follow from a new way of thinking.

Moreover, this endeavour will be assisted by an increased flow of suitable data. Last year, 1993, the first wave of the British Household Panel Study became available providing monthly information on income, benefit receipt and employment status. This year the second annual wave has been released and the best British panel has begun in earnest. Studies are underway to examine the feasibility of conducting a Europe-wide panel that would facilitate cross-national comparisons of social dynamics. The computerisation of administrative records is advancing rapidly in many policy areas which should encourage more sophisticated analyses than those presented in Chapters 8 and 9. Finally, and perhaps most importantly, policy makers and academics are beginning to ask questions that can only be satisfactorily answered by reference to time sensitive data.

In this last chapter we briefly rehearse a few of our earlier conclusions and draw attention to some of the many questions that still require answers. We turn, first, to the conceptualisation and measurement of poverty before considering the causes of poverty and the consequences of poverty dynamics for policy development.

Defining and measuring poverty

Time cannot be ignored even in cross-sectional studies of poverty. The choice of accounting period over which resources and needs are measured and compared will partly determine the level of poverty found in a population and the apparent characteristics of the families that are poor. The longer the accounting period, the lower the incidence of poverty because all but the long-term poor are excluded.

There is no correct answer to the choice of accounting period. A persuasive case can be made for basing the selection on the needs of each particular study but it is then important to take care when comparing results derived from different studies that use different measures. Moreover, the problem does not go away when panel data is used. Chapter 2 demonstrated that the annual accounting period used in the pioneering US Panel Study of Income Dynamics meant that it understated the number of ever-poor families because most spells of poverty last for less than twelve months. The most obvious strategy is to use the shortest possible accounting period and then to present estimates of the extent of poverty based on different duration thresholds. Unfortunately the implications for data handling, not to mention the tolerance of respondents, severely constrain what can be achieved in practice.

But the main reason for taking explicit account of time has less to do with the bias or uncertainty attaching to cross-sectional estimates of poverty than with the realisation that time is inherent in the poverty experience. Not only does the poor population change as spells of poverty begin and end, but the fear of falling into poverty, and the hope that poverty will one day end - a hope which may sustain poor people but fade over time - are among the ingredients that make poverty the potent social force it is. Moreover, most people would probably agree that a long period of poverty is inherently worse than a short transient spell and perhaps, also, that the experience of repeated spells of poverty differs from permanent poverty or from a one-off spell.

In Chapter 2 we experimented with various measures that sought to take account of both the severity and duration of poverty. These revealed that childhood poverty, in the USA at least, is very inequitably distributed even among those children who are ever poor. Moreover, severity is positively correlated with duration. Those who are poor for the longest periods have fewer resources when they are poor and less time to make up for the shortfall when they are not so.

However, the measures used were far from perfect. None took account of the sequencing of periods of poverty and relative prosperity except in so far as a family's money income reflected the effects of past savings. In reality, families are probably most likely to be able to cope with poverty after a long period of affluence because of the consumer assets and durables that they would have accumulated, although such families might find the transition to a frugal existence more difficult to manage than families who had made the adjustment on previous occasions.

The measures also implicitly assumed that a given shortfall in income was equivalent regardless of the period over which it occurred. This is again at odds with common sense. An income deficit that is highly concentrated, meaning for example that a family has to go without any income at all for three months, is likely to have very different repercussions from the situation were the same deficit is spread over a year and the family has a weekly income 25 per cent below their needs threshold.

This failure of measures that combine severity and duration to take account of the sequencing of spells of poverty and relative affluence is of more than passing importance. Throughout this volume it has been argued that the nature of poverty changes according to the way in which spells of poverty are distributed over time. In Chapter 6, six different patterns of poverty spells were identified among children in the USA and shown to be associated with a different level of economic welfare, when measured over all of childhood, and with a unique pattern of socio-economic characteristics. Again, in Chapter 7, different sequences of visits to a hostel are interpreted as evidence of the various functions performed by hostels and may even be indicative of different life-styles among hostel users.

In both the above examples the temporal patterns were derived by a combination of inspection and low level theory but this is not satisfactory as a long term procedure. However, as was noted in Chapter 2, there is as yet no clear guidance as how best objectively to classify temporal patterns. Traditional methods for analysing time series data, such as harmonic and spectral analysis, are not well suited to the analysis of the comparatively short runs of data associated with panel surveys. The standard classification techniques are also unsatisfactory because of their rigid treatment of time. It may be that various forms of factor analysis could provide a route forward, either by factoring a matrix comprising descriptive indicators of the poverty profile of each individual, as proposed by Ray (1992), or by treating the waves of a panel study as cases or variables in the matrix to be factored (S and T-mode analysis) as suggested by Ashworth and Walker (1992).

It is also important further to investigate the sensitivity of temporal patterns to the level at which the poverty line is drawn. Raising or lowering the poverty line in cross-sectional studies increases or reduces the recorded incidence of poverty. In longitudinal studies it is likely to result in longer or shorter average durations and may change the relative importance of various types of poverty. Sensitivity analyses conducted on the typology presented in Chapter 6 showed some sensitivity but much robustness: while the most severe forms of poverty became less prevalent as the threshold was lowered, the rank order was retained; children who moved categories tended to appear in an adjacent one; and the pattern of socio-demographic characteristics associated with each category was retained (Hill, Walker and Ashworth, 1993).

Despite limitations in the explicitly temporal measures of poverty, the analysis in Chapter 2 is important in drawing attention to the distribution of poverty not only within the population at large, but also among poor people themselves. It emphasised that poverty is very unequally distributed with certain people experiencing far more severe poverty than others. It is evident, too, that, in the USA at least, some families are still living at levels close to subsistence. But, again, there is scope for improving the measures and concepts used, and a need to integrate dynamic and static conceptions of poverty.

The analysis used techniques more often employed in the study of income distributions. In this case, shortfall in income, rather than income itself, was arrayed as a Lorenz curve and the Gini coefficient used as the measure of equality. The Lorenz curve provides a measure of shortfall in income suffered by individual poor families relative to the average shortfall in income experienced by poor families as a group and, thus, inequality measures derived from it take no account of the total volume of poverty. Given that policy is likely to be concerned to reduce the total level of poverty, and perhaps to lessen absolute differences in the living standards suffered by poor families, there is a strong case for moving to measures based on generalized Lorenz curves that do take account of the total size of the problem (Jenkins, 1991).

Another possibility is explicitly to build time into Sen's (1982) ordinal measure of poverty which links the measurement of poverty and income inequality. Sen's measure comprises the head-count ratio, H, multiplied by the income gap ratio, I, augmented by the Gini coefficient, G, of the distribution of income among the poor weighted by the ratio of the mean income among the poor to the poverty line income level (1-I):

$$P = H\,[I + (1 - I)\,G]$$

Under this formulation I represents poverty as measured by the proportionate gap between the mean income of the poor and the poverty threshold. However, I ignores distribution of income among the poor which is supplied by G. But, besides the poverty gap of the mean income of the poor reflected in I, there is also the 'gap' arising from the unequal distribution of mean income which is reflected by Gini coefficient G of that distribution multiplied by the mean income ratio (1-I).

The income-gap measure, augmented to reflect the inequality among the poor, is normalised per poor person and so does not take account of the number of people who are poor. To achieve this I+(1-I)G is multiplied by the head-count ratio H to yield Sen's composition measure. Setting the accounting period equal to a life stage or, by using simulation techniques, to a life time would represent a considerable advance over the measures experimented with in Chapter 2.

Perhaps the most important realisation to stem from an explicit focus on time is that the distribution of poverty over time helps determine the distribution of poverty within a population and vice versa. If it is assumed that a particular population is afflicted by a given sum of poverty, measured in days, weeks or years, the occurrence of permanent or repeated periods of poverty would mean that poverty affected fewer people than if spells were predominantly short and one off.

Moreover, the nature of poverty is a function of its joint distribution across the population and over time. To return to the population afflicted by a given sum of poverty. If the poverty is largely permanent, and therefore suffered by a small proportion of the population, it is likely to be a very isolating experience. The poor will be experientially distanced from the wider society which they have little chance of ever joining and which, in turn, will have scarcely any appreciation of what it means to be poor.

If poverty is a repeated experience, larger numbers will be affected. However, the people experiencing poverty will have to confront the apparent futility of their efforts ever to break completely free of the curse of insufficient income. Occasionally experiencing relative prosperity may add to the frustration of being poor and conceivably provide a stimulus for political action. Where poverty is exclusively short-term it may present little problem even to those who are poor. Since the risk of poverty will not vary much from one person to the next, and relatively large numbers of people will have experienced poverty at one time or another, there is likely be wide support for collective policies designed financially to support people at times of need.

It may be appropriate, therefore, to think it terms of not one kind of poverty but many that in reality coexist and, perhaps, differ in their relative importance as societies respond to economic and social change. With poverty differentiated in this fashion it becomes appropriate to look for different models of causation and to move away from generic anti-poverty policies to ones that are tailored to specific kinds of poverty.

The causes of poverty

The major contribution to be made by longitudinal studies of poverty will undoubtedly be in the area of causal theory. This is because panel data make it is possible directly to observe cause and effect. At the moment, however, we are still in the ground clearing phase. Simple ideas have been shown to be lacking and the world far more complex than was once believed. Coherent theoretical structures that take full account of studies of poverty dynamics have yet to emerge and, of course, empirical evidence for Britain is still largely lacking.

American studies, reported in Chapters 3 and 4, have found unsuspected volatility in the financial and other circumstances of families in all sections of society. Substantial variations in income-to-needs ratios from one year to the next are almost commonplace. Moreover falls of 50 per cent or more do not always precipitate a spell of poverty. Research has focused on the events that trigger periods of poverty and again the picture is one of enormous diversity. Not surprisingly a fall in the income of the family head is typically the most important factor but the prevalence of other causes, notably ones connected with changes in household composition, is striking.

One important limitation of this work has been the difficulty of establishing precisely when a spell of poverty started and the nature of the lag between the occurrence of a trigger and its financial impact. This reflects the long accounting periods associated with the early panel studies and the need to control for the high risk of error associated with attempts to measure change in a number of variables (Chapter 2).

Other research, reviewed in Chapter 3 and supplemented by new analyses presented in Chapter 6, has examined the characteristics of people who are most likely to suffer the longest spells of poverty. For the most part the factors associated with an enhanced risk of ever experiencing poverty: poor education, limited work experience, marital status, family size, race and residence in rural areas are also implicated in the incidence of poverty in its most severe and long-lasting forms. There is evidence, too, that people who have suffered a spell of poverty, or have ever claimed welfare benefits, are more likely than others to experience additional spells. Whether this is because they are inherently more prone to poverty, or whether the experience of poverty itself makes people more vulnerable, remains a moot point. Likewise, it has been found that the offspring of poor families are themselves more likely than other children to experience poverty in adulthood but no precise pattern of causal links has yet been established.

In fact detailed causal analysis has yet to begin in earnest. This is partly a chicken and egg problem. Existing theory tends to be expressed in rather general terms that does not readily lend itself to empirical testing. It is also often inherently static in form as noted in Chapter 3. On the other hand, because of their expense, panel studies have tended to be multi-purpose in design and to collect insufficient information for the rigorous testing of theory. One deficiency, which the British Household Panel Study is beginning to rectify, is the limited amount of attitudinal information which is available on a longitudinal basis. With the new panel it will be possible, for example, to examine whether respondents who become and remain unemployed have different attitudes to work than people who do not, whether their attitudes change during spells of unemployment and whether their attitudes are consistent with experiencing a greater risk of unemployment.

However, the most important area for theoretical development lies in the scope for contextualising the impact of trigger events. To date few studies have explored why particular events trigger poverty in certain cases but not in others. The answers are likely to lie in the personal capacities of individuals and in the structural circumstances in which they find themselves. Knowing the histories of the individuals, the sequence of events that have impacted on their lives and the changes that have affected others in the population should make it possible to disentangle the effects of personal and structural factors, and to construct theoretical structures that span micro and macro explanations.

These explanations may need to take account of the different patterns or types of poverty experienced by families and individuals and also of their effects. However, before this is possible we have to learn more about the differentiation of poverty. It is important to establish whether similar kinds of poverty are experienced throughout the life-course, and whether the types of poverty are as discrete as they might appear or whether one form is usually a precursor to another. We need to determine whether the sequencing of spells of poverty is important, if the severity and length of spells are dependent on the characteristics of earlier ones and if the severity of poverty varies systematically within spells.

One might then move on first, to consider the nature of the antecedents to spells of poverty both within and across poverty types; secondly, to take poverty types, rather than spells, as the unit of analysis and to examine whether individuals are more prone to experience certain kinds of poverty on account of their prior status; and finally, to focus on the events that precipitate spells of poverty in order to test which characteristics of individuals and their environment make them prone to suffer various forms of poverty as a consequence of experiencing particular events.

Policy development

Accepting the imperative to act against poverty in all its forms, a large part of the book has been devoted to considering the implications for policy of taking an explicitly temporal perspective on poverty. They are substantial and include straightforward warnings of the dangers inherent in relying on cross-sectional data, reassurance that existing systems of social insurance are well adapted to the risks of personal financial hardship faced by individuals, and the creation of a new agenda of proactive policies designed both to prevent poverty and to bring spells of poverty rapidly to an end.

Rather than attempt to paraphrase much that has been said already or prematurely to try and spell out a new policy agenda, we return to the case study mode adopted in the second part of the book and explore, by way of illustration, some of the policy implications of the analysis of poverty types presented in Chapter 6.

It will be recalled that six patterns of poverty were identified among US children defined in terms of the number, duration and spacing of spells:

.	transient	- single one year spells of poverty;
.	occasional	- repeated one year spells;
.	recurrent	- repeated spells, some longer than a year with at least one period of relative prosperity of more than a year;
.	persistent	- a single long spell;
.	chronic	- one year's remission from poverty;
.	permanent	- continuous poverty throughout childhood.

The evidence indicates that for many of the short term poor, resources exceed needs during childhood. This was the case for all the transient poor. In Britain there is increasing interest in the potential value of private unemployment insurance and this might be an appropriate response to those cases of transient poverty - in the US not necessarily the majority - which result from job loss (but see below). In the US context, where only categorical assistance schemes exist, Government loans have been suggested to tide families over short spells and be repaid during times of relative plenty. The Government would be filling the gap in financial markets by allowing temporarily poor people to borrow on their future, thus evening out their consumption over time and eliminating critical shortfalls in meeting basic needs.

The findings also indicate the limitations to a loans strategy. The break-even point between resources and needs during childhood occurs at poverty durations of about eight years. However, the family incomes of many children experiencing shorter durations of poverty, especially when the spells are recurrent, are low even during periods of relative prosperity. Nevertheless, limiting this strategy to transient and occasional poverty could still reduce the annual US poverty rate by about nine per cent and rescue 35 per cent of the children who are now condemned to experience some poverty during childhood. The cost of such a programme would depend on the Government's ability accurately to target loans on the short-term poor.

Persistent poverty apparently strikes more or less indiscriminately. For this reason, and because persistent poverty often constitutes a major departure from accustomed living standards, broadening the scope and coverage of insurance provides an appropriate preventive strategy. However, the long duration of persistent poverty, and therefore the large sums necessary to make up the deficiency in income, may require prohibitive private insurance premiums even allowing for the relatively small numbers of families that would need to claim. Indeed, the contribution to be made by private insurance to eradicating childhood poverty seems quite limited. Although 41 per cent of ever-poor children experienced either transient or persistent poverty, where private insurance could be expected to play a role, taken together they account for rather less than 14 per cent of the total poverty gap, the expenditure required to eradicate poverty by transfers alone.

As noted in Chapter 5 policy makers in the USA are increasingly trying to develop proactive policies that bring spells to an early end. Because these are often expensive, involving remedial education, counselling and support services, it is important to be able to target interventions on those people who would not easily have escaped poverty on their own. This entails developing methods of predicting the likely length of spells from information concerning the aptitudes and circumstances of people that is available when they first become poor. Britain may be moving tentatively in the same direction as the USA for the Department of Social Security has recently commissioned research to investigate the factors that facilitate families moving off Income Support (CRSP, 1993). It is important, however, that proactive policies also help ex-claimants to remain off benefit in the longer term for otherwise the policies will only succeed in replacing persistent poverty with recurrent spells.

Recurrent poverty, the most prevalent, affecting 8.4 million American children at any time, poses tough choices for policy. Since only a third of the children affected live in families with long-term resources significantly exceeding basic needs, a strategy based on recoverable loans would cause living standards to fall close to poverty levels even in relatively good years. While incomplete families are not uncommon among this group, half of the children always lived with two parents. The common factors are unemployment and low wages. In two thirds of families studied in Chapter 6 the head had spent two years or more unemployed or out of the labour market. Less than a fifth of family heads had made twelfth grade while the majority earn less than $12 per hour [1987 prices].

Therefore, policies to address recurrent poverty in the USA would need to tackle low pay and employment prospects by stimulating labour demand and enhancing supply. Measures suggested to increase in-work incomes include raising the minimum wage, refundable tax credits (Ellwood, 1988), and earnings based income supplements akin to Family Credit (Lerman, 1988; Haveman, 1988). Proposals for stimulating demand range from employment linked tax subsidies to employers (Haveman, 1988) to job guarantees (Garfinkel and McLanahan, 1986), while supply side measures under consideration or testing include remedial education and training, transitional childcare provisions and health insurance for welfare recipients (Wiseman, 1993; Corbett, 1993).

The situation for the chronically and permanently poor is more disturbing. Rather than finding that families' resources are persistently just short of the poverty line - a situation that might be resolved by permanent but modest government subsidies either in the form of cash or in kind - the picture emerges of many families being unable to cover even half their needs as a result of long spells outside the labour market. This is indicative of basic structural flaws in the social or economic infrastructure requiring much more radical forms of intervention. Further investigative work is required to determine the factors that exclude such families from the labour market. What cannot be ignored is the fact that four out of five of the children affected are African-American and that the risk of chronic or permanent poverty is 26 times greater among African-American children than among Caucasians.

Whether these kinds of poverty exist at all in Britain is perhaps debatable given the more comprehensive safety net provided by Income Support. The cultural history of racism is, of course, also very different in the two countries although there is growing evidence of extreme economic disadvantage among ethnic minorities in Britain (Amin, 1992). However, the fact that we do not know whether there are families in Britain living in permanent poverty is not a cause for complacency but a constraint on policy development that needs to be rectified. By publishing a book that draws attention to the importance of understanding poverty dynamics, we hope to have made a small contribution to removing this constraint.

ANNEX A

Simulating spell lengths
(see Chapter 2)

Spell durations

The method used by Ruggles and Williams (1988, pp.5-6) for deriving spell durations is as follows: spells are observed from their beginning until they either end or the observation is right-censored. For each month t, the conditional probability of leaving poverty that month given that the case has remained in poverty up to month t is calculated. This probability is equal to

$$h(t,X) = \frac{f(t,X)}{(1 - F(t,X))}$$

where $f(t,X)$ is the probability density function for spell exits at t months for an individual with characteristics X, and $F(t,X)$ is the cumulative probability function for exits to time t for such an individual. The survival function, which is essentially the probability that an individual will still be in poverty at time t, is simply the denominator of the expression above:

$$s(t,X) = (1 - F(t,X))$$

Spell distributions

Bane and Ellwood (1986, p.10-11) explain three distributions that can be derived from exit probabilities as follows: if the probability that a person who has been poor for t years will not be poor in the next year is given by the exit probability $p(t)$, then three important distributions are easily derived.

Let $D(t)$ describe the fraction of the number of people who have spells which last exactly t years. Then

$$D(1) = p(1)$$

$$(1) \quad D(t) = p(t)[1 - \sum_{j=1}^{t-1} D(j)], \text{ for } T>t>1$$

$$D(T) = 1 - \sum_{j=1}^{T-1} D(j), D(T) \text{ where T is maximum length of spells}$$

The first term in equation (1) is simply the exit probability, the second is the fraction surviving to year t - 1.

251

The distribution of completed spells at a point in time can be derived provided one assumes a no-growth steady state. If F(t) gives the fraction of the number of all persons on the program at a given time who will be poor for exactly t years, then

$$(2) \quad F(t) = tD(t)/ \sum_{j=1}^{T} jD(j)$$

Finally the distribution of uncompleted spells for persons poor at a given time, G(t), is derived by calculating the fraction of the number of persons who began spells t years earlier who would still be on the program (and renormalizing) assuming a steady state.

$$(3) \quad G(t) = [1 - \sum_{j=1}^{t-1} D(j)]/ \sum_{s=1}^{T} [1 - \sum_{k=1}^{s-1} D(k)]$$

ANNEX B

Modelling correlates with poverty type
(see Chapter 6)

A forward selection strategy was used in the log linear modelling, building up the model at each stage with the set of higher order interactions until a saturated model was achieved. Attempts to enhance parsimony by removing selected effects proved to be unsuccessful since each interaction term proved significant (see Table B1).

Working with saturated models - which merely serve to replicate all the complexity of reality - poses problems for interpretation and presentation since the conclusion is that all the component interactions are important. The associations reported in Chapter 6 are those which appear most germane in the context of current policy interest.

Table B1
Likelihood ratio tests of loglinear models

	Model	L^2	d.f	L^2(diff.)	d.f(diff.)	P
1.1)	1	3885	55			
1.2)	P,Ra,Re,C	12079	46			
1.3)	P.Ra,P.Re,P.C, Ra.Re	2025.8	25			
1.4)	P.Ra.Re,P.Ra.C, P.Re.C,Ra.Re.C	293.5	6			
1.5)	P.Ra.Re.C.	0	0			
	(1.1) - (1.2)			26776	9	P<.01
	(1.2) - (1.3)			10054	21	P<.01
	(1.3) - (1.4)			1732	19	P<.01
	(1.4) - (1.5)			293.5	6	P<.01

Key: P   =   Poverty type
     Ra   =   Race of head
     Re   =   Region of birth
     C   =   Urbanicity

	Model	L^2	d.f	L^2(diff.)	d.f(diff.)	P
2.1)	1	59488	5			
2.2)	P,L,E,Re	16436	46			
2.3)	P.L,P.E,P.Re, L.E,L.Re,E.Re	1144	25			
2.4)	P.L.E,P.L.Re,C, P.Re.C,Ra.Re.C	298.4	7			
2.5)	P.L.E.Re	0	0			
	(2.1) - (2.2)			43050	9	<.01
	(2.2) - (2.3)			15293	21	<.01
	(2.3) - (2.4)			845.3	19	<.01
	(2.4) - (2.5)			298.4	6	<.01

Key: P   =   Poverty type
     L   =   Labour market
     E   =   Earnings
     Re   =   Region of birth

	Model	L^2	d.f	L^2(diff.)	d.f(diff.)	P
3.1)	1	54556	55			
3.2)	P,Re,F,Ra	9718	46			
3.3)	P.Re,P.F,P.Ra, Re.F,Re.Ra,F.Ra	1144.6	25			
3.4)	P.Re.F,P.Re.Ra, P.F.Ra,Re.F.Ra	195.1	6			
3.5)	P.Re.F.Ra	0	0			
	(3.1) - (3.2)			44838	9	P<.01
	(3.2) - (3.3)			85733	21	P<.01
	(3.3) - (3.4)			949.5	19	P<.01
	(3.4) - (3.5)			195.1	6	P<.01

Key:
P = Poverty type
Re = Region of birth
F = Family stability
Ra = Race of head

	Model	L^2	d.f	L^2(diff.)	d.f(diff.)	P
4.1)	1	55789	83			
4.2)	P,F,Ra,Ea	1234646	73			
4.3)	P.F,P.Ra,P.E,, F.Ra,F.E,Ra.E	1131.4	44			
4.4)	P.F.Ra,P.F.E, P.Ra.E,F.Ra.E	117.37	12			
4.5)	P.F.Ra.E	0	0			
	(4.1) - (4.2)			43444	10	P<.01
	(4.2) - (4.3)			11214	29	P<.01
	(4.3) - (4.4)			1014	32	P<.01
	(4.4) - (4.5)			117.4	12	<.01

Key: P = Poverty type
F = Family stability
Ra = Race of heady
E = Education of head

256

ANNEX C

Modelling durations on Family Credit
(see Chapter 8)

The modelling strategy

The duration of Family Credit receipt was analysed by regressing the log-odds of those exiting at each time point to those eligible to leave on the predictor variables listed above. This analysis ignores calendar time and uses the first claim period as the starting point. The first two spells were analysed separately, and the model derived from analysis of the first spell was used on the second spell. Further spells were ignored because numbers were considered too small to give reliable estimates.

The coefficients derived from the logistic models are in themselves difficult to interpret thus they have been relegated to this Annex. In order to facilitate an understanding of the model the average length of time spent in receipt of Family Credit was calculated for the distributions of those starting a spell of Family Credit, and for those on Family Credit at any point in time. This was done by taking the exit probabilities from the logistic model according to the particular combination of characteristics for each individual and using these exit probabilities to calculate the proportion of those exiting at each time point over a six year period. It was assumed that the last observed exit probability was constant over later time periods, and that a steady state, no growth system was operative.

A risk set of unity was assigned to each member of the sample and this was used in conjunction with an individuals exit probability to estimate the proportion exiting at each time point. Therefore, the average proportion over the sample at any given time point provides an estimate of the population proportion exiting at that time point. However, this is not constant across individuals in the data set, because of their varying combinations of characteristics, and by breaking down the averages by group membership, differences in the time spent in receipt of Family Credit can be examined. This formulation has the advantage that estimates are not restricted to the assumption that all else is held constant. Thus variables which tend to co-occur, and are related to the duration of Family Credit receipt, can be identified. Ceteris-paribus estimates can be derived from the coefficients given below. However, this is not recommended because of the interdependencies between the predictor variables.

One caveat is that in estimating the risk of duration for individuals information about their first time point was used to initialise each persons risk set. Individuals' circumstances may change over time and whilst this is taken into account in the logistic model it is not for the calculation of the distributions.

Coefficients for the models discussed in the text[a]

Variable	Spell 1	Spell 2	Unconditional Return	Conditional Return
Constant	3.553*	3.771*	-1.595*	9.529*
Couple:				
female main earner	1.017*	2.245*	0.437	0.847
Lone father	0.541	0.190	0.275	0.056
Lone mother	-0.035	0.420	0.155	0.454
Public sector	0.063	0.292*	-0.035	0.198*
Private sector:				
Professional	0.047	0.163*	-0.002	0.180*
Catering	0.031	0.158	-0.013	0.011
Manual	0.107*	0.285*	-0.157*	0.007
Miscellaneous	-0.005	0.193	-0.118	-0.030
One move	-0.604*	-0.041	-1.493*	-1.979*
Two+ moves	-0.912*	-0.324*	-1.915*	-2.861*
Time 2	-0.419*	-0.506*		
Time 3	-0.502*	-0.672*		
Time 4	-0.716*	-1.198*		
Time 5	-0.592*	-1.518*		
Time 6	-1.015*	-2.729*		
Time 7	-1.733*			

Average hourly earnings	-0.140*	0.039	0.275*	0.062
Weekly hours worked	-0.001	-0.008	-0.006*	-0.000
Weekly earnings	0.005*	0.005*	-0.009*	0.002
Pre-FC family income	-0.020*	-0.028*	0.032*	-0.008*
Child benefit	0.008*	0.004	-0.025*	0.012*
Weekly amount FC	-0.065*	-0.079*	0.075*	-0.018*
Age of youngest child	-0.007	-0.048	0.053*	0.011
Number of children	0.453*	0.635*	-0.531*	-0.114
Age of claimant	0.031*	-0.012	0.018	0.002
Female couple x FC	-0.001	0.004	0.003	0.005
Lone father x FC	-0.001	0.025	0.010	0.005
Lone mother x FC	0.013*	0.008*	0.004	0.006
Female couple x Pre-FC income	-0.006*	-0.004	0.005	0.002
Lone father x Pre-FC income	0.003	-0.033	-0.016	-0.002
Lone mother x Pre-FC income	0.001	-0.002	-0.001	-0.002
Female couple x weekly earns	0.001	0.000	-0.002	-0.002
Lone father x weekly earns	-0.001	0.051	0.019	0.025

Lone mother x weekly earns	0.003*	0.005	0.001	0.003
Female couple x age youngest	-0.010	-0.126	-0.136*	-0.189*
Lone father x age youngest	0.087	-0.318	-0.169	-0.110
Lone mother x age youngest	-0.018*	-0.073	-0.053	-0.106*
Female couple x age claimant	0.006	-0.049	-0.024	-0.023
Lone father x age claimant	-0.027	-0.040	-0.017	-0.015
Lone mother x age claimant	-0.029*	-0.032*	-0.008	-0.031*
Age youngest x FC	0.001*	0.001	-0.001*	-0.000
Number of children x FC	0.004*	0.004*	-0.002*	0.002*
Hourly earns x FC	-0.003	-0.003*	-0.003*	-0.001
Age claimant x age youngest child	0.001*	0.002*	-0.000	0.002*
Hourly earns x number of children	0.002	0.005	0.007	0.030*
Hourly earns x age claimant	0.004*	-0.002	-0.006*	-0.004
Number children x age of youngest child	-0.002	0.017	-0.022*	-0.010*
Female couple x age claimant x age youngest	-0.000	0.004	0.003	0.004*
Lone father x age claimant x age youngest	0.003	0.006	0.004	0.003

Lone mother x age claimant x age youngest	0.003*	0.002	0.001	0.003*
Scale				1.373
Likelihood ratio-null	107593	17580	41137	-26213[b]
Likelihood ratio-difference	10976	1678	5954	410
Degrees of freedom	50	49	44	1

[a] Analyses were carried out using the SAS 6.07 procedures LOGISTIC and LIFEREG. All models use a logarithmic link between the response variable and the vector of predictors.

[b] The Likelihood ratio for the model assuming duration is exponentially distributed.

* Significant at P<0.05

Model selection

The initial model was derived from the analysis of the first spell lengths. The Likelihood ratio-difference between the main-effects model and the null model was found to be significant. Thus, the main-effects model was considered as the model against which to compare the Likelihood ratio reduction achieved by the inclusion of interaction terms. The model given above was that which was finally accepted after testing a number of interaction terms by a step-wise procedure. The final model derived from the analysis of first spell lengths was re-applied to each later dataset. This allows a comparison with effects across data sets under the assumption that similar processes are occurring in each instance. The effects of date of first entry into Family Credit and length of first spell were included in the model estimating the length of time between the first and second spell. These effects were included to examine how changes in economic factors (date of entry) and stability of circumstances (length of first spell) affected the propensity of families to return. The effects were not included in models analysing spell lengths for technical reasons which would have greatly complicated the estimation of spell lengths. Both effects proved significant (P < .01) with a longer first spell related to a longer time out of the system; and a later first entry into the system relating to a shorter period before returning. Other coefficients in the model were virtually unchanged by this inclusion.

Formulae used to derive distributions

The following distributions were extrapolated from the analyses:

1. $P(e)_t$: the exit probability, or hazard function, at time t, conditional upon surviving until time t.

2. S_t: the survivor function, or risk-set, at time t.

3. PDF_t: the probability density function, i.e. the proportion exiting, at time t.

4. F_t: the summed proportion exiting by time t

(which is equal to (1-St) or $\sum_{t=1}^{K} PDF_t$)

$P(e)t = \exp(y_t)/(1+(\exp(y_t))$ where y_t is the coefficient for the tth time indicator variable derived from the logistic model

$S_{t+1} = P(e)_t * St$ (where $S_1 = 1$)

therefore,

$PDF_t = S_{t-1} - S_t$
and,

$E(PDF) = \sum_{t=1}^{K} t*PDF_t$ where E(PDF) is the mean of the distribution exiting over a period of K time points (K = max (T))

The above formulae can be used to calculate the distributions of the proportion exiting at each time point and, therefore, the average length of completed durations for those starting a spell of Family Credit. In order to estimate the average length of completed distributions for those families in receipt of Family Credit at any given point in time, the following formula was be used:

$$Q_t = tS_t / E(PDF)$$

and,

$$E(Q) = \sum_{t=1}^{K} t*Qt$$

Bibliography

Adams, K. and Duncan, G. (1990), *Closing the Gap: Metro-Nonmetro Differences in Long-term Poverty Among Blacks*, Ann Arbor, Survey Research Center, University of Michigan.

Amin, K. (1992), *Poverty in Black and White: Deprivation and Ethnic Minorities*, London, CPAG.

Ashworth, K. (1993), 'Family Credit: taking account of time', *Briefings*, Centre for Research in Social Policy, 2, 1.

Ashworth, K. and Walker, R. (1992a), *Reflections on the Role of Time in the Definition and Measurement of Poverty*, Loughborough, Centre for Research in Social Policy, Working Paper 154.

Ashworth, K. and Walker, R. (1992b), *The Dynamics of Family Credit*, Loughborough, Centre for Research in Social Policy, CRSP Working Paper 154.

Ashworth, K. and Walker, R. (1992), *The Classification of Temporal Patterns: New Perspectives on Poverty*, Loughborough, Centre for Research in Social Policy, PP42.

Ashworth, K., Hill, M. and Walker, R. (1991), *The Severity and Duration of Childhood Poverty in the USA*, Loughborough, Centre for Research in Social Policy, CRSP Working Paper 144.

Ashworth, K., Hill, M. and Walker, R. (1992), *Economic Disadvantage During Childhood*, Paper presented to the Population Association of America Annual Conference, Denver, Colarado, May.

Ashworth, K., Hill, M. and Walker, R. (1994), 'Patterns of Childhood Poverty: New Challenges for Policy', in *Journal of Policy Analysis and Management,* forthcoming.

Ashworth, K. and Walker, R. (1992), *Family Credit: Aspects of a Changing Caseload.* Loughborough, Centre for Research in Social Policy, CRSP Working Paper 192.

Atkinson, A. (1982), *Poverty and Social Security*, Oxford, Oxford University Press.

Atkinson, A., (1984), *The Economics of Inequality*, Oxford, Oxford University Press.

Atkinson, A., (1989), *Poverty and Social Security*, Brighton, Harvester Wheatsheaf.

Atkinson, A., Maynard, A. and Trinder, G. (1983), *Parents and Children: Incomes in Two Generations*, London, Heinemann.

Auletta, K. (1982), *The Underclass*, New York, Random House.

Bailar, B. A. (1989), 'Information Needs, Surveys and Measurement Errors' in *Panel Surveys*, eds. Kasprzyk, D., Duncan, G. J., Kalton, G. and Singh, M. P. John Wiley & Sons, New York.

Bane, M. and Ellwood, D. (1983), *The Dynamics of Dependence: The Routes to Self-sufficiency*, Cambridge, MA: Urban Systems Research and Engineering Inc.

Bane, M. and Ellwood, D. (1986), 'Slipping in and out of poverty: the dynamics of spells', *Journal of Human Resources*, 21, 1, 1-23.

Bane, M. and Ellwood, D. (1989), 'One Fifth of the Nation's Children. Why are they poor? *Science*, 245, 1047-1053.

Becker, S. and Silburn, R. (1990), *The New Poor Clients*, Wallington, Community Care and the Benefits Research Unit.

Benus, J. (1974), 'Income Stability', pp. 277-303, in J. Morgan et al (eds.) *Five Thousand American Families*, Vol. 1, Ann Arbor, Survey Research Center.

Beveridge, W. (Chair) (1942), *Social Insurance and Allied Services*, London, HMSO.

Bound, J. et al (1989), *Poverty Dynamics in Widowhood*, Ann Arbor, Department of Economics, University of Michigan: Mimeo.

Buck, N. and Scott, S. (1990), *She's Leaving Home: But Why? An Event History Analysis of the Home-Leaving Process*, Paper presented at the PSID Event History Analysis Conference, Stanford University, 30 June-2 July.

Buhr, P. and Leibfried S. (1994), 'What a difference a day makes', Submitted to *Time and Society*.

Buhr, P., et al (1991), *Passages Through Welfare*, Bremen, Centre for Social Policy Research, Discussion Paper 3.

Burkhauser, R. and Duncan, G. (1989), 'Economic Risks of Gender Roles: Income Loss and Life Events over Life Course', *Social Science Quarterly*, 70, 1, 4-23.

Burkhauser, R. and G. J. Duncan (n.d.), *Life Events, Public Policy and the Economic Vulnerability of Children and the Elderly*, Ann Arbor, Survey Research Centre: Mimeo.

Burkhauser, R., Holden, F., Feaster, D. (1988), Incidence, Timing and Events Associated with Poverty: a dynamic view of poverty in retirement, *Journal of Gerontology*, 43, 846-52.

Burkhauser, R., Holden, K. and Myers, D. (1986), 'Income transitions at older stages of life: the dynamics of poverty', *Gerontologist*, 26, 292-7.

Burstein, N. R. and Visher, M. G. (1989), *The Dynamics of Food Stamp Participation*. Cambridge MA: Abt Associates for the US Department of Agriculture, Food and Nutrition Service.

Carr, T., Doyle, P. and Lubitz, I. (1984), *Turnover in Food Stamp Participation*, Washington DC, Mathematica Policy Research, prepared for US Department of Agriculture, Food and Nutrition Service.

Christiano, L., Eichenbaum, M. and Marshall, D. (1991), 'The permanent income hypothesis revisited', *Econometrica*, 59, 2, 397-424.

Cmnd 9519 (1985), *Reform of Social Security: Background Papers*, London, HMSO.

Cmnd 9691 (1985), *Reform of Social Security: Agenda for Action*, London: HMSO.

Coe, R. (1988), 'A Longitudinal Examination of Poverty in the Elderly Years', *The Gerontologist*, 28, 4, 540-544.

Cohen, Y. and Tyree, A. (1986), 'Escape from poverty: determinants of Intergenerational Mobility of Sons and Daughters of the Poor', *Social Science Quarterly*, 67, 803-813.

Corbett, T. (1993), 'Child Poverty and Welfare Reform: progress or paralysis', *Focus*, 15, 1, 1-17.

Corcoran, M. et al (1987), *Intergenerational Transmission of Education, Income and Earnings*, Ann Arbor: University of Michigan: Mimeo.

Corden, A. (1983), *Taking up a means-tested benefit*, London: HMSO.

Corden, A. (1987), *Disappointed Applicants*, Aldershot: Avebury.

Coulter, F. and Jenkins, S. (1990), *'Differences in Needs and the Assessment of Income Distribution*. Paper presented at the Welfare State Seminar, STICERD, London School of Economics.

Craig, P. (1989), *Costs and Benefits: A Review of Recent Research on Take-Up of Means Tested Benefits*, London: Department of Social Security: Mimeo.

Cross, M. (1993), 'Generating the 'New Poverty': In R Simpson and R Walker (eds.) *Europe: For Richer or Poorer*, London: CPAG.

CRSP (1993), *Barriers to People Moving Off Income Support*, Loughborough: Centre for Research in Social Policy, Paper PP70.

CSO (1991), 'The effects of taxes and benefits on household lives, 1988', *Economic Trends*, 449, 107-149.

Danziger, S. and J. Stern, (1990), *The Courses and Consequences of Child Poverty in the United States*, UNICEFF, International Child Development Centre.

Danziger, S. and P. Weinberg, (1986), *Fighting Poverty: What Works and What Doesn't,* Cambridge: Harvard University Press.

David, M. and Fitzgerald, J. (1987), *Measuring Poverty and Crises*, Madison, Wisconsin: Institute for Research on Poverty, Discussion Paper 843.

Davies, C. and Ritchie, J. (1988), *Tipping the Balance*, London: HMSO.

Deacon, A. (1987), DHSS, *Resettlement Units: A review of research findings*, Leeds: Department of Social Policy: Mimeo.

Deacon, A., Walker, R. and Vincent, J. (1992), *Alvaston Resettlement Unit: A brief history of closure*, Loughborough: CRSP Working Paper 188.

Dean, H. and Taylor-Goodby, P. (1992), *Dependency Culture*, Hemel Hempstead: Harvester Wheatsheaf.

DeParle, J. (1993), 'Clinton aides see problem with vow to limit welfare', *The New York Times*, 21 June.

Department of Employment (1989), *Family Expenditure 1987*, London: HMSO.

Department of Social Security (1993), *The Growth of Social Security*, London: HMSO.

DHSS (1988), *Low Income Statistics: Report of a Technical Review*, London: Department of Health and Social Security.

Dippo, G. S. (1989), *'The Use of Cognitive Laboratory Techniques for Investigating Memory Retrieval Errors in Retrospective Surveys'*, in Proceedings of the International Association of Survey Statisticians Conference, Paris, 1989, Vol. II.

Donohew, L., Tipton, L. and Haney, R. (1978), 'Analysis of information-seeking strategies', *Journalism Quarterly*, 15-31.

Duncan, G. J. (1988), The volatility of family income over the life course, pp. 317-357, in P Balters, D. Featherman and R. Lerner (eds.), *Life-Span*

Development and Behaviour, Hillsdale, NJ: Lawrence Erlbaum Associates.

Duncan, G. J., Hill, M. and Hoffman, S. (1988), Welfare dependence within and across generations. *Science*, 239, 467-71.

Duncan, G. J., Coe, R. D. and Hill, M. S. (1984), 'The Dynamics of Poverty', pp.33-70, in G. J. Duncan (ed.) *Years of Poverty, Years of Plenty*, Ann Arbor: Institute for Social Research.

Duncan, G. J., Coe, R. and Hill, M. (1984), 'An overview of family economic mobility' pp. 9-32, in G. Duncan (ed.) *Years of Poverty, Years of Plenty*, Ann Arbor: Institute for Social Research.

Duncan, G. J. and Hoffman, S. (1986), 'Welfare Dynamics and the Nature of Need', *The Cato Journal*, 6, 1, p. 31-54.

Duncan, G. J. and Hoffman, S. (1981), 'Dynamics of Wage Change', in G. M. Hill, D. Hill and J. Morgan (eds.), *Five Thousand American Families*, Vol. 9, pp. 45-91, Ann Arbor: Institute for Social Research.

Duncan, G. J. and Morgan, J. (1981), 'Persistence and change in family status and the role of changing family composition', Pp. 1-44, in M. Hill, D. Hill and J. Morgan (eds.) *Five Thousand American Families*, Vol. 9, Ann Arbor: Institute for Social Research.

Duncan, G. J. and Morgan, J. (1985), 'The Panel Study of Income Dynamics', Pp. 50-74, in Elder, G. (ed.), *Life Course Dynamics*, Ithaca: Cornell.

Duncan, G. J. and Rodgers, W. (1990) *Has Poverty Become More Persistent?* Ann Arbor: University of Michigan, Mimeo.

Duncan, G. J. and Rogers, W (1988), 'Longitudinal Aspects of Childhood Poverty', *Journal of Marriage and the Family*, 50, 1007-1021.

EG (1991), Employment Gazette, June, p. 5.26.

Elam, G. (1992), *Survey of Admissions to London Resettlement Units*. London: HMSO.

Elder, G. (1988), 'Preface', Pp.15-20 in Elder, G. (ed.) *Life Course Dynamics: Trajectories and Transitions*, Ithaca: Cornell University Press.

Ellwood, D. T. (1986), *Targeting "would-be" Long-Term Recipients of AFDC*. Princeton, NJ: Mathematica Policy Research, Inc.

Ellwood, D. T. (1988), *Poor Support*, New York: Basic Books.

Ellwood, D. T. (1988), *Understanding Dependency: Choices confidence or culture*, Cambridge Mass: Harvard University: Mimeo.

Ellwood, D. T. (n.d.) *Poverty through the Eyes of Children*, Cambridge Ma: Mimeo.

Field, F. (1989), *Losing Out: the Emergence of Britain's Underclass*. London: Blackwell.

Friedman, M. (1957), *A Theory of the Consumption Function*, Princeton: Princeton University Press.

Fry, V. and Stark, G. (1992), *The Take-up of Means-tested Benefits in the UK*, York: Beveridge Conference, September.

Garfinkel, I. and McLanahan, S. (1986), *Single Mothers and the Children: A New American Dilemma*, Washington DC: Urban Institute Press.

George, V. and Howards, I. (1991), *Poverty Amidst Affluence:* Britain and the United States, Aldershot: Edward Elgar.

Gilder, G. (1982), *Wealth and Poverty*, Buchan and Enright.

Glendinning, C. and Millar, J. (1987), *Women and Poverty in Britain*, Brighton: Wheatsheaf.

Goldberger, A.S. (1989), 'Economic and Mechanical Models of Intergenerational Transmission', *The American Economic Review,* June 1989, pp 504-518.

Gottschalk, P. (1982), 'Earnings mobility: permanent change or transitory fluctuations', *Review of Economics and Statistics*, 64, 450-56.

Green, D. (1992), 'Liberty, Policy and the Underclass', in D Smith (ed) *Understanding the Underclass*, London: PSI.

Harding, A. (1990), Talk based on 'Dynamic Microsimulation Models: Problem and Prospects', London: Sontory Toyota International Centre for Economics and Disciplines.

Haveman, R. (1988), *Starting Even: An Equal Opportunity Program to Combat the Nation's New Poverty*, New York: Simon and Schuster.

Heady, P. and Smyth, M. (1989), *Living Standards During Unemployment*, London: HMSO.

Hernandez, D. (1993), *America's Children: Resources from Family, Government and the Economy*, New York: Russell Sage Foundation.

Hill, M. S. and Ponza, M. (1983), 'Poverty and Welfare Dependence Across Generations', *Economic Outlook*, Summer, 61-4.

Hill, M. S. and Ponza, M. (1989), *Intergenerational Transmission of Welfare Dependency*. Paper presented to Population Association of America, March/April.

Hill, M. S. (1983), 'Trends in the Economic Situation of US Families and Children: 1970-1980', pp.9-58 in R. Nelson and F. Skidmore (eds.) *American Families and the Economy: The High Costs of Living*, Washington DC: National Academy Press.

Hill, M. S. (1985), 'The Changing Nature of Poverty', *The Annals of the American Academy of Political and Social Science*, 479, 31-47.

Hill, M. S. (1981), 'Some dynamic aspects of poverty' in Hill, M., Hill, D. and Morgan, J., (eds.), *Five Thousand American Families: Patterns of Economic Progress*, Vol. 9, Ann Arbor: Institute for Social Research, University of Michigan.

Hill, M. S., Walker, R. and Ashworth, K. (1993), *'Defining Types of Poverty: A Sensitivity Analysis'*, Paper presented to the Western Economic Association International Conference, Lake Tahoe, Nevada, 20-4 June.

HMSO (1985), *Reform of Social Security, Background Papers*, London: HMSO, Cmmd. 9519.

Hofferth, S. (1985), 'Updating Children's Life Course', *Journal of Marriage and the Family*, 47, 93-113.

Hughes, M. (1988), *The Underclass Fallacy*. Princeton: Woodrow Wilson School of Public and International Affairs.

Hurd, M. and Wise, D. (1987), *The Wealth and Poverty of Widows Cambridge. Mass:* NBER Working Paper W2325.

Hutton, S. (1991), *'Men's and Women's Income: The Evidence from Survey Data'*, York: Social Policy Research Unit, Working Paper 780.

Hutton, S. and Walker, R. (1988), *Quasi-Cohort Analysis of the Changing Financial Circumstances of Young People*. York: Social Policy Research Unit, ESRC Research Proposal.

Jenkins, S. (1989), 'The Measurement of Income Inequality', in L. Osberg (ed.), *Readings on Income Inequality*. Armonk NY: M. E. Sharpe.

Jenkins, S. (1991), 'Income Inequality and Living Standards: Changes in the Seventies and Eighties.' *Fiscal Studies*, 12, 1.

Johnson, P. and Webb, S. (1989), 'Counting People with Low Incomes: the Impact of Recent Changes in Offered Stability, *Fiscal Studies*, 10, 67-82.

Jones, H. (1987), *The Problem of Single Homelessness in West Yorkshire*, Leeds: University.

Joseph, K. (1972), Speech to the Pre-School Playgroups Association, 29 June.

JSP (1987), *Journal of Social Policy*. Poverty Issue, 16, 2.

Kerr, S. (1983), *Making Ends Meet*, London: Bedford Square Press.

Lawton, J. (1986), 'Surface availability and insect community structure: the effects of architecture and fractal dimension of plants', In B. Juniper and T. Southwood (eds.) *Insects and the plant surface*, London: Edward Arnold.

Leeming, A., and Unell, J. (1992), *Benefit Information Needs of Lone Parents*, Loughborough: Centre for Research in Social Policy, CRSP Working Papers 171 and 176.

Lerman, R. (1988), 'Non-welfare Approaches to Helping the Poor', *Focus*, 11, 1, 24-28.

Lewis, G. and Morrison, R. (1988), *Interactions Among Social Welfare Programs*, Madison: Institute for Research on Poverty, Discussion Paper 866.

Lewis, O. (1966), 'The Culture of Dependency', *Scientific American*, 215, 4.

Lilley, P. (1993), *Benefits and Costs: Securing a Future for Social Security*. Mais Lecture, 23 June.

Lister, R. (1990), *The Exclusive Society: Citizenship and the Poor*. London: CPAG.

Lodemel, I. and Schulte, B. (1992), *Social Assistance: A Part of Social Security or the Poor Law in New Disguise*, Paper presented at the Beveridge Conference, York, September.

Long, S., Beebout, H. and Skidmore, F. (1986), *Food Stamp Research: Results from the Income Survey Development Program and the Promise of the Survey on Income and Program Participation*, Washington DC: US Department of Agriculture, Food and Nutrition Service.

Mack, J. and Lansley, S. (1985), *Poor Britain*, London: George Allen and Unwin.

Mandelbrot, B. (1982), *The Fractal Geometry of Nature*, New York: W. H. Freeman.

Marsh, A. and McKay, S. (1992), *Families, Work and the Effects of Family Credit*, London: Policy Studies Institute.

Marsh, A., McKay, S. (1992), *Supplementing Low Wages*, Paper presented to the York Beveridge Conference, September.

Mayer, S. and Jencks, C. (1989), 'Poverty and the distribution of material hardship', *Journal of Human Resources*, 24, 88-114.

McLanahan, S. and Garfinkel, I. (1988), 'Single Mothers, the Underclass and Social Policy, *Annals of the American Academy of Political and Social Science*.

McLaughlin, E. (1989), *A Study of Invalid Care Allowance: Final Report,* York: Social Policy Research unit, Working Paper 626.

McLaughlin, E., Millar, J. and Cooke, K. (1989), *Work and Welfare Benefits*, Aldershot: Gower/Avebury.

McLaughlin, E., Walker, R. and Ritchie, J. (1990), *The Claiming of Social Security Benefits*, York: Social Policy Research Unit, Working Paper No. 673.

Mead, L. (1986), *Beyond Entitlement: The Several Obligations of Citizenship*, New York: Free Press.

Mead, L. (1989), 'The Logic of Workfare: The Underclass and Work Policy', *Annals of American Academy of Political and Social Science*, 501, 156-69.

Mincer, S. (1974), *Schooling, Experience and Earnings*, New York.

Mitchell, D. and K. Cooke (1988), 'The Costs of Childrearing', Pp. 27-45 in R. Walker and G. Parker (eds) *Money Matters*, London: Sage.

Moore, J. (1987), *Welfare and Dependency*, speech to the Conservative Constituency Parties Association, September.

Murray, C. (1984), *Loosing Ground: Amercian Social Policy 1950 - 1980*, New York: Basic Books.

Murray, C. (1986), *According to Age*, Washington: America Enterprise Institute for Public Policy Research.

Murray, C. (1989) 'In Search of the Working Poor', *Public Interest*, 1989, pp3-19.

Murray, C. (1990), *The Emerging British Underclass*. London: IEA Health and Welfare Unit, Choice in Welfare Series, No. 2.

Nicholson, J. L. (1979), 'The assessment of poverty and the information we need', in *Social Security Research: the definition and measurement of poverty*, London: HMSO.

O'Higgins, M., Bradshaw, J. and Walker. R, (1988), 'Income Distribution over the Life Cycle', Pp. 227-253, in R. Walker and G. Parker (eds.) *Money Matters,* London: Sage.

O'Muircheartaigh, C. A. (1977), 'Non-Response Error' in C. A. O'Muircheartaigh and C. D. Payne (eds.), *The Analysis of Survey Data*, Vol. 2. London: John Wiley and Sons.

O'Muircheartaigh, C. A. (1986), 'Correlates of Interviewer-Reinterviewer Reliability', Proceedings of the US Bureau of the Census Conference II.

O'Neill, M. (1989), *Users of Resettlement Units: A Report of a Survey.* London: Resettlement Agency.

OECD (1989), *National Accounts 1960-87*, Paris, OECD.

Orshansky, M. (1969), 'How poverty is measured?' *Monthly Labour Review*, 92, pp.37-41.

Pahl, J. (1969), *Money and Marriage*, London: Macmillan.

Piachaud, D. (1987), 'Problems in the Definition and Measurement of Poverty', *Journal of Social Policy*, 16, 2, pp. 147-164.

Pieters, D. (1991, *Social Security in Europe*, Brussels: Bryant.

Rawls, J. A. (1973), *A Theory of Justice*. Oxford: Oxford University Press.

Ray, J. C. (1975), *Les pauvres et l'argent*, Nancy: University: thesis.

Ray, J. C. (1992), *Describing Longitudinal Profiles Using Multivariate Procedures and Hierarchical Clustering*, Paper presented to the Third

International Conference on Social Science Methodology, Trento, Italy, June.

Ray, J. C. et al (1991), *Aux Franges du RMI*, Paris: Report CNAF (Caisse Nationale des Allocations Familiales).

Ritchie, J. and England, J. (1988), *The Hackney Benefit Study*, London: Social and Community Planning Research.

Ritchie, J. and Matthews, A. (1982), *Take-Up of Rent Allowances*, London Social and Community Planning Research.

Rogers, E. and Shoemaker, F. (1975), *Communication of Innovations*. Glencoe: Free Press.

Rowntree, B. S. (1901), *Poverty: A Study of Town Life,* London: Macmillan.

Ruggles, P. (1988), *Short-term Fluctuations in the Income and their Relationship to the Characteristics of the Low Income Population: New Data from SIPP*, Washington DC: US Dept. of Commerce, Bureau of the Census, No. 8802.

Ruggles, P. (1989) *Short term and long term poverty in the United States: Measuring the American Underclass*, Washington: The Urban Institute.

Ruggles, P. (1990), *Drawing the Line*, Washington: Urban Institute Press.

Ruggles, P. and Williams, R. (1988), *Measuring the Duration of Spells*, Washington: The Urban Institute, Working Paper 3375.02.

Sen, A. (1982), *Choice, Welfare and Measurement*, Oxford: Blackwell.

Sen, K. (1961), *Hinduism*. Harmondsworth: Penguin.

Shea, M. and Short, K. (1993), *Food Stamp and AFDC Participation: Characteristics of Recipients and the Dynamics of Program Participation*, Paper presented to the Western Economic Association: Lake Tahoe, Nevada, June.

Simpson, R. and Walker, R. (1993), *Poverty and Europe*, London: CPAG.

Smail, R. (1988) 'Non wage benefits from Employment', Pp.132-148 in R. Walker and G. Parker (eds)., *Money Matters*, London: Sage.

Smeeding, T. (1986), 'No money, Income and the Elderly: the case of 'tweeners', *Journal of Policy Analysis and Management*, 5, 707-24.

SSRC (1988), *A Proposal for the Establishment of a Program of Research on the Urban Underclass*, New York: Social Science Research Council.

Thirlway, M. (1989), *Review and Evaluation of Partial Incapacity Provision: Final Report*, York: Social Policy Research Unit, Working Paper 536.

Tienda, M. (1989), *Poor People and Poor Places: Deciphering Neighbourhood Effects on Behavioural Outcomes*, Paper prepared for the American Sociological Association, August.

Townsend, P. (1979), *Poverty in the United Kingdom*, Harmondsworth: Penguin.

US Department of Commerce, Bureau of the Census (1989), 'Money Income and Poverty Status in the United States: 1988', *Current Population Reports*, Series P-60, No. 166.

US Department of Health (1988), *Social Security Bulletin, Annual Statistical Supplement*, Washington: US Department of Health and Human Services.

US Department of Health (1993), *Social Security Bulletin Annual Statistical Supplement*, Washington: US Department of Health and Human Services.

van Oorschot, W. (1991), 'Non-take-up of social security benefits in Europe', *Journal of European Social Policy*, 1, 1, pp. 15-30.

Vincent, J., Ashworth, K. and Walker, R. (1991), *Taking account of Time in the Targeting and Administration of Benefits*, Loughborough: Centre for Research in Social Policy, CRSP Working Paper 141.

Vincent, J., Deacon, A. and Walker, R. (1992), *'One for the Road': Interviews with residents at Alvaston Resettlement Unit before it closed*, Loughborough: Centre for Research in Social Policy, CRSP Working Paper 182.

Vincent, J., Deacon, A. and Walker, R. (1992), *Ten Ducks out of Water: Interviews with ex-Alvaston residents*, Loughborough: CRSP Working Paper 184.

Voges, W. and Rohwer, G. (1991), *Receiving Welfare in Germany: Risk and Duration*, Bremen: Zentrum für Sozialpolitik, Working Paper, 12/91.

Walker, R. (1978), 'Temporal Aspects of Claiming Behaviour', *Journal of Social Policy*.

Walker, R. (1980), *Thoughts Provoked by the Paper on Take-Up*, Note delivered to a Department of Environment Seminar, 13th April.

Walker, R. (1985), *Housing Benefit: The Experience of Implementation*, London: Housing Centre Trust.

Walker, R. (1991), *Poverty and Poverty Dynamics*, Loughborough: Centre for Research in Social Policy, CRSP Working Paper 135.

Walker, R. and Lawton, D. (1988), 'Social Assistance and Territorial Justice: the Example of Single Payments', *Journal of Social Policy*, 17, 4, 437-476.

Walker, R. and Hill, M. (1990), *Poverty Episodes and the Distribution of Poverty: Towards a Research Strategy*, Loughborough: Centre for Research in Social Policy, CRSP Working Paper 128.

Walker, R. and Huby, M. (1989), 'Social security spending in the United Kingdom: bridging the north-south Divide', *Environment and Planning C: Government and Policy*, 7, 321-340.

Walker, R. and Hutton, S. (1988), 'Costs of Ageing and Treatment', in R. Walker and G. Parker (eds.) *Money Matters*, London: Sage.

Walker, R. and Lawton, D. (1988), 'Social assistance and territorial justice: the example of single payments', *Journal of Social Policy*, 17, 4, 437-476.

Walker, R., Ashworth, K. R., and J. Vincent (1991). *Social Security Objectives: Taking Account of Time*, Loughborough: Centre for Research in Social Policy, CRSP Working Paper 136.

Walker, R., Brittain, K., Deacon, A. and Vincent, J. (1993), *Shelter for the Night, A Home for Life: The Dynamics and Functions of Alvaston Resettlement Unit*, Loughborough: Centre for Research in Social Policy, CRSP Working Paper 201.

Walker, R., Dix, G. and Huby, M. (1992), *Working the Social Fund*, London: HMSO.

Walker, R., Dix, G. and Huby, M. (1991), 'How Social Fund officers make decisions', pp.152-165, in P. Carter, T. Jeffs and M. Smith (eds), *Social Work and Social Welfare Yearbook 3*, Milton Keynes: Open University Press.

Walker, R., Hardman, G. and Hutton, S. (1989), 'The occupational pension trap: Towards an empirical specification', *Journal of Social Policy*, 18, 4, 575-593.

Walker, R. and Hutton, S. (1988), 'Costs of Ageing and Treatment', in R. Walker and G. Parker (eds.) *Money Matters*, London: Sage.

Walker, R., Lawson, R. and Townsend, P. (1984), *Responses to Poverty: Lessons for Europe*, London: Heineman.

Williams, F. (1991), *Somewhere over the Rainbow: Universality and Selectivity in Social Policy*, paper given to Social Policy Association Conference, July, Nottingham.

Wilson, W. J. (1991), 'Studying Inner-city Social Dislocations: the Challenge of Public Agenda Research'. *American Sociological Review*, 56, 1, 1-14.

Wiseman, M., 1993, 'Welfare Reform in the States: the Bush Legacy', *Focus*, 15, 1, 18-36.

Index

transient poverty
    see *poverty types*
transition 44, 47
transmission
    see *intergenerational*
    transmission
triggers 3, 43-49, 65, 245-246
Trinder C, 61, 64, 266
Tyree A, 267
UK 7
underclass 21, 42, 53, 58, 117,
    128
Unell J, 107, 272
unemployment 14, 53, 55, 92,
    110, 171-172, 246
unemployment insurance (US)
    112
unit of observation
    see *measurement unit*
USA 4, 6, 12, 14-18, 21-27, 29-
    30, 31-32, 33-36, 44-52, 55-56,
    58-60, 61-65, 66, 69-73, 74-79,
    95-99, 100-101, 110, 117-139,
    176-178, 247-249
US social security administration
    7,8

van Oorschot, W, 102, 277
Vincent J, 14, 141, 150, 160, 165,
    168, 169, 268, 275
Visher M, 27, 49, 58, 100, 119,
    267
Voges W, 56, 275

wage
    minimum 249
    supplement 172
Walker R, 13, 14, 26, 28, 34, 39,
    40, 42, 49, 67, 82, 83, 85, 93,
    94, 102, 103, 109, 120, 123,

127, 141, 150, 160, 165, 168,
    169, 182, 200, 213, 219, 265-
    266, 268, 271, 275-276
war pensions 68
Webb S, 14
Weinberg P, 117, 268
widows 44, 51-52
Williams F, 66, 276
Williams R, 15, 251, 274
Wilson W, 40, 58, 128, 276
Wisconsin 97
Wise D 51
Wiseman M, 249, 277

York 61, 75